D0758207

DATE DUE

Lestrade

and the
Kiss of Horus

Lestrade

and the
Kiss of Horus

Volume XV in the
Lestrade Mystery Series

M.J. Trow

A Gateway Mystery

 REGNERY
PUBLISHING, INC.
Since 1947 • An Eagle Publishing Company

Library of Congress Cataloging-in-Publication Data

Trow, M. J.
　　Lestrade and the kiss of Horus / M. J. Trow.
　　　　p. cm. — (Lestrade mystery series ; v. 15)
　　"A Gateway mystery."
　　ISBN 0-89526-214-2
　　1. Lestrade, Inspector (Fictitious character)—Fiction. 2. Carter, Howard, 1874–1939—Fiction. 3. Police—England—London—Fiction. 4. British—Egypt—Fiction. 5. Archaeologists—Fiction. 6. Egypt—Fiction. I. Title.

PR6070.R598 L476 2001
823'.914—dc21   00-066497

Published in the United States by
Regnery Publishing, Inc.
An Eagle Publishing Company
One Massachusetts Avenue, NW
Washington, DC 20001
www.regnery.com

Distributed to the trade by
National Book Network
4720-A Boston Way
Lanham, MD 20706

Printed on acid-free paper
Manufactured in the United States of America
Originally published in Great Britain

10 9 8 7 6 5 4 3 2 1

Books are available in quantity for promotional or premium use. Write to Director of Special Sales, Regnery Publishing, Inc., One Massachusetts Avenue, NW, Washington, DC 20001, for information on discounts and terms or call (202) 216-0600.

The character of Inspector Lestrade was created by the late Sir Arthur Conan Doyle and appears in Sherlock Holmes stories and novels by him, as do some other characters in this book.

To Tali, for his patience

1

Thebes, the Eighteenth Dynasty of the New Kingdom

The boy-king sat in the shadows, his almond eyes shining in the guttering candle-flames. His wife sat beside him, as patient as she was ever likely to be with her husband, her stepbrother, the Living Image of Amun, ruler of Upper Egyptian Heliopolis. She sighed, patted the clammy hand idling in his lap and half turned in the darkness.

'It's all right,' she whispered to him, stroking the smooth expanse of his shaven head, 'I'm not going far – and Ay will be here soon.'

'Horemheb,' he said, his voice not as deep as hers. She saw the full lips tremble, the gold shimmer in the pierced ears. She looked across to where the statuette of the great general sat, cross-legged, grinning with his monkey-jowls at the royal couple, his breasts hanging over his paunch.

'It's only a piece of limestone,' she said, shaking her head. 'I'll have it taken away.'

'No,' her husband said quickly. 'No. What if he should find out? It was a present . . .'

'What if the moon is made of sycamore figs?' She shook his gold-ringed fingers and let the hand fall. Then she'd tired of the game, of humouring him, and she stood up straight, towering over the intercessor between man and the gods. 'Horemheb is a soldier,' she said. Her voice was as cold as his limestone likeness. 'A servant. Why don't you kick him as you would a dog?'

The boy-king whimpered. 'Oh,' she said, 'I forgot. The last time you kicked your dog, it bit you, didn't it? Well,' the disgust on her painted face said it all. 'You win some, you

7

lose some. Or in your case, little Tutankhaten, you just lose some.'

'Don't call me that!' He was on his feet, shouting at her with that pubescent squeak that always escaped his lips when he'd lost his temper. She looked at him in the acrid sulphur smoke where the great hawk-headed god loomed at his shoulder, gleaming in basalt and gold. He looked younger than his sixteen years. She wondered idly if his testicles had dropped yet. Certainly she hadn't seen them lately, but she really had little desire to. When you've got eight Nubian slaves to carry you everywhere and every one of them is hung like a donkey, what lies under the Pharaoh's thingy is more or less by the by. Still, she thought it was a *bit* forward of the royal embalmer to comment in her presence the other day that the only time he'd see the king erect is when he taped his organ of Ankh to his navel. She'd giggled at the time, but with hindsight, she must have the man's tongue cut out.

She crossed the cold of the marble hall to where Ay, her husband's man, stood in the shadows. He moved like a cat and only his shorn head was visible as she reached him.

'Majesty,' he muttered with a voice like the gravel of the Nile. 'How is he tonight?'

'One of his turns,' she hissed. 'He's panicked for days about the Hittites and the Mittani and whatever the hell's happening below the Fourth Cataract. Now it's Horemheb.'

'Tut, tut,' Ay nodded.

'Speak to him, Ay.' The queen held the man's shoulder. 'You're his most trusted adviser. He'll listen to you . . . Gods, I can remember the time he wouldn't let a slave wipe his bottom unless he checked with you first.'

'Ah,' Ay smiled. 'The good old days. By the way, great and magnificent Ankhasenamun, are you available tonight?'

She clicked her tongue and shook her head. 'You dirty old adviser,' she said. 'A man of your age should know better. Kindly', she lifted his fingers, 'take your hand off my breasts. You'll just have to wait.' And she caught him a nasty one in the groin with her fly-whisk as she slid into the dark.

Ay sank to his knees in the royal presence. Marvellous what a bit of the old genuflection did for the lad's ego. Tutankhamun, Lord of the Nile, Ruler of the Delta, Master of Upper and Lower

Egypt still stood, up to his knees in cushions, still quivering with rage at the exit of his queen and in his fear at the likeness of his general.

'She!' he screeched, pointing into the blackness. 'She called me Tutankhaten, Ay. That's heresy.'

The royal adviser knelt back on his heels. 'It is, divine one,' he growled. 'Shall I summon the executioner?'

'Yes!' The boy's eyes flashed in the candle-flame. 'No! Oh, I don't know, Ay. What do you think?'

'Er . . .?' The adviser spread his arms wide, glancing down at his knees.

'Oh, please.' The boy-king crossed to him on his spindly, barely haired legs. 'Get up.'

'Thanks, Majesty,' Ay grimaced. 'You know these marble halls play merry hell with my sciatica. How are we today?'

'Horemheb, Ay,' the boy whispered. 'What's he doing? Where is he?'

The adviser took the boy's hand and walked him back to the low throne and sat him down where the golden lions yawned under the royal elbows. 'Well,' the older man said. 'He was last heard of in Sulb. That's for definite. But I have heard reports he's making for Tushka.'

'Oh, my God.' The boy sank back into his throne, his gilded fingers caressing the lions' heads for reassurance. Perhaps, somehow, he'd absorb their strength. 'That's getting nearer, isn't it?' He suddenly jerked forward and grabbed the retainer's robe. 'Well, isn't it? You taught me geography, for God's sake. Is it getting nearer?'

Ay patiently removed the boy's hand. 'Yes,' he said, smiling at the hysterical demi-god. 'Yes, Tushka is nearer to us than Sulb.'

'What's he doing? What's he doing?' the king blurted.

Ay held his master's hands firmly in his own. 'What does Horemheb do?' he asked. 'For a living, I mean?'

'He kills people.' The king knew the answer to that one only too well.

'Right. And where is he? Assuming he's reached Tushka by now, I mean?'

'Er . . .' The king was less sure now. 'Upper Nubia.'

'*Lower.*' The old tutor tapped the boy's knuckles. '*Lower* Nubia. So who's he killing?'

There was a pause. 'Nubians?' the king hazarded.

Ay smiled and patted the boy's cheek. 'Got it in one,' he said. 'So, what's your problem?'

'It's when he stops.' The boy-king tried to concentrate, to clear his head. He couldn't find the words with Ankhasenamun. He never could. But with Ay, it was different. He'd always been there, like the father he'd never known. Firm, but fair. A bastard, but not a mean one. Ay always understood. Always knew. Always cared.

'When he stops?'

'Yes. When he's finished killing Nubians. What if . . . what if he wants to kill me?'

Ay chuckled and shook his head. 'Now, why should he want to do that?' he asked. 'Why, little one?'

The boy sat, blinking back the tears. 'I don't know,' he said. 'Perhaps . . . perhaps he wants this throne.' He glanced across to the giant doors of the robing room where all his regalia lay. 'My crown. The crowns of Upper and Lower Egypt. Perhaps he's after them.'

Ay let the king's ringed fingers go. He looked into the face of the Pharaoh and saw no wrinkled lip nor sneer of cold command. Only a poor, pathetic little idiot who'd had the bad luck to be born to the great Akhenaten of the Eighteenth Dynasty of the New Kingdom and his sixth wife. He rose to his feet, driven by his incipient sciatica and a more pressing urge and crossed briefly into the shadows. He lit a taper from a candle and lit another to give himself better light.

'Perhaps he is,' he said softly as he reached down to the base of a pillar. 'Perhaps Horemheb does want your throne, oh wise Lord of the Desert and of the River and of the Sea. But it doesn't matter, really, does it?'

'It doesn't?' Tutankhamun's heart soared with hope. The worst terrors of his young life were being confirmed, but his oldest counsellor, his truest friend, was telling him that it didn't matter, it would be all right.

'Why not, Ay?' the boy-king asked. 'Why doesn't it matter?'

He sat upright on his gilded throne of the yawning lions. He was staring at the sullen, monkey-scowling limestone face of General Horemheb. He didn't see Ay with a deft movement snatch up the cherry-wood club studded with silver. He didn't hear the whirr of it as it came at him through the air. And no one could say whether he knew what hit him as the weapon crunched through the back of his skull and the bone fragments bit deep into his brain.

Ay watched the boy-king's blood arc crimson to spatter on the basalt beak and torso of the hawk-god. He saw the boy-king's narrow shoulders hunch and his fingers flutter uselessly on the lions' heads. He watched him slump to the floor among the pile of cushions and he knelt tenderly beside him, stroking the sleek, dead head.

'It doesn't matter, little Tutankhamun,' he crooned, 'because Horemheb is in Lower Nubia. And *I* am here. That's why it doesn't matter.' And he stooped to plant a last kiss on the shattered skull.

The royal embalmer muttered when he saw the dead king laid out. Then he said nothing as his team got to work to prepare the body for the afterlife. Leaning over the newly washed body and wearing the jackal-head of his calling, he twisted his iron hook up the king's nostrils to poke for his brain and teased it out, collecting it carefully before placing it in an urn, the canopic jar to his left, the lid of which resembled a hawk. His servants held the boy upside-down briefly while he poured his potion into the nasal cavity and rinsed out the empty skull. The resin would come later. He heard the curiously empty click as the boy's head rested on the wooden pillow again. He washed the mouth out and carefully placed inside the gums the oil-soaked wads of linen. Then he reamed out the nostrils of their contents and plugged them with wax. He took the camel-hair brush from a servant and began to coat the dead boy's face with resin. Finally, he placed a piece of linen over each dull eye and pulled the eyelids down over them.

'Well, 'e can't be more than seventeen, Kat, eh?' the embalmer's number two speculated, peering at the expressionless face.

'Indeed. It's a crime, isn't it? Go on, then, call the bastard in.'

The nameless one stood outside the tent, the flat, black Ethiopian stone gleaming dully in his hand, honed to a razor's

11

edge. He entered to the rhythmic chanting of the priests. Again, the jackal head bent over the body, Kat in the likeness of the great god Anubis, and drew with his rush pen a five-inch line of ink down the dead king's left flank.

There was a rip and a squelch as the Ethiopian stone sliced through skin and muscle. Kat's numbers two and three buried themselves in the open abdomen and removed the organs they found there. The nameless one placed them in the jars with the lids of the dog's head and the jackal's and the man's.

'Right,' Kat had joined the body on the slab again. 'Palm wine.' He clicked his fingers and an assistant brought a ewer. He poured it into the body cavity. 'Just a quick rinse, I think. That'll do nicely. Pounded spices. Now.'

At a signal from the royal embalmer, the priests turned on the nameless one, spitting at him, hurling abuse. He turned on his heel, in the time-honoured way, rivulets of phlegm running down his sinewy back.

'Who'd have his job, eh?' Haph asked.

'Somebody's got to do it,' Kat said.

He clicked again and another servant slapped the spices firmly into his right palm. 'Hmm,' Kat breathed them in. He began to probe inside the body with his practised fingers. 'You can't beat a bit of infusion, that's what I always say. Gentlemen, over to you now. And Haph, go easy on the pure bruised myrrh, there's a good embalmer's mate, only I'm still reeling from Nefertiti, Gods bless her amulets.'

'And I remember Nepherkheprure-Waeare,' Kat's number two chipped in.

The embalmer looked at him. 'That's easy for you to say,' he said. 'Right. Bit of cassia in the thorax now and I think we've finished. Where's my needle?'

Haph, up to his wrists in viscera, looked down wistfully at the dead king's face. 'Talking of which,' he said, 'I'd say somebody stitched him up good and proper, wouldn't you, Kat?'

The embalmer glanced up and grinned under the mask. 'You know what they say, Haph,' he said. 'The king is dead. Long live the king. Know what I mean?' And he tapped the side of the jackal's snout.

Haph nodded. 'Nod's as good as Ankh to a blind camel,' he said. 'Natron?'

Kat nodded. 'Three gallons should do it. And then we'll stand watch for seventy days in the time-honoured tradition. Who's doing grave goods for this one, Haph?'

'Dunno. Merymery, I s'pose.'

'Oh, Gods, no.' Kat paused in mid stitch. 'Better get the papyrus out then. It's going to be a long night.'

Virginia Water, 17 March 1923

He lay with his arms flexed at the elbow, in the manner of long dead Egyptian kings, the forearms across his chest, the left above the right. In his hand lay the fly-whisk, its white horsehair trailing elegantly over his waistcoat.

'Daddy!'

The head came up and with it the body. He blinked, not sure, for the moment, of his surroundings.

'Daddy? Are you awake?'

The opening of the door sent a ray of sharp sunlight into the room, the dust particles dancing in the air.

'Oh,' the voice was softer. 'You were asleep. I'm sorry.'

The fly-whisk snaked out, hissing through air, spraying the dust into the sunbeam. 'Got you, you little bastard.'

He let his feet find the slippers and tottered over to the murder scene. But there was no corpse. The little bastard must have fallen somewhere behind the curtains.

'Not sleeping, my dear,' he said, crouching with the whisk at the ready. 'Just lulling our little buzzing friend into a false sense of obscurity. The first flies of the season are little buggers, aren't they? Damned if I know where they go in winter, but I'm bloody certain where they are every spring – swarming around my ears.'

'That was Fred Wensley,' she told him.

'What was?'

She looked at her father. She knew he was too old for all this. Too old for the rough and tumble. He should have retired years ago. Come to think of it, he *had* retired years ago; yet here he was, staring his three score years and ten squarely in the face, still chasing shadows, still listening to the testimony of ghosts. She smiled at him. To be fair, ex-Detective Chief Superintendent Sholto Lestrade OM didn't look a day over sixty-five. And he'd looked like that since he was nineteen.

'The telephone,' she told him. 'That was Fred on the telephone. There's been some trouble at St Bart's. A nightwatchman has been killed.'

Lestrade got to his feet. The girl in front of him was his Emma, a woman grown. He wasn't happy about the daringness of her hem-line, the cut of her cloche or the rakish angle of her cigarette holder, but this was 1923. And if Emma Bandicoot-Lestrade was a *little* on the mature side for a flapper . . . well, it was hardly his place to say so.

'Well, why didn't you call me?' he asked her.

'I did.' She put her hands on her hips and shook her head at him. 'Will you take the train? Or shall I drive?'

He didn't like that, either. His little girl should still be in frothy dresses and mutton-chop sleeves, lashing out with her ping-pong bat or tying up the Bandicoot boys in the old orchard at Bandicoot Hall. Instead, here she was, smoking and driving like a man. Still, the war had caused all that. Deciding her breasts would let her down in the Light Infantry, she'd elected to drive a tram instead. For nearly two years passengers in Croydon and Thornton Heath went in fear of their lives.

'Why doesn't Fred send a car?' Lestrade asked her.

'Why doesn't Fred send a policeman?' she countered. 'A *real* one, I mean.'

'Thank you, daughter dear.' Lestrade ferreted in the wardrobe. 'Where are my spats?'

'You know what I mean, Daddy.' She patted his shoulder and kissed his forehead.

He looked at her. 'Yes,' he said, 'I do. You think I'm too long in the tooth for all this, don't you? Better I'm put out to grass, I suppose. From Scotland Yard to knacker's yard. I wish it was that simple.'

'It *is* that simple,' she told him. 'Frank Froest, Edward Henry, Abberline; they've all gone, Daddy.'

'Fred's still there.'

'Yes,' she conceded, 'he is, but he's fifteen years younger than you.'

14

'And Walter Dew.' Lestrade had found his spat. Now all he needed was the other one. 'He's still going strong.'

'But he's snow white.'

'No,' Lestrade shook his head. 'More like Dopey.' He saw that she wasn't smiling. 'Emma,' he took her hands in his, the spat thrown on the bed, 'don't you see? I can't sit around here all day, moping. Now that Fanny's gone, life is . . . well, it's empty. You know me . . .'

She did. Only too well.

'Give me the thud of size elevens on the pavement, the rattle of the keys, the click of the cuffs. It's like a drug, I suppose. The battered corpse in the alley. The body in the library. Murder at the manse.'

She clicked her tongue and shook her head. 'I know,' she said, 'I know. I'll get the car. Why are you putting those things on? You know you hate spats.'

'They were the last thing Fanny bought me,' he told her. 'The last present. It's what she would have wanted.'

'Daddy,' Emma Bandicoot-Lestrade raised an eyebrow. 'You know perfectly well your good lady wife is having a whale of a time on the Riviera with cousin Val. You were supposed to be going with her. Letitia and Harry Bandicoot also asked you to go on safari to Africa with them.'

'Too busy,' he shrugged. 'Besides, cousin Val and Fanny may get on like a house on fire, but to me she's the kiss of death. One whiff of her aftershave and I'm reaching for my revolver – well, I would if I had one. Talking of which, what's that smell I can smell?'

'It's me,' she beamed. 'Coco Chanel's new perfume. Number Five. Do you like it?'

He shrugged. 'Vaguely better than Number Two, I suppose. Oh, all right.' He tossed the spat back into the recesses of the wardrobe. 'A bloke can't go around in one spat – people would talk about him.' And he hauled out his second-best Donegal, the one fashionable people had stopped wearing in 1895.

There were once three chapels in the precincts of the ancient hospital of St Bartholomew. Only one still stands – the Holy Cross, known to all and sundry as St Bartholomew-the-Less. St

Bartholomew-the-Great stands outside the hospital walls, with its front to Smithfield, where armoured knights once clattered down Giltspur Lane to joust at the tilting yards there and Queens Mary and Elizabeth, God Bless Them, burnt people with religious zeal and lots of firewood. As for St Bartholomew-the-Inbetween, only God knew where that once stood.

Emma wanted to go with her old dad through the gateway they'd put up in 1702 when they'd realized it was time for some Queen Anne architecture, but her old dad had said no. It might be grisly. And his words were punctuated by the dull thud as another bullock dropped like a stone in the meat market behind them.

'Pick me up from the Yard, later,' he said. 'And don't talk to any strange men.'

There was as strange a group of men as Lestrade would care to meet standing in a huddle in the gloom of the underground passages that ran like rabbit runs, criss-crossing Smithfield, linking wards and medical school. Two of them Lestrade recognized.

'Inspector Macclesfield.' The ex-Detective Chief Superintendent tipped his bowler.

'Mr Lestrade.' The Inspector's finger snaked along his trilby-brim. Macclesfield was built like a Brixton privy, without the green-and-cream tile covering of course, and had a face like a dray horse. There were those, like Emma Bandicoot-Lestrade for instance, who called him handsome. The other one was Wilhelmina Macclesfield, his mum. Good copper, though, was Macclesfield; recently promoted, and rightly so, for his work on the Hard case.

Standing next to Macclesfield was a bad copper, Inspector McNulty, of the City Force, that strange band of no-hopers the late Home Secretary, Mr Robert Peel, had never *quite* had the balls to deal with. McNulty was the one who'd put the 'un' in unpleasant.

'Didn't you see the blue tape?' he growled at Lestrade. 'The police cordon?'

'Tsk,' Lestrade shook his head, 'these old eyes of mine. Missed it completely.'

'Well, you couldn't have,' McNulty said. 'Because it's waist high, see, and would've hit you at waist level.'

'Good God.' Lestrade recoiled a step or two. 'The old faculties

16

are more diminished than I thought. I didn't feel a thing down . . . there. Still,' he sighed. 'At my age, you don't.'

'Now, look . . .' Gerald McNulty might have been an oaf of the worst water but he knew when he was being sent up. It happened to him most days. But he didn't like the way Norroy Macclesfield turned away, chewing the rim of his trilby to stop himself guffawing.

'Fred Wensley called me in, Inspector,' Lestrade said to the City man. 'Where are we, Norroy?'

The big Inspector turned back to Lestrade. Surely the old boy wasn't *really* gaga, was he?

'St Bart's Hospital, Mr Lestrade,' he told him.

'Yes.' Lestrade was patience itself. 'But where vees-ah-vee the City boundary?'

'Ah, I see.' Macclesfield had caught his drift. There was to be a jurisdiction dispute and Lestrade needed ammunition. 'Well,' he said. 'If you glance down, sir, you will see the mortal remains of Albert Weez, nightwatchman and boiler man to St Bart's. His nether regions are lying in the City of London, but his torso is in E Division, Metropolitan Area.'

'Bollocks!' snorted McNulty.

'As I said, Gerald,' Macclesfield held his ground, 'they are in the City of London.'

'*All* of him is in the City of London,' McNulty insisted. 'The bloody boundary is a quarter of a mile *that* way,' he waved towards the Bailey. 'No, that way,' he waved towards St Paul's. 'Well, whichever bloody way it is, we're inside City limits here. It's bad enough, Macclesfield, that you come trampling over my manor, but some old fogey . . .'

'Ah,' Lestrade wagged a finger at him. 'But you're forgetting the Whittington Sanction.' He smiled.

'You what?' McNulty blinked in the half-light.

'Tell him, Norroy.'

'Fourteen twenty-three, I think you'll find, Gerald,' the Metropolitan Inspector began. 'In the gift of the then late Mayor of London, Richard Whittington – he who kept having the turns – St Bartholomew's Hospital – and the Bailey, come to think of it – was granted to the Priory of St Greavsey-at-Westminster. That Sanction has never been revoked. In other words, this is our turf.'

'But you just said . . .'

'Oh, his legs are yours, yes. That's because, of course, the place has expanded a bit since fourteen twenty-three and whoever brought an untimely end to Mr Weez had the awkwardness to fell him precisely on the borderline. It's a bitch, isn't it?'

'Think about this positively,' Lestrade urged. 'With things as they are, you've only got half the paperwork to do. Now, a man is dead, Inspector. Can we get on with this?'

McNulty wasn't at all sure about the Whittington Sanction. But he'd crossed the great Fred Wensley before and Lestrade was a legend in his own life-style. Better bite the bullet and do as the old man said.

'Who found the body?' Lestrade could get down on his knees all right; as to the getting up, somebody else might have to shift for him.

'Some kid poking about.' McNulty riffled through his notepad. 'Here we are. One Cedric Keith Simpson.'

'Patient?' Lestrade asked.

'Dunno,' McNulty shrugged. 'I didn't spend that long with him. He seemed affable enough.'

'No.' Lestrade's head was down, checking the corpse. 'I mean, is the lad Simpson a patient here at the hospital?'

'No, he's an intending medical student, sir,' Macclesfield told him. 'We've got him upstairs.'

'Upset?' Lestrade asked.

'Upstairs,' Macclesfield repeated, louder this time.

Lestrade sighed and looked up at both inspectors. There wasn't much to choose between them, really, IQ for IQ. 'Cause of death?'

'Well . . .' McNulty began, but Macclesfield cut in.

'Uh-uh.' He wagged a warning finger at his oppo. 'Cause of death is to the head, Gerald,' he said. 'My patch, if you remember our previous conversation.'

McNulty frowned.

'Blunt instrument, sir,' Macclesfield went on. 'I counted three blows.'

'Four,' Lestrade corrected him. 'Delivered from which side?'

'The left.'

'Attack from in front? Behind?'

18

'The side.'

'You wouldn't care to impound the type of instrument?'

'Life preserver would be my guess.'

'Inspector?' Lestrade wanted a second opinion.

'I'd go along with that.' McNulty thought it best to concur.

What was left of Albert Weez lay on his right side, the arm pinned beneath him pointing along the darkened passageway to the door beyond. His mouth hung open and his grey eyes stared lifeless and dull, sunken in their sockets as though shrunk back from the sight they saw before somebody demolished his skull. His jacket had been wrenched back over his shoulders, pinning one arm behind him. The other he'd obviously torn free in the struggle before he'd gone down.

'He didn't die here,' Lestrade muttered, peering along the corridor. 'Constable?'

'Yessir.' The Metropolitan instinctively clicked to attention.

'What size boots do you take?'

'Ten, sir.'

'My man takes eleven,' McNulty chipped in, rather gratuitously, Lestrade thought.

'Show me.' Lestrade was still talking to the Met officer.

He lifted a single sole.

'Which way did you come in?'

'From there, sir,' the constable told him. 'Same way you did.'

'No blood,' Lestrade mumbled, half to himself. 'Which means he was dragged that way – and by the wrist, I'd say. Norroy, have you got Fingerprints on the way?'

'On the way, guv,' Macclesfield nodded.

'So are mine,' McNulty assured the assembled company.

'Well, then.' Lestrade flapped his arms in the air until both Inspectors caught him and hauled him upright. 'This place is going to get like Piccadilly Circus in a minute. Where's this lad Simpson?'

The lad Simpson was seventeen, though he looked older. He had the kind of ears, downturned at the top, that looked as though someone had swung him round by them shortly after birth. That same rather vicious assault had produced a loosening of the jowls so that the post-pubescent Simpson could have passed for a bloodhound. Nature had given him a superfluity of teeth, too. Quite a bitch, Nature.

'Cedric?' Lestrade peered at the lad.

'People call me CKS.' He stood up and extended a hand. 'Oh, I'm sorry.' And he put the pathological specimen back in its jar.

'Do they, Cedric?' Lestrade was still peering. 'I am Ex-Detective Chief Superintendent Lestrade, attached fairly loosely to Scotland Yard.'

'Gosh.' The boy grinned so that all his teeth were on show.

'I understand that you found the body.'

'That's right,' Simpson smirked. 'Bit of a facer, isn't it?'

For the first time, Lestrade took in their surroundings. They stood facing each other in a museum of the macabre, where indescribable bits of dead people floated in formalin. Anything with eyes appeared to be staring directly at Lestrade. And this was one time when staring back probably wouldn't have much effect.

'Tell me', Lestrade scraped a chair forward and ushered the boy into another one, 'how you came to be in the passageways beneath this building. What, in short, are you doing at Bart's, Simpson?'

'Ah,' Simspon beamed. 'Yes, I thought you'd ask that.'

'You did?'

'Oh, yes. You see, I know a little of police procedures. First, Mr McNulty asked me that question. Now he's the nasty policeman. Called me Simpson and assumed I'd done it.'

'And then?'

'Then Mr Macclesfield asked me the same question. Now, he's the nice policeman, called me CKS and assumed I didn't do it.'

'And where does that leave me?'

'Well.' Simpson leaned back, cradling his right knee in his clasped hands. 'You're the guv'nor,' he said. 'You're walking a a very clever middle road. You've asked me the same question and you've called me Cedric *and* Simpson, knowing I prefer CKS . . .'

'And who do you think I think did it?' Lestrade asked him.

'Er . . . Ah.' Collapse of precocious kid.

'Actually,' Lestrade leaned forward and whispered, 'it could very well be Mr McNulty, but we'll draw a veil over that for the moment. You'd better follow procedure, then, and answer my question.'

'What I was doing in the underground passages, you mean? Well, Mr Lestrade, I was visiting the hospital this morning . . .'

'Visiting a patient?'

'No, the hospital. Giving the place the once over. You see, I'm hoping to be a doctor. I've been to Tommy's and to be honest, I wasn't very impressed. I'm off to Guy's tomorrow. I really can't decide whom to honour with my presence.'

'What school do you go to, Cedric?' Lestrade asked.

'Brighton and Hove Grammar School, Mr Lestrade. Do you know it?'

'Mercifully, no,' Lestrade scowled. 'Tell me, are they all as bright as you are?'

'Oh, Lord no,' Simpson grinned. 'I was voted Chap Most Likely To last term.'

'And have you?'

'What have you got on the cause of death?' Simpson ignored him.

'What have you got?' Lestrade threw it back at him.

'Well.' Simspon looked about him conspiratorially. 'If you'd like my help . . .'

'Oh, I would,' Lestrade humoured the lad. 'I would.'

'Five blows to the left side of the head.'

'Five?' Lestrade frowned. 'I only counted four.'

'Ahah,' Simpson grinned. 'That's because you forgot to use your thumb for counting.'

'What?' Lestrade said levelly.

'No, seriously though,' Simspon chuckled. 'The first swipe was to the parietal region.'

'Where?' Lestrade blinked.

'Up here.' Simpson pointed to the top of his head. 'That would have caused loss of balance, quite severe bleeding and an absolute blinder of a headache. The second blow was like unto it, as they say in chapel readings – only lower. A horizontal biff that caught the temporal and parietal suture.'

'And the third?' Lestrade wasn't sure he was hearing all this from a seventeen-year-old Brighton and Hove schoolboy.

'The poor old duffer – oh, begging your pardon, Mr Lestrade – must have been rolling around now and the third was delivered as he fell, at the base of the occipital region. That's where the neck bone's connected to the head bone.' Simpson could sense that Lestrade was seriously out of his depth. 'The fifth blow – the one that in the darkened recesses of the passageway you understandably missed – was delivered virtually over the fourth, but by this time the deceased was on the ground and the impact caused a compound fracture of the zygomatic arch – as I think you'll find when they X-ray.'

There was silence. 'And the weapon?' Lestrade eventually found his voice.

'Heavy. Blunt. An iron bar, I would think . . . Oooh, eight or nine inches long, tubular, perhaps with a two-inch diameter. Conjecturally I would suggest a crowbar.'

'He didn't die in the passages, of course,' Lestrade said.

'Lord, no. In the pharmacy next door.'

'The . . . May I ask you, Mr Simpson, how you know that?'

'Blood-stains on the stairs, Mr Lestrade,' the boy answered. 'And a particularly interesting cluster of blood on the carpet in front of the poisons cabinet. That's where his cheek was smashed – where the last blow was delivered.'

Silence again.

'You never actually answered my question,' Lestrade told him, as if in a dream. 'Why were you in the underground passageways?'

'Oh, didn't I?' Simpson frowned. 'Sorry. I was lost. Got a head like a sieve, you know.'

It was a relief to Lestrade to talk to someone who wasn't seventeen and sieve-headed. Just your ordinary run-of-the-hospital pharmacist. While he was doing it another jurisdiction row broke out between the fingerprints boys from the Yard and the City; then another between their respective photographers. It hadn't been like this since the good old days of the Ripper. Lestrade didn't intervene. Norroy Macclesfield was big enough and ugly enough to hold his own. And if he chose to hold anybody else's, they'd know about it soon enough.

William Pargetter was a lean, pasty-faced boffin who looked

as though he went to bed in his white coat. Assorted shades of litmus paper burst like a buttonhole from his top pocket and his lapels and cuffs were canvases of chromatography. He also owned the most ill-fitting set of dentures in the world.

'I really can't understand it,' he clicked, as his upper set refused to be parted for long from their lower cousins.

'What?' Lestrade was peering into huge carboys of purple and amber liquid. The pasty head of the pharmacist swam mauvely into his vision on the other side.

'Old "Whizzo". Didn't have an enemy in the world.'

'Old "Whizzo"?'

'Albert. Albert Weez. Everybody knew him as "Whizzo". Salt of the earth type. Dressed up as Santa for Christmas and did the children's ward. Pity, really, he was due to retire next month.'

'What would he have been doing up here? In the pharmacy, I mean?'

Pargetter shrugged and shook his head. 'No idea,' he said. 'He came on duty at eleven, if my memory serves, and checked the boiler in the basement. You're sure he died in here?'

Lestrade crossed to the tell-tale stain, brown and sticky on the floor. 'The trail leads that way,' he said. 'Down the stairs to the passage under the courtyard where we found him. What's in this cabinet?'

Pargetter peered through the shattered glass and felt more of it crunch under his feet. 'Poisons,' he said.

'Anything missing?'

Pargetter nodded. 'I've checked the inventory. One bottle of potassium cyanide. That's all.'

'Who's responsible for security in this building?'

'Well, in this room, I suppose I am. There's only one key to the poisons cabinet.'

'And where's that kept?'

'Around my neck.' Pargetter lifted his tie to reveal the little brass key.

'Any doctors have access to it?'

'Not without signing the book – and not without using the key.'

'What if you're off sick?' Lestrade asked.

Pargetter pulled himself up to his full height. 'Please,' he

23

said, his incisors clashing. 'I haven't lost a day in sixteen and a half years.'

'But if you had . . .?'

'Then whoever needed access would need to contact me. I am not on the telephone.'

'You live . . .?'

'Frugally enough,' Pargetter clicked.

'No, I mean, where do you live?'

'Eighty-three, Splendesham Villas, Norwood.'

'Alone?'

'With my sister, Miss Pargetter.'

'What about during the day?' Lestrade asked.

'Beg pardon?'

Lestrade mechanically checked the windows. 'I mean, what happens if someone wants the cabinet while you're at lunch?'

'They'll have to wait.'

'And while you're . . . er . . . answering the call?'

Pargetter looked at the ex-Superintendent oddly. 'I'm not a religious man, Mr Lestrade,' he said.

'This is where they got in,' Lestrade muttered, half to himself and prised up a piece of twisted windowframe. He looked out of the lower pane. It was a first-floor window. 'Quite agile,' he mused.

'Beg pardon?'

'I was thinking, whoever broke in must have a certain agileness.'

'Agility,' Pargetter corrected him.

'Probably,' Lestrade nodded, pressing his blunt old nose against the blunt old glass. 'He'd need to haul himself up by the drainpipe and then fiddle about with that overflow pipe. Not a climb for an old man.'

'But why kill Whizzo?' Pargetter rattled.

Lestrade looked at his man. 'He was in the wrong place at the wrong time, Mr Pargetter,' he said. 'Sometimes that just happens, I'm afraid.'

It was the third time they'd called it Scotland Yard – a little place by the river, crammed from floor to ceiling with shoe boxes, files, fingerprints, murder weapons, death masks. The lunch-time shift was just marching out in column of twos when the cab dropped Lestrade off. One by one, the older hands flew up to helmet rims, saluting the old guv'nor. He knew them all, by nickname at least – Grinder, Hoof, Methuselah, Dimples; fine lads whose collective shoe size was 160. As for their collective IQ, better leave that stone unturned. And they in turn knew him. He'd been part of the furniture at the Yard when the oldest of them cut his teeth on a Metropolitan Water Trough. He was a man you reckoned, a man you rated. Keep wide of him if a case wasn't breaking, if the cocoa wasn't hot, if the Freans were less Peakish than usual; but when the chips were down and your back was to the wall, there was no one they'd rather have there.

He took the lift to the third floor. In the old days, he'd have bounded up the stairs three at a time, but he'd loosened too many teeth doing that and he wasn't sure his knees would still be with him by the time he reached the top. The door of the Chief Constable was open wide and the Chief Constable himself sat facing it, his large ears lit by the spring sunshine streaming in through the window.

'Fred?' Lestrade instinctively paused in the doorway. The Chief Constable had gone a funny colour. He was changing like a chameleon through puce to mauve and the veins stood out on his forehead. Lestrade hurtled in through the door. In two bounds he'd crossed the room and had wrestled the Chief Constable to the ground. He pinned his man to the floor, wrenching at his tie, ripping the studs from his collar.

'Constable!' he roared. 'Quick! The Chief Constable's having a heart attack.'

The Chief Constable looked up at him and raised an eyebrow. '*Au contraire*, Sholto,' he said, 'I was merely conducting an experiment.'

Size eleven boots had clattered to Lestrade's side. The ex-Detective Superintendent looked up at the anxious young man whose feet were inside them. 'Not bad,' he nodded. 'But, had this been a real emergency, five seconds is a long time. See if you can do better in future.'

'Yes, sir,' the constable promised he would.

'Thank you for helping us in that little test, Chief Constable,' Lestrade smiled. 'Er . . . get me up, lad, will you?'

The constable got him to his feet and Lestrade found the chair by himself.

'Tea, Rockliffe,' the Chief Constable ordered while he vaguely searched for his collar stud. 'And you'd better break into the Bath Olivers. I've a feeling this is going to be a long day.'

'Experiment, Fred?' Lestrade placed his bowler on the corner of the desk.

'Forty-two seconds,' the Chief Constable said.

'What?'

'I'd managed to hold my breath for forty-two seconds.'

'Ah,' Lestrade mused. 'Not much going on at the moment, then, Yard-wise?'

'It's a case I'm working on, Sholto,' the Chief Constable was retying his tie. 'It all hinges on the man's ability to stay underwater for one and a half minutes.'

'Underwater?' Lestrade repeated. 'But you were in the open air, over water, so to speak.'

'Little by little, Sholto,' the younger man said. 'Anyway, you assumed I was having a turn as it was. If I was upside down in a bucket of water, no doubt you'd have instantly thought "suicide" and rushed to my aid, yet again.'

'Well, Fred,' Lestrade smiled. 'We *do* go back a long way.'

Indeed they did. Lestrade remembered Frederick Porter Wensley as a rather earnest young constable from Dorset way back in the days of Whitechapel and the Ripper. He was the first detective to be given the King's Medal and both of them had done their share of ducking and diving, especially under anarchist fire in the Siege of Sidney Street. 'Mister Venzel' the Chosen People called him. Coppers called him 'Sir'; crooks called him 'Fred'; journalists called him 'The Ace'. But Lestrade knew his man too well. The strain around the eyes, the crook of the smile on the thin, almost furtive lips. The Ace was in a hole.

Rockliffe arrived with the tray. Lestrade was impressed. None of his lads had ever made tea so fast. He was less impressed as the sienna nectar hit his lips. Quality appeared to have floated out of Fred Wensley's window.

'Would you take a biscuit, sir?' the constable asked.

'He always did.' Wensley grinned as Lestrade began the exact science of dunking. 'Thank you, Rockliffe. We're not to be disturbed.'

Young Rockliffe had rarely seen two men so disturbed in his life, at least not in the same office, but it wasn't his place to say so and he made his exit.

'Fine brew, Fred,' Lestrade lied.

'Don't lie to me, Sholto.' Wensley was smoothing down what little was left of his hair these days. 'I've found no one to make a decent cup of tea since Walter Dew.'

'How is Walter?'

'Chapter Four.'

'Er . . .?'

'Of his great work. *I Caught Crippen*.'

'Ah, yes,' Lestrade chuckled. 'He finished Chapter One in 1912 if I remember aright. Not bad in two years. Still . . .' he did the necessary mental arithmetic, 'three more chapters in twelve years – I have to deduce he's slowing up a little.' Lestrade leaned forward to his man, ignoring the plop as his Bath Oliver disintegrated and plummeted into his tea. 'What's the matter, Fred?'

'Matter?' the Chief Constable did his best to be nonchalant.

Lestrade gave him an old-fashioned look. 'I've been retired now for five years officially; four unofficially and I haven't had a call from you other than to invite me out to the Police Ball, for three. Then suddenly, there's a cree-de-cur, as the French have it, and I'm up to my fob in jurisdiction disputes with the City Force.' Lestrade waited for a sign from Wensley. He wasn't going to get one. 'I *am* right, Fred?' he queried. 'St Bartholomew's *is* in the City of London?'

'It is,' Wensley nodded.

'So I *was* out of my manor?' Lestrade badgered him further.

'As out as the Eddystone Lighthouse during the candle scandal,' Wensley admitted. 'But I had my reasons.'

'Ah,' Lestrade leaned back. 'Now those are things I'd like to hear.'

Fred Wensley nodded, the cold grey eyes not leaving Lestrade's for an instant. 'Yes,' he said. 'You have a right to know.' He rummaged in his waistcoat pocket and produced a key. A click to the left, then to the right and the mysterious little cupboard by his left knee swung open. He leaned over, at a rather brave angle, Lestrade thought, for a man who must be all of fifty-five, and straightened again with a piece of evidence in his hand.

Lestrade peered at it. 'Looks like . . . looks like the corner of a warrant card,' he said.

'It is,' Wensley nodded.

'I don't follow.'

The Chief Constable stood up, grating back the chair and crossed to the window. 'I've never really liked this place, you know, Sholto.' He was talking to the river, sparkling and brown in the spring sun.

Lestrade knew that. The view was altogether wrong for Fred Wensley. It wasn't facing east, to his beloved City. Not for the first time, Lestrade realized that Wensley had joined the wrong force. 'The warrant card?' he asked.

Wensley turned back to him. 'The warrant card', he repeated, 'was found near the body of one Edward Jones on Hounslow Heath two months ago.'

'Dropped by the investigating officer?'

Wensley shook his head. 'Dropped by the murderer,' he said.

Lestrade's eyebrow rose, just a threat – always a sign that something was in the wind. 'How do you know?'

'I was there when the Coroner found it.'

'The Coroner?'

Wensley nodded. 'It was wedged in the turn-up of his trousers.'

'Snappy dresser, then, the deceased?'

'For an old fogey, yes.'

Lestrade narrowed his eyes. 'Old?' he asked.

'Edward Jones was sixty-four.'

'A mere shaver.' Lestrade dismissed it with a click of his fingers.

'The first of three,' Wensley told him.

'Of which Albert Weez was the third?'

The Chief Constable nodded, slipping into his chair again. 'The second was Jacob Hoare, aged sixty-nine. His body was found floating near Greenwich last month.'

'Tell me,' Lestrade said, 'were all three blokes clubbed to death?'

'Seems likely,' Wensley said. 'There was some doubt about Hoare because of the time he'd been in the water.'

Lestrade smiled. 'So you've called me out of retirement so that an old fogey can catch a killer of old fogeys, eh?'

'No, Sholto.' The Ace's face remained poker-straight. 'I called you in because you're the one man I know I'd trust with my life. The only one whose warrant-card corner that couldn't possibly be.'

'Because I no longer have a warrant card,' Lestrade nodded wistfully.

'Precisely,' said Wensley. 'Besides, didn't you handle a similar case a few years ago? One in which old men were dying?'

'The Brigade Case, yes,' Lestrade nodded. 'That was '91. You hadn't finished shitting yellow then.'

'I was a constable,' Wensley bridled. 'Four years in the Force.'

'That was different,' Lestrade said. 'All those men had served in the same regiment in the Crimea and they were all poisoned. What's the link between your victims?'

'That's just it,' Wensley sighed, 'there isn't one.' He passed a ledger across the desk to Lestrade. 'There's the file. Different backgrounds, different addresses, different jobs – no common ground at all that I can see. But after the first one I made a point of putting different officers on the case – in view of that.' He pointed at the warrant card.

Lestrade squinted at the torn fragment more closely. 'Looks like a "1",' he muttered. 'Can't you trace that?'

'There are nine figures on a Metropolitan warrant card, Sholto.' Lestrade didn't need Wensley to remind him. 'I've traced five that end in a figure one. You'll note it's pale blue – detective inspectors and above.'

'One belongs to Colin Smedley.'

'"Deadly" Smedley? He whose breath could stop a hunger march?'

Wensley nodded, 'But he's been in the London Free for nine weeks with inverted testicles.'

'Best place for him, then,' Lestrade winced. Even at sixty-eight the prospect brought tears to his eyes.

'Another to Dicky Tickner, P Division.'

Lestrade didn't know him.

'And that leaves the remaining three.'

'Go on.'

'You don't know the first two, but they're my own boys in the Flying Squad. One is Walter Hambrook. The *Daily Telegraph* called him "the ideal officer".'

'One to watch, then,' Lestrade nodded grimly.

'The other is Bob Fabian. Nice enough lad, but he put the bish in ambitious.'

'And the third?'

'Norroy Macclesfield.'

Lestrade's mouth sagged a little. 'Now, come on, Fred. There I have to draw the line. I've worked with Macclesfield before. He's a good copper.'

'They're all good coppers, Sholto,' Wensley said. 'But I have to face the fact that one of them might be a murderer. Hambrook took the first case; Fabian the second; Macclesfield the third. I've got all of them but Tickner in the spotlight. If there's a fourth, I'll send him. What I'd like you to do is to shadow them. Macclesfield you know already. Get to know the others.'

Lestrade sighed. 'Looking for bent coppers isn't my idea of a cosy retirement, Fred,' he felt compelled to say.

'I know, Sholto,' Wensley took back his piece of incriminating evidence and slipped it into the secret drawer whence it came, 'but I don't know who else to turn to. You know how it is. We've got the finest police force in the world in the Met, but I wouldn't turn my back on some of the buggers – and those are the ones I like. No, I want a fresh mind on this. Somebody who's on the outside, but who knows the system. That's you, that is. Will you help me, Sholto?'

Lestrade looked at his man, the most popular policeman since Sergeant Getty had inherited a fortune from some American relatives a few years back. 'All right,' he said. 'Where do I start?'

2

Two floors below the office of the Chief Constable, two detectives of the newly formed Flying Squad were making their way to the stairs. Outwardly impervious to the sniggers of their colleagues, the fact that both were dressed as Yeomen Warders of the Tower rankled with each of them.

'Tell me, Inspector Fabian,' the taller of the two said under his enormous moustache, 'do I look as big an idiot as you do?'

Fabian looked his oppo up and down. The man had no calves at all and Tudor tights did nothing for him.

'I fear you do, Inspector Hambrook. At least the Old Man didn't insist on those codpieces. I'd have had to get fairly unpleasant with that woman in wardrobe if she'd persisted. A chap on the up like me can't go around looking *totally* ludicrous, you know.'

'What is the Chelsea Arts Ball exactly?' Hambrook wanted to know.

'Buggered if I can tell you,' Fabian shrugged. 'Bunch of ponces dressed up in funny clothes. D'you think the Old Man's got it right; about the whole thing being a cover for white slavery, I mean?'

Hambrook shook his head. 'I've got a lot of time for the Ace, but I think he's out on a limb over this one. I say!' The detective had stopped on a turn of the stair to stare out of a window.

Fabian whistled at his elbow.

'I saw her first, Bob,' he said. 'Finders keepers.'

'In a pig's ear,' Fabian retorted. 'What a smashing piece of hors-d'oeuvres. Is my ruff straight?'

And they spun on their Tudor heels and clattered back down the stairs. The object of their attention was Emma Bandicoot-

Lestrade who had just driven her Austin Seven into the court-yard below Fred Wensley's office. She hauled on the handbrake and stepped out, with the intention of fetching her father. Her coat had hooked itself on to a bumper however and just as she was bending over to extricate herself, two Beefeaters had appeared at an upstairs window and had nearly done themselves a mischief craning their necks to the appropriate angle.

Now Walter Hambrook was no slouch. In the Metropolitan Inter-Divisional Sports, he had twice won the hurdles and three times the Hundred Yards Dash. He would have won the Egg and Spoon outright had he not collided with Streaker Jenkins of F Division three yards from home. So on the second turn, he was clearly ahead of the rather dumpier Bob Fabian. But the rather dumpier Bob Fabian had the instincts of a born climber. In fact, had he and Hambrook been running *up* the stairs, he'd have been well ahead. As it was, he cocked his leg over the bannister and slid past his friend with a triumphant whoop, gambolling nimbly over that nasty knob at the bottom and colliding solidly with an elderly gent just emerging from the lift.

'My God, I'm terribly sorry, sir. Are you all right?' Fabian helped his target up.

'All right? All right?' the elderly gent parroted. 'I'm careered into by twelve stone of Beefeater and you ask me if I'm all right. Look at my nose.'

Fabian did. 'Good God' he gasped. Its tip had gone. Just a flattened end. 'Did I do that?'

'What the hell do you think you're doing?' the old boy wanted to know. Fabian had apologized once. This ancient mariner was beginning to irk him somewhat. And Bob Fabian had never suffered irks gladly.

'Undercover work,' Fabian said, hearing Hambrook arrive at his back. He narrowed to the old boy. 'Do you know who I am?'

The damaged gent peered back. 'Not a clue,' he said. 'But I think I should tell you that if you thought that fancy-dress costume was unique, you're in for a bit of a shock.'

'I'm Inspector Robert Fabian,' Fabian said. 'Fabian of the Yard. No doubt you've heard of me.'

'No doubt at all', said the old boy, 'I haven't. And who's this?'

'Inspector Walter Hambrook.' Hambrook could be as officious as Fabian when the mood took him. 'Hambrook of the Yard.'

'Well, I never.' The old man shook his head. 'Take that ridiculous moustache off, sonny, it does nothing for you whatsoever.'

Instinctively Hambrook felt below his nose. 'How dare you?' he said. 'It's a humble thing, but mine own.'

'That's funny,' said the old boy. 'I thought moustaches at the Yard went out with tipstaves and wooden rattles.'

'Yes, well,' Fabian smirked, enjoying his friend's discomfiture. 'That's as may be, but at the moment, you're hindering the police in the pursuance of their enquiries. Now you've collected for the *War Cry* or whatever it is you're doing, on your wheelchair, grandad.'

And the uniformed inspectors spun on their heels and made for the door, elbow to elbow and ruff to ruff.

'Excuse me,' they chorused as they stepped into the April sunshine.

'Ah,' Emma looked at them in surprise, 'it's a Beefeaters' Excuse Me.'

'Hambrook.' The leaner inspector doffed his hat. 'My friends call me Wally.'

'Naturally,' Emma beamed.

'I'm Bob Fabian.' The plumper one doffed his. 'Bob Fabian of the Yard.'

'I'm Emma Bandicoot-Lestrade,' she told them.

'Lestrade?' Hambrook raised a quizzical eyebrow. 'I know that name.'

'Pity you don't know the face,' a voice snarled behind him.

'Ah, Daddy.' Emma squeezed between the Beefeaters and kissed him.

'Does my nose look red to you? Broken even?'

'Oh, God.' Fabian's face fell and his hand leapt up to catch it. He'd heard it wasn't like Lestrade to break even.

'Mr Lestrade, I . . .' Hambrook began.

'That's ex-Detective Chief Superintendent to you, sonny,' Lestrade snapped. 'I can only assume that old Fred Wensley is suffering from overwork. Mental strain. Well, it can happen.'

'Why, sir?' Hambrook asked.

'Because he told me you two were officers in the Flying

33

Squad. Either that or I'm deafer than I thought I was. First you knock me flying – perhaps that's what Fred had in mind – then, you browbeat me with a rank I last held nearly a quarter of a century ago. Now you have the infernal cheek to make passes at my daughter.'

'Sir, we . . .' both Beefeaters began.

'Please,' Lestrade bellowed. 'You've already done enough today to get yourselves back on the Horse Troughs. One more word and it'll be a pleasure to have you two sent to the Tower. After all, you're dressed for the part.'

'Yes sir.' Hambrook put his hat back on and saluted. Fabian did the same. They marched smartly back inside to be about their business.

'Ooh, Daddy,' she patted his cheek, 'you are an old bear.'

He smiled ruefully at her. 'And what if I told you, daughter mine, that one of those two idiots is a murderer?'

She frowned at the entrance way through which they'd disappeared. She took her head. 'I wouldn't believe you,' she said.

'No,' he climbed on to the running board of the Austin, 'neither would I. Can you manage the crank? Only I think Fabian of the Yard just ruptured my clavichord.'

Sholto Lestrade was still muttering about arrogant little whipper-snappers and assuring his daughter that he'd been collaring criminals while Messrs Hambrook and Fabian were still shitting yellow, when a telegram arrived for Emma Bandicoot-Lestrade. It was from Highclere, from Evelyn Herbert who was an old school chum. And her father, the fifth Earl of Carnarvon, was dead.

The Lestrades, father and daughter, took the Great Western to Newbury, that hideous little market town which stands on the banks of the Kennet. Its church was built, appropriately enough, by Jack of Newbury, who led 150 men north to fight for his king at Flodden. At Newbury, they milled and they malted, pumped and made machine engines; and within its borough boundaries lay Speenhamland, renowned for its System and its racecourse, well known to the Flying Squad through the activities of its touts. Its market day was Thursday. So it was just as well that the Lestrades got there on Tuesday.

'Tell me about the fifth Earl,' Lestrade chewed the end of his cigar as the motor-taxi rattled south across the bleak expanse of Greenham Common. He noticed some rough-looking women loitering on its fringes, as though waiting for something.

'Daddy,' Emma looked sharply at her father, 'I've told you already.'

'I know,' he nodded. 'Tell me again.'

'Ah,' she raised an eyebrow under her cloche, 'it's the old "Make 'Em Say It Again" ploy, isn't it? Will I never be anything but a suspect to you?'

'Of course not, chummy,' he scowled. 'Now you cough like a good 'un or it's the bracelets for you.'

'Oh, goodie.' She clapped her hands together. 'Coral is particularly "in" this year.'

'The fifth Earl?' He blew smoke rings at her.

She knew when she was beaten. 'The fifth Earl,' she repeated, clearing her throat. 'George Edward Stanhope Molyneux Herbert, born 1866. Nice old boy, although I suspect your Berkshire colleagues may disagree with me.'

'Oh? He's got form, you mean?'

'Hardly that,' Emma giggled, 'The late Earl fancied himself as something of a . . . what did people call them? . . . "automobilist"? Up before the beak more often than a baby cuckoo. He nearly killed himself a few years ago.'

'Really?'

'It must have been about the turn of the century. Evelyn was staying with us at Bandicoot Hall and I remember Harry coming in very grey-faced to breakfast one morning. Oh, I couldn't have been more than seven or so, but you know how some things stay in the mind?'

Lestrade did. He'd only ever seen his old friend Harry Bandicoot grey-faced once and that was when someone had suggested they demolish Eton. Other than that, he was the overgrown schoolboy who had brought up his daughter for him. The Lestrades owed the Bandicoots a lot one way or another.

'Anyway, he said that Evelyn's pa had been hurt. Oh, of

course he played it down for us children, but I heard him talking to Letitia afterwards. It was that apparently that persuaded the fifth Earl to go to Egypt.'

'Better roads?' asked Lestrade, never having been further east than the Dymchurch levels.

'Better climate. I must say when I first met the old duffer some years later, he didn't look at all well. Eight stone twelve in his combinations – and that wringing wet. He became a prey to our good old British winters and found solace in the Winter Palace Hotel in Luxor. It was there he met Howard Carter.'

'Howard Carter, the Whistling Flasher of Bury St Edmunds?'

'No.' She cuffed him round the ear with the beaded end of her scarf. 'Howard Carter the archaeologist. Honestly, Daddy, do you *never* read a newspaper?'

'The *Police Review*,' he countered sulkily.

'Howard Carter', she told him patiently, 'is the man who has discovered the lost tomb of Tut-Ankh-Amen, in the Valley of the Kings.'

'Ah,' Lestrade nodded.

'It's the most exciting find in the world,' she enthused. 'What a heartbreak for the fifth Earl that he didn't live to see its glories unfold.'

The glories of Highclere unfolded as the taxi swept through the great gates. A long gravel drive ran between cedars of Lebanon to the vast Queen Anne house with its red brick and its Dutch influence, as though its architects had been heartily miffed that Dutch William was dead and his unprepossessing sister-in-law had come to the throne. A huge pair of stone staghounds bayed at the front door and a liveried flunkey stood at the top of the steps.

'Mr Lestrade?'

'Perhaps.' Years on the job had taught the ex-Superintendent circumspection.

'Oh, Daddy,' Emma hissed quietly. 'Yes,' she said to the flunkey. 'This is Mr Lestrade. I am Miss Lestrade.'

'Ravishing!' a voice called from behind her and a tall, good-looking young man was running across from the gazebo. She was struck by his lovely blond curls and his dark-brown eyes and stood there with her mouth open.

'I'm Jack Holinshed. You have to be Emma.'

'Do I?' She stared at him. 'Do I really?'

He took her hand and kissed it. Lestrade cleared his throat. Here was his daughter, around whom men buzzed like bees on red hot pokers, going googly over an overdressed layabout in a blazer. What were people calling them nowadays? Bright Young Things? He noted the buttons. Some hunt or other? Or was it a yacht club? He'd never really mastered the Gothic script.

'Ah.' Holinshed gripped his hand fervently. 'I thought so,' he said.

'Did you?' Lestrade's eyes narrowed.

'I knew your eyes would be hazel.'

'Really?' Lestrade felt himself pulling away.

'The mark of the hunter,' Holinshed beamed. 'Isn't that what you do, Mr Lestrade? Hunt men?'

'I used to,' Lestrade said. 'But all that was some time ago. I'm retired now.'

'And I'm Fatty Arbuckle!' Emma snorted. 'Mr Holinshed . . .'

'Jack.' He turned to her, placing an arm around her shoulders and leading her up the steps.

'Jack,' she repeated. 'Where's Evelyn? We got her telegram . . .'

'Ah.' He jerked his head in the direction of the taxi and the flunkey scuttled off to get the bags. 'Well, there I'm afraid I have an eensy-weensy confession to make.'

'Oh?'

He led her into the vast marble hall where a huge fire roared and crackled in the grate.

'The telegram was actually from us.'

'Us?' Lestrade followed, looking for somewhere to put his bowler.

'Oh, dear,' Holinshed laughed. 'I'm doing this very badly,' he said. 'Come into the library and I'll explain all.'

The library was a fraction larger than the Bodleian and nearly as dusty. Lestrade had stood in more of these than Jack Holinshed had had hot dinners. He'd always suspected the aristocracy of buying their books by the yard. Unlike the ex-Superintendent himself who always visited Lost Property and bought his books *from* the Yard.

A striking-looking girl, perhaps a year or two younger than Emma, stood framed in the light of an oriel window. A more romantic soul than Lestrade's would have seen in her the last glimmer of the Lady of Shalott, but when she moved, the spell was broken and her heavily fringed dress shimmered as she walked. The resemblance however was uncanny. The same curly blonde locks, but the eyes hidden behind the newly fashionable dark glasses that many Bright Young Things were sporting these days. She crossed to Lestrade.

'I'm Tilly,' she smouldered, running her fingers across Lestrade's palm and a little way under his cuff. Any minute now, Lestrade thought she might start reciting 'Round and round the garden'.

'My sister,' Holinshed didn't need to announce. 'Tilly, this is Superintendent Lestrade . . . and Miss Lestrade.' He placed an arm across Emma's view of the room, so that she was forced to look into his face. She didn't object.

'Charmed,' Lestrade said, rubbing his ticklish wrist on the rough tweed of his Donegal. 'You two sent the telegram?'

'We did,' Holinshed said, reaching across Emma and pulling the bell-pull. 'Please . . . have seats.'

The Lestrade family collapsed into the bottomless chintz. Jack Holinshed stood by the fireplace, warming his Oxford bags.

'Ever since George was taken ill, we've been here, comforting Lady C and Evelyn.'

'George?' Lestrade needed help. 'Lady C?'

'Lord and Lady Carnarvon,' Tilly purred, lighting a black cigarette in an ebony holder. 'Emma, darling, do you?'

She smiled at her father. 'Only when Daddy isn't looking,' she said and accepted one.

Daddy ignored her. 'Then why the subterfugue?' he asked.

'The what? Oh, I see.' Holinshed perched on the arm of Emma's chair. 'Well, we weren't sure if Evelyn had spoken to you of us, Emma. I thought if I sent a telegram under my name you wouldn't come. We discussed the whole thing at some length with Lady C. She suggested we call you in. It was very important that you came.' He looked into her eyes for so long she had to look away.

'May I ask why?'

Holinshed looked at his sister. 'Because,' he said, 'because George, Lord Carnarvon, was murdered.'

Emma looked at her father. 'Where is Evelyn?' she asked.

'In the Valley of the Kings by now,' Tilly said.

'You'd better tell me all you know, Mr Holinshed,' Lestrade said.

'Well,' he sighed, raising his hands. 'I'll try. Tilly, darling, could you see where that wretched butler has got to? Either he's deaf as Lon Chaney's parents or that bell-pull has to go.'

She smiled and swept from the room.

'George left for Aswan at the end of February,' Holinshed told the Lestrades. 'He'd exhausted himself at the finding of the tomb . . . Are you an *aficionado*, Mr Lestrade?'

'No,' the ex-Superintendent told him. 'Church of England.'

'Well,' Holinshed went on, 'as far as we could gather from the telegram Evelyn sent us from Cairo, her father cut himself shaving, whether at Aswan or before, we don't know. He'd been bitten by a mosquito, here on the cheek.' He held an elegant finger up to his handsome face. 'Apparently, the bite was swollen, his cut-throat razor opened up the wound and he was soon running a temperature of 101. Evelyn – you know her, Emma – insisted he went to bed to rest. She'd gone out to visit at the end of March. Anyway, after a seeming recovery, he got worse. Lady C was hysterical. We got her into a Puss Moth with Dr Johnson and off they went.'

'Puss Moth?' Lestrade repeated. He didn't like the sound of that. 'Dr Johnson?' Wasn't he the bloke who wrote a dictionary and thought that a horse was part of a postern?

'It's an aircraft, Mr Lestrade,' Holinshed explained. 'Johnson is the family quack. Lord P got there just in time.'

'Lord P?' Lestrade queried.

'Teddy Porchester,' Emma cut in. 'Evelyn's brother.'

'The poor old aristocrat passed into the void in the early hours of the morning. The fifth of April. He'll be sorely missed, I fear.'

'Probably,' nodded Lestrade, 'but what you've described to me, Mr Holinshed, is a tragic accident, no doubt extrapolated by the heat and the flies. It's a long way from murder.'

'Yes,' Holinshed stood up. 'Will you excuse us, Emma?' He held her hand again. 'There's something I'd like to show your father.'

'Of course,' she smiled.

Holinshed held the door open for Lestrade and then led the

way through the oddly silent house. For all that flames danced in every room, a coldness hung on stairway and hall that made Lestrade pull his ancient Donegal about him. Holinshed took his man down a flight of stone steps into the cellar where bottles of port, cocooned in cobwebs, waited to titillate the palate of a man who would drink no more. A dead dog lay on a table in the centre, its tongue lolling, its eyes glazed.

'This was Susie,' Holinshed said. 'George's favourite terrier bitch.'

'Dreadful.' Lestrade shook his head. 'Bled to death, I suppose.'

'What?'

'The leg,' Lestrade said. 'The animal only has three legs.'

'That's an old loss, Mr Lestrade,' Holinshed said. 'It happened years ago. No, Susie just howled on the morning of the fifth and dropped dead. I didn't want to involve Tilly in all this. The unfortunate beast was on her bed at the time.'

'Just as well she's a bitch,' Lestrade muttered.

'I beg your pardon?'

'The terrier.' He pointed to it. 'It's just as well she's a bitch. Don't know how she'd have managed in the lamp-post department with an injury like that if she'd been a dog.'

'Oh, quite,' Holinshed frowned. 'But that's not all. On the day the antechamber to the tomb was opened, the pet canary of Howard Carter, the resident archaeologist, was swallowed by a cobra.'

'Good Lord.'

'Exactly. And at the very moment Carnarvon died, the lights went out, all over Cairo.'

'Fancy.' Lestrade shook his head.

'Mr Lestrade.' Holinshed stood squarely to his man, holding him by the shoulders. 'All I know is that the Herberts have been friends of ours since I can remember. Evelyn has often spoken to us of Emma and Emma's father, the doyen of detectives. This is no accident, Mr Lestrade. The dog, the canary, the lights. I can't pretend to explain it, but it makes the skin on my scalp crawl.'

'What would you like me to do, Mr Holinshed?'

'I'd like you to find out what *really* happened,' the blond man said. 'I'd like you – and Emma – to come to Egypt with Tilly and me and ask those foreigners a few questions.'

'Come to Egypt?' Lestrade's eyebrows had all but disappeared under his hairline. 'How?'

'Fly, of course,' Holinshed beamed. 'This is 1923, Mr Lestrade. This is the age of the plane.'

'Where?' Fred Wensley was incredulous. First, his old oppo Sholto Lestrade had asked to meet him, not at the Yard, but in the library of the British Museum, a room Wensley always thought Lestrade knew nothing about. Second, they'd drifted upstairs to the Museum Tea-Rooms after an ancient researcher, a somewhat unsavoury chap, had complained about their whispering together. Third, Lestrade was paying.

'Egypt,' Lestrade repeated.

'That's what I thought you said. Are you being mother?' Wensley pointed at the teapot.

'Not at my time of life,' Lestrade said. 'The honour is all yours.'

'Well, well.' Wensley poured for them both.

'You don't mind, do you, Fred?'

'My dear Sholto, you're not under my jurisdiction. You're a free agent. If you've got the folding stuff . . . Personally, I can't afford to get much further east than Rotherhithe, but that's what being a chief constable does for you.'

'Apparently.' Lestrade's tie-end somehow joined his spoon to swirl around in his tea. 'Oh, bugger.' He wrung it out. 'Apparently, money is no object.'

'How nice.'

'No, I mean, it's on the Herberts.'

'I see.'

'No, I just meant . . . well, you did ask me to have a little peep at the Old Fogey murders. No doubt you felt I had a certain entity with the victims.'

'Well, yes, but I . . .'

'Well, I've got an idea.'

'Oh.' Wensley's stirring came to an abrupt end. He had an enormous respect for Sholto Lestrade. And an affection beyond

41

the common. He'd go to hell and back for that man. But as for listening to his ideas, well, that was something else. Lestrade's ideas tended to get you held at knife-point or thrown off a bridge or handcuffed to the buffers of the eight thirty-six from Swanage.

'Why don't I take your suspects with me?'

'What?'

Lestrade closed to his man. The Flying Squad were all masters of disguise. Who was to say that the floozy in the mob-cap wasn't Sergeant Joe 'The Ox' Ledbetter? Or that the old girl in the wheelchair sucking her Bath Oliver wasn't actually Inspector Tom 'Hercules' Bennett? Lestrade kept it low. 'You suspect Macclesfield, Hambrook and Fabian. Am I right? The torn warrant card?'

'Let's say I'm keeping an eye on them,' Wensley nodded.

'Well, let me do that. In Egypt, they're out of your hair. I can work my wiles on them. And if another old fogey bites the dust in their absence, you'll know they're in the clear. At the same time I can use their powers of arrest to affect the Carnarvon murder. If murder it be.'

'Do you think this Holinshed character is on to something?'

Lestrade stroked his moustache. 'I don't know, Fred. I'll be able to tell you more when I've checked the set-up out there.'

'You're keen to go, then?'

'Keen?' Lestrade nearly dropped his cup. 'Fred, I'm absolutely terrified.'

Wensley shook his head. 'It's unprecedented, Sholto,' he said. 'Yard officers going to Egypt. Dear God, we'll be sending them to the Falkland Islands next!'

The rather fetching young lady in the powder-blue uniform made the announcement one more time, bellowing into her loudhailer as she sauntered around the departure lounge in Croydon Airport: 'Imperial Airways are pleased to announce the departure of their flight to Cairo. Will passengers please make their way on to the concourse, preferably before the wind changes.'

'I didn't care for that.' Wally Hambrook picked up his suitcase.

'What?' Bob Fabian grappled with his.

'That wind-changing bit.'

'Ever flown before?' Norroy Macclesfield asked, handling his Antlers with dexterity.

'No,' his fellow inspectors chorused. 'Have you?'

'Not unless you count the hurricane of '21,' he told them. 'I estimate I travelled forty-eight feet at an altitude of six or seven inches before I hit that gate.'

'Well, that's pretty good,' Hambrook nodded, impressed. 'As good as the Wright brothers, anyway.'

'Anybody seen Lestrade?' Fabian asked.

They turned in a body to see an elderly gent in bowler and Donegal crossing the wind-swept tarmac. Perhaps it was the way his ravishing daughter was tugging him from in front, then changing position and pushing him from behind, but something gave them the distinct impression that ex-Detective Chief Superintendent Lestrade was a little reluctant to go.

Ahead of them, the de Havilland DH66 Hercules throbbed on the runway like a great silver bird.

'Isn't she a beauty?' Jack Holinshed sauntered past the struggling Lestrades, his blond hair held in place by a Panama of generous cut.

'If you say so,' Lestrade senior growled above the snarl of the engines.

'She's a prototype.' He helped the ex-Superintendent on to the steps. 'Wide-track undercarriage and slab-sided fuselage mounted on the lower wing. Triple fins and rudders. Cruising speed, just under a hundred miles an hour.'

He'd vanished into that slab-sided fuselage by the time Lestrade's jaw had stopped falling. '*How* fast did he say?' he asked Emma.

'Daddy,' she shouted into his ear, 'we promised to help Evelyn Herbert and that's what we're going to do.'

He clutched her sleeve. 'I've heard people's bodies fall apart if they travel too fast.'

'That's what they said about the motor car,' she told him. 'And before that, about the train. You'd remember both.'

'Thank you, dear,' he said and let her push him inside, tripping ever so slightly and landing in a wicker chair. The cabin was laid out as for a Cheltenham tea-room. The Holinsheds, Tilly and Jack, were chatting to a dashing young man with gold braid on his sleeve. He, apparently, was the pilot and it comforted Lestrade not one jot to discover that he'd flown Camels during the War. Being in the desert with Lawrence of Arabia hardly made for safety.

The three wise policemen, inspectors all, were being wedged into their seats with thick blankets by the girl in powder blue. Then she clapped her hands and made an announcement.

'Ladies and gentlemen, I am Veronica and I am your air hostess for all the legs of this flight. We shall be taking off in a quarter of an hour. Morning coffee will be served at eleven, luncheon at twelve thirty. We expect to reach Paris by two at the latest. Now, may I introduce your captain, Captain Mainwaring.'

'People call me Guy,' he smiled. 'Welcome to Imperial Airways' spanking new bus.'

'Bus?' Lestrade hissed to Emma.

'She may not be as pretty as the Handley Page, but she's got bags of get up and go and that's just what we intend to do. So sit back and enjoy yourselves.' He turned towards the cockpit. 'By the way, you may experience a slight vibration on take-off and a feeling of excessive nausea after that. Veronica will pass among you with bags. And please don't open the windows in case of blow-backs. Incidentally, the usual office is to be found at the rear of the aircraft. Some of you gentlemen may find your style a little cramped, but this aircraft *is* only a prototype, so any complaints, please pass them to Veronica.'

Hambrook winked at Fabian. Veronica appeared to be the kind of girl chaps often passed a complaint to. In the half-a-mile-high club, it went with the job.

'Tally Ho!' shouted Mainwaring. 'Last one in France is a cissy.'

If Lestrade thought the throbbing of the three engines intrusive before, it was nothing to what he experienced now. Ahead, through a partially curtained door, he saw Captain Mainwaring fitting a leather helmet over his head and fiddling about with knobs and levers. The old policeman's ears seemed to collapse inside his head and his brain to explode as Mainwaring wrestled with the throttle. Hedges that ringed the aerodrome became a blur, Croydon a jumble of buildings that hurtled past them.

Lestrade thought it best to concentrate on things inside the cabin. Emma sat beside him, smiling, chatting to Norroy Macclesfield. Hambrook and Fabian were in earnest conversation over a hand of Canasta. The Holinsheds were ordering drinks from Veronica. This was all some mad dream, some terrible nightmare from which he would wake. But he was awake. And suddenly, there was no more land. The comforting landmarks of Surrey were a crazy jigsaw of fields and ribbon roads, snaking away to his right and behind him. He felt his stomach hit the roof of his mouth and then an eerie strangeness as the Hercules climbed through the low cloud. He was in limbo, lost in a way he'd never ever been lost in the streets of London. He shut his eyes and prayed.

Emma and Norroy had morning coffee. So did everybody else except Sholto Lestrade. At twelve thirty on the nose, Veronica, her powder-blue uniform wrapped in a powder-blue apron, served the *noisettes d'agneau et pommes frites*, followed by *blancmange Lafayette*, to remind the passengers they were over France. Lestrade had a glass of water.

He was still sitting with his eyes shut, his moustache curled over the rim of the Imperial Airways blanket, when the aircraft began to lurch to the right and rattle violently. He opened his eyes to see Tilly and Emma casually angling their coffee cups to counter the roll and Walter Hambrook, who was winning at Canasta, neatly catch his winnings and sweep them into his pocket.

'What's happening?' Lestrade grabbed Veronica's arm as she swept past, collecting empties.

'We're banking,' she said.

'On what?' Lestrade's question was rather more falsetto than he would have liked. 'Getting down alive?'

She smiled and patted his hand. 'Wouldn't you like to take your bowler off, Mr Lestrade?' she asked. 'We'll be in Paris in a few minutes.'

'Thank you, no.' He sat resolutely. 'I might catch a chill.'

Lestrade's eyes were closed again as the ground came up to meet them. He didn't see the crowds surging on the runway, nor the large placards held up to the plane by running, gesticulating men on the ground. Nor would it have been very pointful if he had, because the placards were written in French.

Luckily, Captain Mainwaring had been stationed there during the war and he spoke it like a native.

'Strike of airport officials!' he shouted back into the cabin. 'We can't touch down here.'

'What?' Lestrade's eyes flew open. 'What do you mean?'

'We'll have to fly on to Lyons.'

'Where?' Lestrade shouted.

'Lyons,' Veronica repeated for his benefit. 'It's only another two hours in the air.'

'Two hours?' Lestrade thought he said, although no sound had escaped his lips.

'Nothing to worry about,' Mainwaring chirped. 'There's only a slim chance of us running out of fuel.'

Lyons may have lacked the *élan* of Paris and the industrial sabotage of its airport workers, but it was the second largest commercial centre in France, famous for its silk, its Crédit Lyonnais and its spuds of almost the same name. Imperial Airways, ever ready to doubt the support of foreigners, was ready for the argy-bargy on the Orlée Airstrip and had a nice little hotel – L'Aviateur Fatigué – waiting in the Rue de la Guillotière. Lestrade had never been so glad to see terra firma in his life and he even partook of a cognac in the hotel bar – Macclesfield was paying. He collapsed into his bed a little after midnight, but the damned thing kept banking and diving through the clouds of his sleep and it was a wreck who staggered down to breakfast the next morning.

While Hambrook and Fabian demanded in loud English their bacon and eggs, Jack Holinshed nipped out to the runway to check that all was well. The de Havilland had been duly washed and polished and refuelled and all was in order.

'Where to today?' Lestrade was almost afraid to ask as he crossed the concourse. A warm wind lifted the flaps of his Donegal, and for all it was April, he felt peculiarly mellow – for a man staring death in the face, that is.

'Rome,' Veronica smiled. 'But before that we have a little treat.'

All the passengers except Lestrade were delighted to discover that the tables had been stashed to one side of the fuselage and all the seats were facing forward. Pinned up across Mainwaring's cockpit door was a white canvas screen. On a jardinière-type thing at the narrow end stood a black contraption that looked for all the world like Arlt and Fricke's Improved Hair Drying Apparatus, the Mark Three version of 1905. In fact, it turned out to be a cinematograph projector.

'On a prototype aircraft', Mainwaring beamed, 'you would expect prototype entertainment. No expense has been spared in bringing you a cinematic delight. We have *The Cabinet of Dr Caligari* on the flight to Rome and tomorrow, on the flight to Cairo, *Il Duce Pulls It Off*, a documentary with English subtitles about everyday Fascist folk.'

There were murmurs of approval all round.

'Now, while I get "Olivia" into the air, Veronica will pass among you with the petit fours. And the vomit bags. All hell's likely to break loose over the Dordogne. I'm expecting turbulence with a capital T.'

And as Lestrade stole a glance out of the window, the sun kissed the great dome of the church of Notre Dame de Fourvière, sliding away out of sight on the dark green hills below.

Because the de Havilland 'Olivia' was only a prototype, Imperial Airways had not had time to solve the problem of the in-flight cinematic delight. The projector could be housed satisfactorily and Veronica wore a more revealing cutaway uniform in order to sell her ices. It was generally agreed, however, that a silent film was nothing without the music. And the problem remained, where to put the piano? In the short term, Veronica provided a solution there too. She was not only an air hostess, it transpired, but a *siffleuse* of some note. Lestrade had obviously misheard in the rumble of the engines and assuming the unfortunate young lady to have acquired a social disease, moved his seat a little further back. It only confirmed his suspicions that she wasn't well when she began to purse her lips and flap her hands around them. Peculiar symptoms, Lestrade frowned amid the engines' roar; it looked for all the world as if she was whistling.

A thick carpet of fog lay over Rome's airport and Captain Mainwaring had to circle a few times. Hambrook and Fabian were deep in conversation, trying to unravel the complexities of *The Cabinet of Dr Caligari*. Emma and Macclesfield were pointing out of the window, swearing they could see the sun glinting on the dome of St Peter's and the Palazzio Venezia. For a brief moment, as the de Havilland shuddered and groaned, Lestrade thought he was going to die. Then they were buffeting along the runway and newspapermen were racing with them, cameras popping and flashing in the noonday Italian sun.

'Look at this, Wally.' Fabian pointed. 'We're famous!' And he rummaged in the luggage rack for his Yard trenchcoat. Veronica opened the door and Bob Fabian was first out on to the steps, pipe in hand, fedora at a rakish angle. And when the papparazzi rushed past him, hats and notepads waving, his lip only trembled for a moment with disappointment.

'What's going on?' Hambrook joined him at the door.

'Buggered if I know,' Fabian muttered, relaxing his careful pose. 'Some bloody Wop VIP over there by the look of it.'

'That's Mussolini.' Holinshed squeezed past them. 'Il Duce himself. Take a good look at him, gentlemen. That's the next ruler of the world.'

'What?' Fabian frowned. 'That fat little bloke? All boots and bald head?'

'That's the one,' Holinshed beamed. 'He flies into the airport now and then just to raise a crowd.'

'What a poser!' Fabian growled.

'Maybe,' said Holinshed. 'But at least in this country, the planes run on time.'

Someone once said when a man is tired of Cairo, he's tired of Fife. Lestrade couldn't remember who it was exactly or what the precise connection. Certainly, beyond the confines of the little airport there was no sign of a Scotsman anywhere.

'The temperature', Captain Mainwaring informed his passengers as he hauled off his helmet and passed among them, 'is a pleasant 68°. Over there', he pointed through the port windows, 'is the Bab-el-Nasr, the gate of victory. And beyond that, the tombs of the Caliphs. I should keep your hands on your wallets and purses from now on, ladies and gentlemen. You will find yourselves surrounded by street urchins of every

48

complexion. If you'll take my advice, you'll clip 'em round the ear. And gentlemen . . .' he lowered his voice and raised his eyebrows, 'keep close to the walls in the Old Native Quarter. Hunnish practices.' He would say no more.

They were shepherded quickly through customs, eyed closely by tall men in fezes. Already Lestrade was making enquiries about the sea route home. The smell of camels hit them as they crossed the Ismailiyeh Canal *en route* to the Egyptian Museum of Antiquities.

'I am Kalil,' their tall, fierce-eyed guide had told them. 'The Sirdar is waiting.'

'Sirdar?' Lestrade said out of the corner of his mouth.

'Sort of High Commissioner,' Holinshed explained. 'Our Man in Cairo. It's not every day an English aristocrat dies in their desert. He'll have all the facts by now.'

'Then', Tilly said, 'we must go and find Evelyn.'

'Oh, yes,' Emma agreed. 'The poor dear.'

Some yards away on the street called Sharia El-Kubri, two Egyptian fellahin rested on their shovels.

'Bitch of a day, Hassim,' the taller one murmured.

'Working here has its compensations, though, Mubarak. Look at the pyramids on that.'

Hassim spat into the dust that lay like a Persian carpet everywhere in those mean streets. 'White women!' He followed his friend's gaze. 'I wouldn't give you a thank you.'

'Well,' Mubarak shrugged, 'to each his own. Allah, look at that one in the funny hat. Why is he wearing that coat?'

'White men!' Hassim spat again, this time behind him, so that his aim plopped into the sluggish brown waters of the Nile.

'Allah created the English mad,' Mubarak nodded, watching the one in the funny hat fanning himself frantically. 'My old donkey to your pet cobra he passes out before he gets to the door.'

'You must be joking,' Hassim scowled. 'There's no sport in that. Oops, there he goes now.'

And they watched, nodding and shaking their dark-brown

hands, as the gentlemen in the English party carried the one with the funny hat into the cool of the Museum of Egyptian Antiquities.

'How was the flight into Egypt?'

Lestrade sat bolt upright. Ahead of him, in the shadows, a basalt jackal leered at him, his ears erect, mouth gaping, every sinew of the neck taut and rigid. The jackal looked quite relaxed by comparison. A rather pallid face appeared between the statue and Lestrade. 'Hello,' it said. 'Are you with us again?'

'That all depends on who you are.' Lestrade squinted in the cool of the darkness.

'Oh, sorry, old boy. I'm Aubrey Herbert.'

'Of the Carnarvon Herberts?'

'The same.' He extended a sinewy hand.

'I thought you'd have a trace, at least, of a Welsh accent. Ooh.' The ex-Superintendent's head throbbed like the de Havilland engines.

'Daddy!'

'Ah,' Lestrade smiled. 'My daughter's voice.'

'We were so worried.' Emma was suddenly beside him, patting his hand, stroking his head.

'The last thing I remember', he said, 'was shooing away those little boys who were buzzing round us. I fainted, presumably?'

'It's the heat, Daddy,' Emma told him. 'As well as the flies.'

'Actually,' Herbert produced Lestrade's headgear, 'it's the demon bowler.'

'Oh?'

'Too stifling for Cairo. And as for this . . .' Herbert held up Lestrade's Donegal, 'six Merinos must have died to make that.'

'I don't think they actually kill the sheep these days, do they, Mr Herbert?' Lestrade had the strength to snatch back his belongings, as Emma helped him to sit upright.

'Take my advice,' Herbert said. 'Get yourself a lightweight galabieh and a Panama. Oh, and if you're going up-country to the tombs, you'll need plenty of Keating's Powder.'

'Who is this Keating?' Lestrade had been a passenger long enough. It was time he took command of the situation. He had

50

three inspectors of the Yard who collectively couldn't inspect a bus ticket, a couple of socialites who would be as much use in a murder enquiry as umbrellas under Niagara Falls and . . .

'The johnnie who invented the powder, I suppose.' Herbert lit his pipe, his jaundiced face flashing yellow in the eerie light. 'Fleas are a huge problem out here, Mr Lestrade, along with tomb robbers and terrorist murder.'

'Terrorist murder?'

An alien voice echoed through the marble halls of the Museum of Antiquities. 'Excuse me, Herbert Pasha, you are not permitted to smoke in the Museum.'

'Oh, bugger off, Mahmoud, my brother dug most of this stuff up. And don't give me any of the old acid about your birthright. If it weren't for us British, you lot would have been overrun by the mad Mahdi years ago.'

The attendant scowled in the shadows, and exited, muttering.

'Ungrateful johnnie, your average fellah,' Herbert commented, getting comfortable on a stool of the Sixteenth Dynasty. 'Mind you, his ancestors knew a thing or two about creature comforts. Fits the bum like a glove, this . . . oh, beggin' your pardon, my dear. We Carnarvons call a spade a spade.'

'That's all right,' Emma smiled. 'So do we Lestrades.'

'My condolences for your late brother, Mr Herbert.' Lestrade was almost his old self now, the hum in his ears having lessened to an acceptable level.

'Now, Daddy . . .' Emma warned.

'I'm all right, darling.' He patted her knee. The look on old Herbert's face suggested that he rather wanted to do that. 'Where are the Three Wise Men?'

'If you mean Norroy, Wally and Bob . . .'

Lestrade groaned.

'. . . As soon as it was obvious you hadn't had a stroke, they went off with the Holinsheds to book in at the hotel.'

'Where are you staying?'

'Shepheard's,' she told Herbert.

'Ah.' His face fell. 'Don't have the *mouton à la Grecque*.'

'Really?'

'Awful lot of *Grecque* and not much *mouton*, if you catch my drift.'

'Now.' Lestrade patted his daughter's hand this time. 'I'm perfectly all right. You go and soak up some culture in the Museum while Mr Herbert and I have a little chat.'

She looked sideways at him, stood up and kissed him on the forehead. 'You know,' she said, 'I never thought it would happen to you.'

'What, that I'd pass out in the heat?'

'That you'd become a patronizing old bugger!' And she swiped him round the head and clattered away into the Nineteenth Dynasty.

The grey Arab pawed the sand in the purple haze of the twilight. The Frenchman pulled his galabieh round him, for night was the Winter of the Tropics and it was suddenly cold.

'She is a magnificent animal, Le Clerk Pasha,' the fellah said, patting the animal's warm neck and steadying the stirrup. 'It is nearly dark, but she will carry you faithfully. Has she not the eyes of the stars and the heart of the lion?'

Alain Le Clerk was no judge of horseflesh. He was his country's leading Egyptologist and, if he said so himself, a pretty dab hand when it came to the old bicyclette. He appreciated, however, that the old bicyclette was damned hard work in the desert, and at least a horse was preferable to a camel.

The fellah with the fez barked orders to the fellah without and the latter dropped to his hands and knees so that Le Clerk could mount. He put his left foot into the stirrup, his right on the fellah's back and the fellah grunted to take the strain. Then he rose up, lifting the Frenchman to saddle height. The grey shifted under his sixteen stone and tossed her head as she felt the bit ease back against her soft mouth.

'Thank Mr Carter for his hospitality,' Le Clerk said. 'I'll meet him at Luxor tomorrow as we agreed.' And he nudged the Arab with his heels and the two of them cantered off into the desert night.

Howard Carter was waiting at Luxor at the appointed hour. Le Clerk was late. The Frenchman would be late for ever now. In the rising gold of the dawn, against the ever changing ripples of the sand, the grey Arab pawed the ground in its search for scrub grass. Some yards away, the galabieh flapping in the wind, lay the body of France's greatest Egyptologist. Above him, circling with hungry eyes and razor beaks, the vultures of the desert came to dine.

3

So Lestrade took Aubrey Herbert's advice, or at least part of it, by buying a Panama at Messrs Netherby and Netherby, in the Rue Nueve. He baulked at the galabieh however. They only sold those in the Old Native Quarter and having walked past a few of them, he suspected that the old natives didn't give any quarter at all. Besides, they were all blues and whites and didn't match his eyes, not even the whites.

He sat the next afternoon in the lounge of Shepheard's Hotel, supping a rather fine brandy and facing a rather mystified policeman.

'You look mystified, Norroy,' he said, smiling at the ox-like inspector whose hair lifted rhythmically as the ceiling fan caught it. Beyond the shadowed awning of the window, Cairo slept in the noonday heat, the demon sun glaring off dome and minaret. As the muezzin called the faithful to prayer, echoing and re-echoing over the silent city that Allah was great and that Mohammed was his prophet, Lestrade noticed all the waiters turn sideways and nod in the same direction, then carry on about their business.

'I don't really know what I'm doing here, sir,' Macclesfield confessed. 'One minute I'm working on an old boy, battered to death in the basement of St Bart's, the next I'm sitting in a hotel in Egypt, drinking . . . whatever this is.'

'Think yourself lucky,' Lestrade chuckled. 'Whatever it is, it's not available out there,' he nodded to the city. 'Alcohol is apparently taboo to the Mohammedans. They cut their hand off for touching it.'

'I'm still mystified,' Macclesfield shrugged.

'Show me your warrant card, Norroy,' Lestrade said.

The Inspector frowned. 'All right,' he said. He'd worked with Lestrade before, as a sergeant on the Magpie case. You didn't ask questions of this man. You just did what he said. There was always a reason. A rhyme. He yanked it out of his inside pocket.

'Looks new,' Lestrade commented. 'That'd be because of your recent promotion.'

Macclesfield chuckled. 'That'd be because I lost the original,' he said. 'Bit embarrassing, actually. It was only my second day as Inspector and I couldn't find it.'

'Where did you lose it?'

Macclesfield shrugged. 'Damned if I can remember,' he said. 'It was a routine day. I don't think I left the Yard.'

'Canteen?'

'Canteen,' Macclesfield nodded. 'Urinals. Garage. That was about it.'

'Garage?' Lestrade frowned. 'You mean you have a motor? In my day, inspectors walked.'

'In my days too,' Macclesfield nodded grimly. 'I sometimes wonder what the police strike was all about a few years back.'

'It was all about being abandoned by the great British public,' Lestrade shook his head ruefully, 'and by the top brass. I went to the wall because of it.'

'I know, sir,' Macclesfield nodded. 'It's funny, I never had you down for a militant.'

'Liberal,' Lestrade corrected him. 'Life long. Still, now women have the vote . . . God, Emma will become illegible in two years . . .' He shuddered at the thought of it. 'But I egress. The matter in hand . . .'

'The warrant card, sir?' Norroy Macclesfield's eyebrow was arched in a silent question. Not for the whole world would he have asked Lestrade why he wanted to know. Not for the whole world would Lestrade have told him to mind his own business.

'Oh,' Lestrade bluffed. 'I'd heard they'd issued a new pattern recently. But no, it's the same as mine used to be. Well,' he was happy to change tack, 'keep it handy. You might need it later for this Carnarvon business.' He looked into Macclesfield's calm dark eyes. Good lieutenants like him deserved better. 'You're here', said Lestrade, 'because the family suspect that Lord Carnarvon's death was not the accident it appears. You're here to use your considerable powers of arrest. I don't have any.'

'Won't we be treading on a few toes, sir?' Macclesfield asked.

Lestrade chuckled. 'I expect so, Norroy,' he said. 'So what's new? Why do you think they appoint you blokes with size-eleven feet? What have we got on Carnarvon?'

'Little enough, really.' Macclesfield let the unaccustomed claret swirl once more around his tonsils. 'Bit of a facer, the family leaving like that.'

'Yes, it was odd, wasn't it? Evelyn and Lady C having invited me out, you'd think they'd hang about for a bit.'

'I tried to speak to Sidney Smith.'

'Who's he?' Lestrade wanted to know.

'The Tabeeb el Sharah, as they say in these parts.'

'All right, Norroy,' Lestrade humoured him. 'So I didn't have the benefit of a Board School education. Enlighten me.'

'It means legal doctor, guv. He's a sort of Home Office pathologist.'

'Any good?'

Macclesfield shrugged. 'I don't know. I was passed on to the Sirdar.'

'Who?' Lestrade had had that explained to him already, but he hadn't been at his most receptive then.

'Local army commander. Bloke called Lee Stack.'

'Useful?'

'No,' Macclesfield said. 'Seemed to think I was a small-arms dealer. Sent me on to the Procurator-General.'

'What does he do?'

'Well, from what I saw, as little as possible. Bloke called Hughes. Head of the Parquet.'

'Isn't that a floor?'

'Apparently it's the Ministry of Justice.'

'Ah.' Lestrade blew smoke rings to the spinning fan. 'We clearly have a lot to learn about this country, Macclesfield.'

'Their criminal law is based on the Code Napoleon, you know.'

'Get away!'

Macclesfield nodded. 'As I live and breathe.'

'So why did you want to see this legal doctor chappie?'

'Well, he knew Carnarvon – and all of them involved in the tomb. I thought he might have some ideas on the cause of death.'

Lestrade sighed. 'We could certainly do with some of those,' he said.

While Inspectors Hambrook and Fabian acted as escorts to Miss Bandicoot-Lestrade, the three of them taking in the fabulous sights of Cairo, a deputation called at the Shepheard's Hotel to see a man who was legend west of Port Said.

'You want my what?' Lestrade asked the three.

'Your autograph, sir, please.'

Lestrade looked at Macclesfield, but the Inspector had turned away in an effort to keep his chuckling shoulders under control.

'Well, I'd be delighted, Constable . . . er . . . ?'

'Guest, sir,' the tallest said. 'Tom Guest. Of the Parquet, Camel Patrol.'

'I see.' Lestrade scrawled his name on the outstretched pad. 'And . . . er . . . ?'

'Keen, sir.'

'Yes, I can see that; but what's your name, lad?'

'Keen, sir. Reginald. Parquet, Camel Division.'

'Ah, of course.' He scribbled on his piece of paper. 'And?'

'Nettlefold, sir, Pomeroy Nettlefold. Parquet, Matrimonial Disturbances Squad.'

'Get a lot of that, do you, in Cairo?' Lestrade asked, affixing his monica. Then he wrote his name.

'Ooh, bags, sir,' Nettlefold told him. 'In Islamic Law a man is allowed four wives, but you know how it is – wife number four is a luscious piece of crackling who has taken the place of wife number one, shrivelled to the constituency of a dried prune. Motive enough for the old poisoned-fig ploy.'

'Poisoned figs?' Lestrade repeated. 'Ingenious. Personally, I find figs so repulsive, I wouldn't know if they were poisoned or not. Well, thank you, gentlemen, I'm entirely flattered . . .'

'Mr Lestrade,' said Keen, 'we . . . well, we're all hoping to make a name for ourselves in the Egyptian service. We all speak

57

fluent Arabic and don't take bribes and so on. We're . . . well, frankly, unspeakably ambitious and we'd like to know more about your famous cases.'

'My . . .?'

'The Baskett Case, for instance . . .' Nettlefold began. 'Old Beelzebub Baskett . . .'

'Was guilty as sin, whatever the newspapers said,' Lestrade answered him. 'Though I concede we were lucky to have a judge who was more than a little parmesan. Now, gentlemen, please. I hate to be rude, but Mr Macclesfield and I have work to do.'

'Aha,' said Guest. 'So this isn't a holiday, Mr Lestrade?'

'Let's say a working holiday. I'm curious to know, gentlemen, how you knew I was here at all.'

'Ah, the jungle drums,' Guest smiled. Nobody crosses the Sharia El-Kubri without the Parquet knows about it. Do you mind if we ask if your visit has anything to do with the late Lord Carnarvon?'

Lestrade looked at his men. Three fresh-faced rookies, who, were it not for the copper of the Egyptian sun on their cheeks, might have come straight out of their first day on the beat. The uniform was different, but the shining zeal was the same.

'It might,' he said, charily. 'Why do you want to know?'

'Because the damnedest thing has happened,' Guest told him. 'Up-country. A Frenchman called Le Clerk has been found with a broken neck. Fell off his horse.'

'What's damnedest about that?' Lestrade asked. As a copper in the Mounted Division he had regularly fallen off his.

'Well,' Guest checked that no fellah lurked in the lounge's shadows. 'This Le Clerk had just visited the tomb of Tut-Ankh-Amen too, like Lord Carnarvon. Coincidence, wouldn't you say?'

Lestrade would. But he wouldn't say anything at all until he'd had a second opinion. Jack Holinshed knew where the morgue was. Egypt to him was a second home. So were Syria and Palestine. He didn't like to brag of it, of course, but he'd been at Allenby's elbow when the great general thundered into Jerusalem, riding knee to ham through the trenches of

Megiddo. And he hoped that Lestrade would excuse him, but he'd seen enough corpses for a lifetime. He'd wait in the rooms above.

So it was that Sholto Lestrade stood alone but for the dead in the mortuary basement. He was grateful for the relative cool of the cellar, even if the uneven flagstone floors threatened to play merry hell with his tarsals. Shafts of Cairo sunlight streamed in through the wooden slats, illuminating the naked woman who lay there.

For a while he tried to avoid her, listening to the hubbub of noises from the Old Native Quarter in the street above – the braying of donkeys and the haggling of merchants. Then, professional curiosity got the better of him and he found himself staring death in the face, as he had so often before.

'Who the devil are you?' The English bark made him turn.

'Sholto Lestrade,' he said. 'Scotland Yard.'

'Scotland Yard.' All he saw at first were laced shoes on the uneven stair, topped by a dusty white coat. 'Let me see your papers.'

The feet clacked down the steps and their owner stood in the light shaft. 'I'm Sidney Smith.'

'The legal doctor,' Lestrade nodded. 'My papers are in my hotel room.'

'Always a mistake,' Smith said, placing his sandwiches and a flask on the dead woman's slab. 'How do I know you're not some Peeping Tom?'

Lestrade glanced down at the deceased. 'She was about forty years old,' he said. 'Led an outdoor life. She'd had children. And whoever killed her choked the life out of her with a ligature.' He squinted at the purple bruising on the neck. 'Hemp, I'd imagine, with the knot to the left. Probably struck from behind.'

'All right,' Smith was too wily a character to be impressed, 'so you're a knowledgeable Peeping Tom. What did she do for a living?'

Lestrade blinked. He checked the hands. The fingernails were good. Then the feet. Likewise. But the skin of the soles was hard and calloused. 'She walked a lot,' was the best he could do.

'A knowledgeable Peeping Tom who knows nothing about

Egypt,' Smith continued with his diagnosis. 'Look at her repro-
ductive organs, man.'

'Er . . . I don't really like to,' Lestrade said.

'Tsk, tsk.' Smith shook his head. 'Still, that doesn't prove you
aren't a detective, just that you're a typical bloody Englishman.
Standing there like some blushing girl. She's got pubic hair.'

'So she has . . .' Lestrade was out of his depth.

'Well, I know its existence shocked the burnt sienna out of
old John Ruskin, but we men of the world shouldn't be
surprised by it. In Egypt, however, it speaks volumes.'

'It does?'

Smith nodded. 'It means she was a doxy, Mr Lestrade or
whoever you are. A prostitute. You were right to look at her
hands. No manual labour. Her feet are calloused because of the
beat she walked. Serviced her clients standing up, I shouldn't
wonder. Sandwich?'

Lestrade shook his head.

'In Egypt, good girls shave their pubic hair. It's a sign of
purity. Prostitutes keep theirs, for aphrodisiac purposes, so I'm
told.'

'Told?' Lestrade raised an eyebrow.

'Good God, man,' Smith's eyes widened, 'with Mrs Smith up
at the villa such experiences are bound to be a *little* second-
hand. Now, unless you're the vile sort of chappie who poses as
a policeman in order to stare at women in the altogether, what's
your purpose here?'

'Alain Le Clerk,' Lestrade said.

'Ah, the flying Frenchman.'

'Do you have him here?'

'I have what's left of him here.'

'Some constables of the Parquet told me he died as a result of
a fall from his horse.'

Smith turned to the far corner. Then he turned back to
Lestrade. 'Just a minute,' he said. 'Do you have any jurisdiction
here?'

'None whatsoever,' Lestrade assured him. 'Just a nose for an
accident that wasn't an accident.'

'You mean, he didn't fall; he was pushed.'

'Something like that,' Lestrade nodded.

'Well,' Smith slid open a metal drawer that grated like the

bars in hell, sending myriad dust particles flying into the sunbeam, 'you're misinformed. The fall was accidental all right.'

'Oh.' It wasn't the first time Lestrade had got it wrong.

'But that's got bugger all to do with it. In my not inconsiderable experience, a man whose stomach contains three grains of henbane often does tend to fall off his horse.'

'Henbane?' Lestrade peered down as Dr Smith whipped back the grey winding sheet.

'Hyoscyamus Niger; a pretty little plant that grows fairly furiously all over the Nile Delta. It has a rather lovely yellow flower and its seeds are quite commonly used in seasoning here abouts. Has a root a bit like a parsnip. Mind you, mistake it for one, and I'll guarantee you won't live to sample the cheese and biscuits.'

'That fast?'

'It can be.' Smith was busy rummaging in a cupboard above the mortal remains.

'Is there an antidote?'

Smith paused in mid-rummage. 'My dear fellow, he's dead. Pathologist of extraordinary brilliance I may be. Jesus Christ I most assuredly am not. Oh, I don't say if I'd got to him in time, pumped his stomach out and shot him full of tannic acid . . . maybe even morphine or pilocarpine. Even so, it would have been touch and go. As it is, of course, there'll be a devil of a stink.'

'The climate?' Lestrade pulled a distasteful face.

'No, I mean politically. You know it's Zagloul, don't you?'

'Zag . . .?'

'Here.' He found a glass jar with amber liquid in. 'Pass me that cat, will you?'

'Aarghh!' Lestrade had put his Panama down on what he assumed was a hat, curled up in the darkened corner. As it turned out, he was wrong by one letter and the slightly bemused beast was just coming to in the total blackness, staring into a hatband that said six and seven eighths.

'Go on, man, it's only Nefertiti.'

'It may only be Nefertiti to you . . .' Lestrade muttered. Then he whipped off the Panama and grabbed the grey, sinuous creature before it could uncoil. 'Why am I doing this?' he said. 'Other than that you asked me so nicely, I mean?'

'You'll see.' He took the animal by the scruff of its neck and tilted its head to the light. 'Watch the pupil.' And he poured some of the amber liquid into the cat's eye. The pupil shrank to a pinprick and the animal leapt clear, hissing and taking a slice out of Lestrade's hand as it bolted for the steps.

Smith shrugged. 'It goes with the territory for a laboratory cat,' he said. 'You should see the tests she undergoes when I'm using gelignite. She's not really an Egyptian Rex – it's just that all her fur has burnt off over the years. No, don't feel sorry for her.'

'I'll try not to.' Lestrade licked the agonizing lacerations and began rummaging for his handkerchief. 'What did that little experiment prove?'

'The presence of henbane.' Smith slid the bottle back whence it came. 'The liquid is a sample of urine I took from the deceased this morning. Any of the solanaceous plants contain an element of atropine – that's what caused the pupil dilation. Sandwich?'

'No, thank you,' Lestrade declined again. 'Did you know him?'

'Le Clerk? Yes, I met him once. A few months back. Rather a ladies' man, I understand. I didn't care for him much. Too much of a gigolo, if I'm not mixing my races.'

'What do you suppose happened?'

Smith sniffed. 'I thought that sort of thing was what you chappies did,' he said.

'Oh, we do,' said Lestrade. 'But I have to admit I'm on alien ground here.'

Smith smiled and tapped the side of his nose. 'You'll have to go up-country,' he said. 'Visit the murder scene. The Pyramids and beyond.'

'Beyond?'

Smith chuckled. 'There are more things in heaven and earth, Lestrade, than are dreamed of in Scotland Yard. Look, I'm pretty busy now, or I'd offer to take you.'

'I daresay Mr Holinshed will do the honours.'

'Holinshed?'

'Yes. Do you know him?'

'Never heard of him. Unless he's that bloke that Shakespeare based his plays on. Still, you'll need a native guide.'

'I will?'

'Oh, yes. Unless Holinshed has some Egyptian blood in him, he'll take you round in circles out there. It's not like Margate, you know, Lestrade. Here we have serious sand. You stray a yard or two from the river and nobody will be responsible. I know a chappie who's pretty reliable. Of course, you won't be able to start until tomorrow.'

'Too hot?' Lestrade asked.

'No, no. I've just got to bail out the reliable chappie. He's in jail at the moment. Now, is there anything else, only I've got to lock up shop and get some zizz. Siesta, you see. Sandwich before you go?'

'When Smith said "ship of the desert",' Lestrade said, 'I naturally assumed he meant a boat.'

'I expect he thought you wanted to get there quickly.' Jack Holinshed was busy with his girths. 'Travelling by steamer or felucca would take two days at this time of year. You'd die of boredom.'

'I think that end might be preferable.' Lestrade looked up at the pallid, thickly smelling beast that was to be his companion of a mile. 'Either way, there's likely to be another death on the Nile.'

'This is Mustapha.' Holinshed waved to the scrawny Egyptian in the red-and-gold galabieh. His eyes gleamed over a hawk nose and he could have earned a fortune modelling for the god Horus until he smiled and the evil stare was broken by a gappy grin.

'Ah, Lestrade Pasha, it is an honour on my house to be allowed to serve you. Of the very many and very illustrious personages I have carried up-country, never have I had the honour to carry one who is solving the murders in the Yard of Scotland.'

'You are remarkably well informed.' Lestrade's eyes narrowed. What with the topi cutting a groove in his forehead and the Keating's Powder coating his lips, the morning was not going well. 'How do I get on this thing?'

'Not from that side!' Mustapha screamed. 'Cleopatra, she has the patience of Allah, but it is of singular importance that you do not come upon her from the blind side.'

63

'Um . . . look . . . er . . . you haven't got a horse, have you? Or a donkey, perhaps? I'd even settle for an Austin Seven.'

'Ah, the automobile of Austin Pasha is a veritable triumph of British engineering, but my Cleopatra was made by Allah for traversing the desert. She is a member of that group of even-toed ungulates, the mammals who ruminate. Note her divided upper lip.' Lestrade did, with some distaste. 'Her two pairs of canine teeth.' Lestrade liked the look of those even less. 'If I were to be able to show you her stomach, you would observe that it has three compartments, not unlike the cells I recently vacated. The most remarkable feature of Cleopatra's physiognomy is that the corpuscles of her blood are not circular as in other mammals, but oval as in birds and reptiles. They are also nucleated . . .'

'How do I get on, Mustapha?' Lestrade sensed senility overtaking him and the heat of the sand beginning to burn through his boots.

'On that – if you will excuse the lascivious nature of the word – erect hump, Lestrade Pasha. Put your hand on the pommel of the saddle, thus.'

Lestrade did.

'Your other hand likewise on the cantle, so.'

Lestrade obeyed.

'Now, it is for Lestrade Pasha to mount by placing his illustrious loins astride Cleopatra's hump.'

'Like this?' Lestrade's right leg swung across the ornate leather saddle, but the dromedary bucked upwards with a sickening, hoarse cry and on clambering to its front feet, threw Lestrade right over its head.

'Nearly, Lestrade Pasha.' Mustapha beamed his encouragement. 'Perhaps this time if you put your foot in the stirrup first.'

'Yes.' Lestrade spat sand and allowed the camel driver to dust him down. 'Yes, that would probably increase my survival rate.' He glanced up at Holinshed, already atop his beast, looking like Lawrence of Arabia. 'Done this before, have you?'

'Oh, beginner's luck, old man,' the blond rider grinned. 'You'll get the hang of it.'

Mustapha whispered something Egyptian in the camel's ear

64

and the beast snorted, rolled its left eye and dropped to its knees again.

'She is ready now, Lestrade Pasha,' the camel driver said, his hands outspread. 'Once you are in the saddle, hook your left foot under your legendary fundament, as Holinshed Pasha has done.'

Lestrade glanced across. He stood rather more chance of hooking his left foot under Holinshed's fundament from where he stood. Summoning up what little remained of his dignity, he launched himself for a second time. Cleopatra snorted again, her lips quivering, either with contempt or disbelief, and Lestrade gripped the reins for all he was worth as she lurched upright.

'Is that it?' he called out to Mustapha. 'Am I doing it right?'

'You will be, Lestrade Pasha,' Mustapha said, 'when you sit upright. At the moment you are, by my estimation, at an angle of forty-five degrees to the vertical. It is rather like rowing with one oar on the Lake of the Serpent in London. You will go round in a circle and the view will become very monotonous.'

He reached up and pushed Lestrade upright.

'She will do ten miles an hour when she smells water or a man camel,' Mustapha said. 'She can do without water for three days because of her stomach pouches.'

'How long can she go without a man camel?' Lestrade thought it prurient to ask.

'Fear not, Lestrade Pasha,' Mustapha swung lazily atop his own beast, 'she is not in season. She will not, at the moment, look at a man camel twice, for all they whistle at her. Hutt! Hutt!' Mustapha's beige beast reared up out of the sand.

Holinshed moved his animal in close to Lestrade's. 'Use your crop on her neck,' he said. 'And keep her rein short – you know, like Lady Jane Grey's.' He winked at the former detective. 'She'll roll like a drifter. Why else do you think they call these things ships of the desert? The trick is to roll with her. Try to fight her and you won't be able to stand for a week. Hutt! Hutt!' And he flicked his crop across his camel's ears as the animal loped forward.

'Hutt! Hutt!' said Lestrade. Cleopatra turned her wrinkled old neck and chewed the cud or whatever it is camels chew in the Native Quarter of Cairo. A gang of ragged street urchins was rapidly closing in as the camel bellowed and flicking her fly-whisk tail, thudded off down the road in the wake of the others.

It helped a little, on the two agonizing days of their journey, that Mustapha kept up an almost running commentary on the lush pastures they trotted through. Learning that the area of the country was some 385,000 square miles came as no surprise to Lestrade. His backside felt that he had ridden every one of them. He was a little surprised, however, to learn from their guide that only some 13,600 square miles was habitable. Personally, what with the flies in his mouth and the sand in his eyes, he'd come to the conclusion that none of them was.

Slowly, they left behind the greenery of the Nile and the grey alluvium of its flood plain (Lestrade didn't remember any of this from his days at Mr Poulson's Academy for Nearly Respectable Gentlefolk when Mr Mercator had tried to teach him geography). Perhaps it was the heat or the flies, but Lestrade didn't remember much after they carried him into the oasis at Beni Suef. He lay in the darkness of his tent, the mosquito net wrapped around him like a shroud.

Mounting the next morning was surprisingly easy, for a man who felt as though he'd left his legs in the lagoon at Menzala. Flocks of scrawny sheep met the travellers on their way, the hunched camels of the day; and tall, black-robed Bedouins glided past, born to their tall saddles and silent gazes.

'Apart from the camel,' Mustapha was in full flight, 'the ass, the sheep and the buffalo have been placed for our use by Allah. Among the fauna of the desert you see before you, the hyena and the gazelle may be found in numbers, with the hare, the jackal and the fox.' He turned in the saddle. 'In the valley of the great Nile, the lynx, the ibis and the bats. And Cleopatra in her wisdom will step over the echis, the horned viper and the hooded snake. There are scorpions without number and the fleas are legion.'

Lestrade had already discovered that and his chest was red raw with his scratching. So much for Keating's Powder. Nightfall on the second day, when the stars came out like diamonds above the dying glow of the sun, saw them at Abu Qurgas.

Mustapha was well into the anthropography of his people by noon the next day, when the sun was a demon burning into Lestrade's forehead. On the guide's advice, he'd abandoned his topi and wore the arabic headgear favoured by Holinshed, his face swathed in yards of white cloth and the barrels above his brow flashing gold in the sunlight.

'The Bedouin are the people of the tent,' Mustapha said, pointing at their low black camps that ringed the sandy hills. 'They look down their noses at us fellahin. That is because they are shorter than we are, less rangy and have coarser hair. Were it not for the camels they ride, they would in fact be looking up at us most of the time.' He unhooked a goatskin sack from his saddle bow. 'Camel's-milk elevenses, Lestrade Pasha?'

They carried Lestrade Pasha to a shady grove of pomegranate trees and there he closed his eyes and tried to remember where his feet were. He was just losing the will to live when the sound of a motor klaxon brought Cleopatra to her feet, braying in retaliation. A cloud of dust rose in the shining, wobbling distance as a black speck began to grow before the travellers' eyes.

'What do you make of it, Mustapha?' Jack Holinshed was just finishing his millet and raw vegetable pasty.

'It is one of Mr Ford's motor cars of the type called Model T,' the guide said, shielding his eyes with his hand. 'An inferior marque, of course, to anything made in England.'

'Of course,' Holinshed smiled. 'Can't see who's in it, I suppose?'

'It has the pennon of the Sirdar on its bonnet.'

'The what?' Lestrade croaked through parched lips. Would he *never* remember the meaning of that word?

'The Most Illustrious Commander of the Egyptian Forces,' Mustapha told him. 'Lee Stack Pasha, May His Tribe Increase. A product of your public-school system and your Sandhurst. This man is Alexander, Caesar and Napoleon Bonaparte rolled into one.'

'All right, Mustapha,' Holinshed scrambled to his feet, dusting the sand from his boots, 'he can't hear you yet.' He trained his binoculars on the black speck. 'Lee Stack be buggered,' he said. 'I met Stack at Biarritz last year. If that's the Sirdar, I'm a Buddhist.'

It wasn't the Sirdar. So it followed that Holinshed's Anglicanism was in no doubt. Instead, a rather small, unprepossessing man in a fawn-coloured jacket braked, turned off the ignition and clambered out of the Model T's cab.

'Hello,' he said. 'We heard about you chappies over the wireless. Thought I'd give you a bit of a lift. I'm Clifford Hanger, Publicity Man for the Tomb That Time Forgot.'

'Jack Holinshed.' Holinshed caught his hand. Hanger pumped it vigorously. 'This is . . .'

'Superintendent Lestrade,' Hanger beamed. 'Yes, I know.' He grinned at the recumbent form. 'Is he all right?' he muttered out of the corner of his mouth to Holinshed. 'He looks dead.'

'He'll be fine,' Holinshed told him.

'Ah, yes.' Hanger took one look at Mustapha. 'No roomee,' he said loudly. 'Car full. No room. You go. Go back Cairo. Take camels. Oh God, don't *any* of these buggers speak a civilized language?'

'Oh yes, Effendi,' Mustapha beamed. 'And I think you will find that my English is not at all bad either. I and my camels – oh, pardon – my camels and I – were hired by the Most Illustrious Dr Smith Pasha, the Dissector of Dead Persons, to take Holinshed Pasha and Lestrade Pasha to the Valley of the Kings. I cannot break my word what I have given before Allah.'

'Really?' Hanger beamed at him. He muttered again to Holinshed, 'these people break their word more easily than they break wind. Well, all right,' he called to the guide. 'But on your own fez be it. You'll have to trot along behind. Mr Lestrade, can you walk?'

'Walk?' Lestrade repeated. His eyes flickered for a moment. 'Be gentle with me.' And his head lolled backwards.

The Winter Palace Hotel at Luxor was every bit as plush and comfortable as Shepheard's in Cairo. Hanger's Ford was every bit as uncomfortable as Cleopatra's hump and it was with vast relief that Lestrade allowed himself to be carried from one to the other and to slump in the fan-cooled lounge while white-fezed waiters plied him with cocktails. He sent a telegram down-river to Emma to tell her that they'd arrived and that he was all right. As all right as a man could be who'd just spent the last two hours being talked to by a man in advertising.

Over dinner, which was all in French, the ex-Chief Superintendent sat between Jack Holinshed and Clifford Hanger. Mustapha they hadn't seen since their arrival, but he and Holinshed had kept pace with the Ford all along the indescribable road from Manfalut to Karnak. Above the roar of the engine, Hanger had gestured to the far bank of the Nile that there was Thebes. Lestrade had misheard him and kept an even tighter grip on his wallet.

'Don't you tan at all?' Lestrade asked Holinshed over a plate of something unidentifiable. His own face was brick red except where the cloth whatsit had been wrapped across his nose. He looked like a panda with no sense of colour.

Holinshed shrugged. 'Lucky, I suppose,' he said. 'What news of the tomb, Mr Hanger?'

'Call me Cliff,' the Publicity Man beamed, pouring a little more champagne for them all. 'Well, it's a bit of a bugger at the moment. I don't mind telling you, Lord C's death has left us all in a bit of a pickle.'

'It has?'

'Well, the thing of it is, you see, dear old Howard's no great shakes when it comes to the front.'

'Front?' Lestrade had been listening to this man's conversation since that squiggle in the Nile below Dairut. He hadn't really understood much of it.

'Publicity – you know, salemanship. That's what I was before this. Didn't I tell you? You know "That 'Kruschen' Feeling"?'

Lestrade did, having often been wedged between a rock and a hard place.

' "That 'Kruschen' Feeling"?' Clearly Holinshed had not.

'The advertisement for "Kruschen Salts" – it's in all the best mags. Shows an old boy – oh, begging your pardon, Mr Lestrade – sliding down a banister. Pa Kruschen. "Here's the dear old boy again – just brimming over with high spirits and the sheer joy of living. He gets up every morning feeling he could do the staircase in one." Yes, I know.' Hanger read the faces of his audience. 'Bit Over The Top, isn't it, as we used to say on the Ypres Salient. Actually, there's no scientific evidence that Kruschen Salts do you any good at all and they taste like camel shit. Still, they're made in Manchester, so that explains a lot.'

'And what brought you to Egypt?' Lestrade asked.

'The SS *Dementia*,' Hanger beamed. 'Out of Southampton. Ha, ha! No, seriously though; Lord C advertised for a PR man.'

'A PR man?' Lestrade was grateful for a reason not to put a forkful to his lips.

'Public Relations. That's my job.'

'I heard *The Times* was on that,' Holinshed said.

'Percy Merton?' Hanger sucked on his teeth. 'An amateur, dear boy.'

'Haven't the *Daily Mail* flown somebody out?'

'"Nobody" would be rather more apposite. Arthur Weigall, former Director of the Society of Antiquities.'

'An expert, then, in archaeology, I mean?' Lestrade observed.

'To his own satisfaction, yes.' Hanger sipped the bubbly. 'Personally, I think he is to archaeology what the iceberg was to the *Titanic*. He wouldn't know an Amenhotep from his elbow. But then, my job is to sell the tomb, not get buried in academic claptrap. What do you both think of this?'

He pulled from his pocket a fairly nauseating little model of a cat. 'It's a mummified cat,' he explained. 'Or rather, the original was. I'm having them made by the thousand in Cairo and shipped from Port Said. I think they could catch on. I'm calling it Carnarvon's cat and there'll be a de luxor edition – like it? – with a nodding head to put on the back seat of people's motors.'

'Charming.' Holinshed's grin was frozen.

Lestrade was speechless. But then, half a clove of garlic *had* just reached his taste buds.

'I'm working on copies of the "Carnarvon Cut-throat" at the moment. "Your very own chance to own an exact replica of the razor that killed Carnarvon."' His fingers wrote it in the air. 'Available in mild steel and bakelite. Three bob. What do you think?'

Lestrade closed to his man. 'What do *you* think, Mr Hanger?' he asked.

'Cliff, Cliff,' the ad-man insisted. 'Think about what?'

'About what happened to Lord Carnarvon?'

'Er . . . well, he died, didn't he? Look,' he did so, at them both, 'my understanding was that you'd been sent out, Mr Lestrade, as a security expert for the tomb. And we could certainly do with some of that.'

'I am here at the request of the family,' Lestrade said, 'to investigate the death of Lord Carnarvon. We'll discuss Mr Le Clerk later.'

'Le Clerk?' Hanger frowned. 'Look, Mr Lestrade, Egypt is a rough country. It's full of creepy crawlies of the poisonous variety, burning days and freezing nights. Lord C was never very strong, you know, not since his accident. And Alain Le Clerk, well, let's just say I wouldn't have put my money on him in the Derby. He just fell off his horse, that's all. These things happen.'

'Were you here when Lord Carnarvon died?'

'My dear fellow, I was at his bedside. We all were – Lady C, Lady Evelyn, Howard Carter.'

'Carter?'

'He's the archaeologist,' Hanger explained. 'It's his dig.'

Lestrade pushed away whatever it was on the plate in front of him.

'Is the kebab not to your liking?' a passing *maître d'hôtel* asked.

'No, it's fine,' Lestrade said, patting the table cloth. 'In fact, I've rarely seen a prettier one. Now, Mr Hanger . . .'

'Cliff. Cliff.'

'Now, Cliff Cliff,' years of interrogation had taught him the value of being the nice policeman, 'perhaps you could tell us what happened the night Lord Carnarvon died. And Mr Holinshed, I wonder if you could ask if they do a nice spotted dick anywhere in the hotel? I could eat a horse.'

It was the damnedest thing, Hanger had told them. The lights all went out in Cairo at the exact moment that Lord Carnarvon died. He was staying in the Continental Hotel in the city and cut his cheek with his cut-throat razor, the one with the family crest of the gryphon sejant (an ad-man had to know his family crests). Hanger himself had noticed, in between dreaming up slogans for the forthcoming opening of the tomb, how angry and red the old man's face looked. As though the hawk-headed guardian of the tomb had pecked him on the cheek. The Horus

Kiss. He seemed to rally, then the fever set in and a curious lack of lustre seemed to settle on him, like the sands of the desert settle on everything. In the early hours of the fifth of April, with his wife, son and daughter at his bedside, Lord C's breathing had become ragged, forced. For a moment, his eyelids fluttered to the ceiling. Then he said two words – or what sounded like two words. Soft wings. Nothing more. The Cairo papers had a mourning frame around their next day's editions. Traffic in the Sharia Imad-ed-Din came to a halt. There was a minute's silence as a token of the city's respect for a great man.

'Odd that Lady Evelyn didn't stay to greet us,' Lestrade mused that night as he and Jack Holinshed waved *au revoir* to Clifford Hanger, driving into the night.

'Bodies don't keep in the Egyptian heat, Mr Lestrade.' The blond man pulled a long cigar from an inside pocket of his dinner jacket. 'They wanted to bury him on Beacon Hill, I understand, above his beloved Highclere. You didn't ask Hanger about Le Clerk.'

'One death at a time, Mr Holinshed.' Lestrade pulled out his cigar, rather shorter, from his serge jacket. 'I find it helps keep things in perspective. The Valley of the Kings tomorrow, then?'

The Valley of the Kings was the valley of the dead, a rivulet of shade and sandstone with a dry wadi meandering to the east. Here, with wailing and with sorrow, the ancient Egyptians had brought their dead kings, the Pharaohs who bestrode the known world like colossi. Hatshepsut slept here, Tuthmosis and Rameses, Amenophis and Siptah, Sethos, Yuya and Merenptah. For a little while, the archaeologists had looked on their works and despaired. Then, they started to ransack them, all in the name of science, of course.

4

Lestrade had sat through some pretty bizarre breakfasts in his time. None could compare, however – not even the one at Wigston Guthlaxton – with his first in the Valley of the Kings. The morning goods were unexceptional – curved bits of pastry and a jam-like substance. The coffee was a little too thick for Lestrade's taste. In fact it took eight seconds by his old half hunter for the spoon to slide from the perpendicular in the cup's contents. No, it was the setting. A trestle table, gleaming with silverware and the crested China of the Carnarvons, had been set up in the gloomy passageway that led to the tomb of Rameses XI, Excavation Number Four. The clatter of cutlery echoed back into the recesses where the great Pharaoh had laid in state for thousands of years, before the chisels of grave robbers had robbed him of his peace.

Jack Holinshed and Clifford Hanger, of course, Lestrade already knew. Across the table from him sat the tall, darkly handsome Arthur Cruttenden Mace. Over coffee, he told Lestrade his life story, whether he wanted to know it or not. He was a distant cousin of another great archaeologist, Flinders Petrie. Lestrade had heard of this man. So eminent was he that the Australians had named a mountain range after him and the chemists – or was it the glaziers – a dish. Mace had dug all over the place, at Abydos, Hiw, Dendera, Giza and Naga-el-Der. He'd joined the Metropolitan Museum twenty-two years ago as assistant Curator of Egyptian Art. He was a man of immense common sense, he told Lestrade, but he had to dash, as he was busy on the first volume of *The Tomb of Tut-Ankh-Amen* and he had to bash out a chapter before the Olivetti's keys became red hot in the midday sun.

That left Lestrade talking to Alfred Lucas. Physically, the Chemist of the Antiquities Service reminded Lestrade of his old friend Rudyard Kipling, with his beetling brows and heavy moustache. Sadly, the man had been born in Manchester Lestrade had ascertained, and had none of Kipling's charisma. He was a friend of Sidney Smith's however, and Lestrade might have need of the man's chemistry set before the case was over.

Henry Burton – 'Call me Harry' – to Lestrade's right, had long ago abandoned his native Lincolnshire for the sunnier climes of Florence. Since the outbreak of war, however, he had been digging about in the Valley of the Kings, first for the rich American Theodore Davis and more recently for Carnarvon. He was the photographer of the expedition and as if to prove it, leaped up from the breakfast table several times to take the odd snap of the team breaking croissants, spreading jam, stirring coffee etc., perhaps to prove to a disbelieving world that archaeologists did it sitting down.

Arthur Callender was a bluff, no-nonsense engineer, recently retired from his post as Manager of the Egypt and Sudan Branch Railway Company. To avoid confusion with Mace in what was an over-abundance of Arthurs, he had taken to calling himself 'Pecky' and the other team members had reluctantly taken it up.

Diagonally across from the ex-Chief Superintendent, wrestling with a particularly recalcitrant piece of toast, sat the bulky, white-suited figure of Alan Henderson Gardiner; decidedly the wrong side of forty-five, if Lestrade was any judge. With that ability he had to make the opening of a boiled egg sound as if it were an event of world interest, Cliff Hanger had introduced Gardiner to Lestrade as the foremost philologist of his generation. Lestrade nodded coolly. After all, a man's religion was his own affair. Of all the breakfasters that morning, Lestrade sensed that this man was the most cut up about the death of Carnarvon.

'Lindsley Foote Hall,' the tall American extended a hand as he came late to the table, 'MIT.'

'Sholto Lestrade.' Lestrade shook it. 'L-e-s-t-r-a-d-e.'

'I'm the expedition's draughtsman.' Hall clicked his fingers for a white-jacketed fellah to pour his coffee. 'What's your position, Mr Lestrade?'

'Mr Lestrade has no position,' the last member of the team said. 'He is merely here to observe.'

All eyes turned to Howard Carter, Carnarvon's Field Director. The man's broken nose, immense chin and drooping moustache gave him a somewhat hangdog appearance. Lestrade had met him briefly the night before. In fact his was the first face he had set eyes on after he woke up from his fall. After a day on a donkey, Lestrade's legs had given out entirely and he had tripped over the animal's reins only to fetch himself a concussing one on a huge lump of scree. A bucket of water, thoughtfully hurled by Carter, had brought him round. The hangdog features had smiled at first, but as soon as Carter learned that Lestrade was in the Valley of the Kings to investigate not one, but two suspicious deaths, his demeanour had changed entirely. Throughout breakfast, while Lestrade took the opportunity to size up the killing capabilities of the tomb team, Carter had been drumming his nervous fingers, first on the trestle table, then on his coffee cup. Finally he'd been carving little hieroglyphs into the table cloth with his knife blade. All the time, his dark, deep-set eyes had swivelled from breakfaster to breakfaster. Until now, he had not said a word.

Now was Lestrade's chance to put that right. 'Mr Carter,' he said. 'Could I have a word?'

The Field Director's moustache twitched irritably. Pecky Callender sensed his old friend's mood and led as dignified an exit as he could. 'Well, I've got some fellas to see,' he announced. 'Lindsley, could you show me those sketches.'

'Sketches?' the tall American was only on his first slurp of coffee. 'Uh – oh, sure, sure, Pecky. Right with you.' And he gulped down the thick, brown, Turkish contents of his cup and snatched up his drawing pad. 'I'd like to get one of you, Mr Lestrade,' he said. 'Just for the record. Perhaps tonight?'

'Oh, I don't think . . .'

'Well, now, don't undersell yourself,' Hall patted the man's shoulder, an earnest expression on his face. 'Whether you think or not, you're a visitor to the tomb. And I'm making a point of sketching all the visitors we get.' He leaned over to Lestrade. 'It'll be a cold day in hell afore the camera takes over from the pencil.' And he stood up again, beaming broadly at Harry Burton, who ignored him.

75

'Did you have a chance to sketch Mr Le Clerk?' Lestrade asked him.

'Sure did. Wanna see?'

Callender cleared his throat.

'Later, Mr Hall,' Lestrade said and the lanky American loped off.

'Harry,' Callender was gesturing at those who were left, 'I'd like a shot or two of the entrance this morning.'

'Another?' Burton was about to light his pipe when he felt it taken from him by the waiter. 'Ah, oh, of course. Right. I'll just get another roll of film.'

'Yes.' Holinshed stood up. 'Cliff, you know your way around. Could I see the entrance? If you're not busy, I mean?'

'Delighted, dear boy.' Hanger stuffed a croissant into his pocket for later.

'Come along, Alfred.' Mace helped the man up. 'I'd like you to have a look at some salts I'm oxidizing.'

Lucas looked blank. 'Very well,' he said. 'Gentlemen, would you excuse us?'

Carter dismissed the waiters with a wave of his hand. He poured another coffee for Lestrade. 'Well,' he said, his quiet voice curiously resonant in the echoing chamber, 'what is it you want, Mr Lestrade?'

'Lord Carvarvon.' Lestrade leaned back, watching his man through experienced, half-closed eyes. It was cool in the corridor and the day was a bright shaft of light from the far end through which the silhouettes of Carter's team were busy vanishing in all directions.

'I fear he is dead,' Carter said.

'Indeed,' Lestrade nodded. 'Malaria, some say.'

'Pneumonia is the official cause on the death certificate.'

'You've seen it?'

'I have.'

Lestrade stirred his coffee. Nuts floated on the surface, sluggishly, like ships caught in the Sargasso Sea. 'That's not conclusive,' he said.

'What do you mean?' Carter's dark eyes faltered.

'The symptoms of pneumonia are very commonplace,' Lestrade told the Field Director. 'They cover a multitude of sins.'

'What do you mean?' Carter asked again.

'There seems to be an echo in here,' Lestrade observed. He leaned forward. 'I mean', he said, 'that in my time I have investigated deaths that were apparently caused by pneumonia. Only to discover that the *real* cause was poisoning.'

'Poisoning?' Carter's knife blade stopped in mid-hieroglyph.

'You were with Lord Carnarvon when he died?'

'No. Not exactly. I'd been with him some hours before.'

'Here at the tomb?'

'Yes.'

'How did he seem?'

'In what way?'

'Was his vision blurred?'

'No; at least he didn't mention it.'

'Was his hearing faulty?'

'What?'

'I said . . .'

'Yes, I know what you said.' Carter slammed the knife down. 'No, I don't think so.'

'Was he thirsty? His skin red?'

'One is always thirsty in the desert, Mr Lestrade. Surely you've been in Egypt long enough to know that. The trick is not to give in to it. And *never* drink water that has not been boiled. The tsetse fly, you see.'

'Was his skin red?' Lestrade persisted.

'Only his cheek,' Carter told him. 'What poison are we talking about, Lestrade?'

The former Chief Superintendent paused, frowning. 'I'm beginning to wonder,' he said. 'You didn't gaze into Lord Carnarvon's eyes, I suppose?'

Carter sighed. 'I worked for the man, Lestrade,' he said, with what little patience he could muster. 'I wasn't having an affair with him.'

'Quite.' Lestrade was anxious to reassure him. 'Quite.'

'He had a headache,' Carter remembered. 'He seemed a little tired, that was all. Nothing in that. We all get it. It's an exhausting business, excavating in this heat.'

'Did Lord Carnarvon actually do the digging?' Lestrade asked.

'Usually, no,' Carter told him. 'Most of the time, he supervised from a mesh cage he'd had built. It's out there, near the entrance. Kept mosquitoes away.'

'Mosquitoes,' Lestrade repeated. 'They carry malaria, don't they?'

Carter stood up sharply. 'Mr Lestrade,' he said, 'the Carnarvon Expedition has lost its captain. Until Almina – Lady Carnarvon – returns from home, *I* must perforce be that captain. I have found the most exciting tomb in the world; in the whole history of archaeology. Forget Schliemann – he made most of it up, anyway. The name of Howard Carter will echo down the years. And I don't need that idiot Hanger to dress it up for me. But,' and he placed both hands on the table as if to steady himself, 'all this will come to pass *only* if I can keep this damned team together, keep the meddling Egyptian government out of what's left of my hair and get into that burial chamber. A simple job, you might think? Don't you believe it! So, if you'll excuse me, I really have better things to do than swap sympton stories with a Scotland Yard detective who's been put out to grass! Good morning!'

And he turned on his heel.

Lestrade was grateful for the relative cool of Alfred Lucas's tent later that morning. The chemist had donned his white coat and his glasses were tilted up on top of his head.

'Ah, Mr Lestrade,' he said, waving a hand for the man to sit down. 'Doing a spot of observing?'

'Investigating.' Lestrade eased himself into the canvas seat. Cleopatra's hump had taken its toll of his lower regions.

'Ah, that sounds exciting.'

'Tell me about mosquitoes,' Lestrade asked.

'Mosquitoes?' Lucas looked up from his microscope. 'Well, that's a little out of my league, but I'll do my best. The most common sort carry anopheles maculipennis, the malaria organism. The female picks it up – pick up anything, some females, won't they? – and the parasite lives in its stomach, forming large cysts. These rupture after a while and the parasites are spewed out into the body cavity, then into the salivary glands.

I say, Lestrade, are you all right? You've turned a rather odd shade of green.'

'The coffee, I think' Lestrade said. 'A few too many nuts in mine.'

'Ah, Egyptian tummy.' Lucas wagged a finger. 'We all get it first time out. Tutmoses's Revenge, the archaeologists call it. You came across the desert, didn't you? Damn brave. Damn brave.'

'So the bite of the mosquito passes the malaria organism on to a person?'

'Hey presto!' said Lucas, fiddling with his slides. 'Other species spread yellow fever – that's the most common species over here, of course; Aedes Aegypti. Others – Culex Fatigans, I believe – carry elephantiasis. Come to think of it, they're little buggers, aren't they? If Gibbon is to be believed, they wiped out the Roman Empire, you know. Or was that emperors copulating with their sisters? Anyway, it was something like that. Oh Lor', you're talking about Lord C aren't you?'

'They say he was bitten by a mosquito.'

'Entirely possible,' Lucas said. 'We all are from time to time. But he died from pnenmonia.'

'How do you know?'

'His death certificate said so.'

'And you have faith in that?'

'I have faith in science,' Lucas told him. 'Anyway, I've had long chats with Johnson, the family physician. The man's perfectly competent, I would say.'

'And the symptoms of malaria are not those of pneumonia?'

'Lord, no. Well, come to think of it, some of them are. Sweating, dry skin, intense headache. Nothing pulmonary, though. And of course with malaria, you get rigor and vomiting.'

'Did Lord Carnarvon vomit?'

'I really don't know. I wasn't there. Look, my dear chap, I don't wish to be rude or anything, but I don't think the British public wants to read this sort of sensationalism, whatever newspaper you write for.'

'I don't write for any newspaper,' Lestrade said. 'Not even the *Police Gazette*.'

'Eh?'

'I'm attached to Scotland Yard.'

'Good Lor'. I say!'

'Tell me, Mr Lucas, are Lord Carnarvon's things here? In the camp, I mean?'

'Yes, most of them, I believe. Some of course he took to Aswan with him.'

'Do you know if his razor is here?'

'Have a look for yourself. Howard Carter was in the process of parcelling up his personal effects and posting them to Lady C back home. Out there.' He pointed to a large black tent some way from the others. 'That's Lord C's. Help yourself. By the way, you haven't happened upon my glasses, have you? I could have sworn I had them here a moment ago.' Lucas was rummaging among his souvenirs.

'On top of your head.' Lestrade made for the exit.

'Eh? Oh Lor', yes. Er . . . glad you spotted that one, Lestrade. Well done. If I can be of any further assistance?'

Lestrade paused in the tent-flap. 'If I find a cut-throat razor with the crest of a gryphon, then you most certainly can, Mr Lucas,' he said.

Night lent an eerie silence to the Valley of the Kings. The great, bleak outcrops were black and ominous, looming over the little storm lanterns of Carter's camp, like tiny stationary fireflies on the Valley floor. The temperature fell through the cool of the evening to the near-freezing of midnight.

Lindsley Foote Hall was in his ante-room, the hastily erected shed glowing with a livid blue light by which he sketched after dark. Lestrade wrapped his thin serge around him. His long Bedouin cloak he'd left with Mustapha and Cleopatra at Luxor. He could have done with it now. What ridiculous weather. It was never like this in Virginia Water. He rapped on Hall's door.

'Just a second,' an American voice called from within. 'I'm roughing in at the moment.'

Lestrade raised an eyebrow. He couldn't possibly interrupt that. Then, there was a scuffling of furniture inside and the dry rattle of bolts being undone.

'Ah, Mr Lestrade. Welcome.'

'It's rather late, I'm afraid,' the ex-Chief Superintendent apologized.

'Nah, don't think anything of it.' Hall ushered him into the tiny two-roomed hut. 'It's a bit of a squeeze, I'm afraid. Would you like some bourbon?'

'If that remotely resembles brandy, I'd love some.'

Hall reached down a dark bottle labelled 'Poison' and poured them both three fingers' worth. 'I'll swear I don't know how these Moslem guys manage without the old hair o' the dog. May you buy up all the sketches!' He raised his glass in a toast.

'Good digging.' Lestrade did likewise.

'Well, sit you down. I guess this is what you came to see.' And Hall tossed a drawing into Lestrade's lap.

'Alain Le Clerk?'

'To the life,' Hall nodded.

Lestrade took in the topi, the paunch, the cravat. 'He looks better here than when I saw him last.'

'Oh? And where was that?'

'In Cairo Mortuary.'

'Ah. The end of the line, huh? Say, what did the autopsy reveal?'

'The . . . er . . .?'

'Er . . . post-mortem I guess you'd call it in England.'

'I'm afraid I don't know . . .'

'Uh-huh.' Hall wagged a finger at Lestrade. 'You may be able to fool the others that you're an archaeologist or reporter or whatever, but you're a detective. Trust me, fella, I know. Got a brother-in-law in the FBI. Guy just can't help himself. You buy a new canvas and he wants to know how much tax you paid on it. You go to the ballet and he asks if there were any Undesirables in the audience. It's in the blood, I guess.'

Lestrade chuckled. 'I guess . . . suppose it is,' he said. 'All right, Mr Hall, I'm attached to Scotland Yard.'

'Yeah,' the draughtsman nodded. 'I'm kinda fond of it, too. Drew some pics in London last year. 'Course it rained every goddamn day. So, why your interest in Le Clerk?'

'As I expect your brother-in-law would say, "I'll ask the questions" if you don't mind, Mr Hall.'

The American shrugged. 'Well, aside from the fact that my

81

brother-in-law doesn't call me Mr Hall, yeah; you got that one right. OK. Fire away.'

'When did you make that drawing?'

'Er . . . let me see.' Hall rolled his glass between his fingers and stared at the sketch-strewn ceiling for inspiration. 'Last Thursday. The day he arrived at the camp. He only stayed one day.'

'Not overnight?'

'No.'

'Is that usual with visitors to the tomb?'

'It varies,' Hall told him. 'It depends on how they got here. How many of 'em there are. And how interested in archaeology they are.'

There was something in Hall's tone, something in the way he pursed his lips.

'By which you mean?' Lestrade asked.

'Let me show you something, Mr Lestrade.' Hall rummaged in a sideboard drawer to his left and pulled out an object, wrapped in sacking. 'Take a look.'

Lestrade took it. It lay heavy in his hand. He unwrapped the cloth to reveal a gold statuette of an Egyptian, his arms crossed over his breast, his eyes flashing with red stones.

'Solid gold,' Hall said, with more gravel in his voice than in the Valley outside the hut. 'The stones are cornelian. That little trinket I tend to use as a paperweight. The fact is it's three and a half thousand years old and at today's market prices for gold, it's worth a little over five thousand dollars. That's about ten years' wages for my brother-in-law in the FBI and forty years' wages for the fellahin who found it.'

'I don't follow your drift, Mr Hall.' Lestrade handed the little Pharaoh back.

'This is a ką,' Hall said, putting his glass down and stroking the statuette lovingly. 'The spirit of the dead king Tut-Ankh-Amen whose grave we are now plundering. There were several others in the antechamber. You see, we're all grave robbers, Mr Lestrade. Oh, most of the tombs in this Valley were robbed centuries ago, probably by the guys who built them. Rich Egyptians had a silly habit of parading all these goodies through the streets on the way to the burial chamber. It's likely some dishonest priest or architect left the seals open on the stone block that covered the entrance. And – whammo! A few days later, it's Christmas for any fellahin with a bit of get up and go. Fort Knox is only tricky because as yet no one's been able to buy the guy with the key. And for thousands of years, people have been trying to get inside the vaults again. Just in case. In case one's been missed. And it had. No one had found the tomb of Tut-Ankh-Amen until Howard Carter did it six months ago. And when he did; when that candle lit up that solid wall of gold, the chariots, the statues, the canopic jars, man, that was some hornet's nest!'

'There was a hornet's nest in the tomb?'

'Er . . . no,' Hall frowned. 'I was speaking metaphorically, Mr Lestrade. My point is that we've got what the whole darn world wants – the treasure of the Pharaohs. We get whole charabancs out from Luxor and Karnak, even from Cairo and Alexandria, to gape at a hole in the desert. I guess about ten per cent are really interested. The other ninety have come to see what they can buy, scrounge or steal. We've got two newspaper guys here – Merton of *The Times* and Weigall of the *Mail* – not to mention that shithead Hanger, that PR man. It's sorta difficult to keep a secret when you've got guys shouting with loudhailers from the rooftops, "Gold! Gold!" I tell ya, Mr Lestrade, it's like California and the Forty-Niners all over again.'

'And Mr Le Clerk?' Lestrade said. 'Did he come to rob the grave?'

'Like I said; in a manner of speaking, we all have. The native Indians from my homeland believed that if the white man took their photograph, he was stealing their soul. Maybe that's what Harry Burton's doing by photographing Tut-Ankh-Amen and his grave goods and what I'm doing by drawing them.'

'Did you know Le Clerk?'

'Only by reputation.' Hall refilled their glasses. 'An arrogant sonofabitch by all accounts; but then, you show me an archaeologist who isn't. Must've been kinda lonely out here, though.'

'Lonely?'

'Well,' Hall closed to his man, 'he had a reputation as something of a ladies' man.'

'Really?' Lestrade checked Hall's drawing again.

'Oh, I know, he's no Adonis. But it was rumoured he had a second family in Palermo, a third in Ankara and a fourth in

Akron, Ohio. Look-ee here.' Hall dragged down a weighty tome from his shelves. He riffled through the pages. 'There.' He jabbed a finger down on a photograph of a carefully posed group under the Great Pyramid of Cheops. 'Pretty girl number one.'

She was sitting apparently on Le Clerk's knee. Lestrade couldn't quite see where his right hand was. The other one was draped around the neck of a camel.

'And here.' Hall whizzed on through several erudite chapters. 'Pretty girl number two.' This time he was standing behind an Egyptian girl, beaming over her shoulder. Neither of his hands was visible this time. Lestrade read the caption: 'The great French Egyptologist and friend. Gizeh 1909'.

'Not to mention this one.' Hall reached up for another book and expertly found the relevant page.

Lestrade peered at it. 'Looks like a bloke,' he said. 'A bit effeminate, perhaps, but a bloke none the less.'

'What?' Hall squinted sideways, tilting his head. 'Oh, yeah, that's T. E. Lawrence in his Arab period. No, the other side.'

'I can't tell under the veil.'

'Take it from me, she's all woman. That's the second youngest daughter of King Faisal – the Catherine the Great of Mesopotamia. If Le Clerk was shafting her at the time, believe me, he'd have had to have had the stamina of a mountain goat.'

'Why are you telling me all this, Mr Hall?' Lestrade asked.

The draughtsman leaned back, grinning broadly. 'Because a dick from Scotland Yard doesn't come snooping around if a guy falls off his horse. You think he was murdered, don't you? Well, a guy with wandering hands like Alain "I'm Hung Like A Donkey" Le Clerk picks up quite a few enemies along the way – husbands, fathers, brothers; maybe even sons – I never heard he was *that* choosy. Any one could've fixed his saddle, sawed through his cinch. It'd be easy.'

'No doubt it would,' Lestrade finished his drink, 'except that he didn't die by falling off his horse.'

'No?'

'No. He died by poisoning.'

'No kidding?'

Lestrade took in Hall's open-mouthed expression. 'Never mind, Mr Hall,' he smiled at the doorway, the dangling drawings fluttering in the night wind, 'however Mr Le Clerk died, someone in this camp knows more than they're telling. Thanks for the drink. I'll see myself out.'

The glow of dawn was already in the sky to the east as he crossed the white paths that led back to the tent he shared with Jack Holinshed. Mercifully, the man didn't snore, but then, having spent two nights under the stars with Mustapha and his camels, Lestrade would look on every night to come as a bonus.

He really must see a doctor when he got back to Cairo, he told himself. Do something about that ringing in his ears. Come to think of it, that ringing sounded familiar. Had a ring to it, in fact. It couldn't be, of course, but it sounded for all the world like 'I Wish I Could Shimmy Like My Sister Kate', the smash hit of 1922. It sounded even more like it as he rounded a spoil heap and saw a glow coming from a hole in the ground, yards away across the shale.

Drawn to it like a magnet, Lestrade peered down the flight of uneven stone steps. There was a new concrete lintel holding up the roof above it, but there was definitely a faint light through the door at the bottom and the muffled ragtime tune seemed louder here. There was no one in sight. The small army of fellahin, engaged all day in hauling rocks and sieving sand under the merciless sun, were huddled under canvas, already pointing to the east for morning prayers. Somewhere, a camp dog whined and turned over in its sleep, chasing hares under its moon of dreams. Lestrade could see Hanger's Ford and Carter's Oakland axle deep in the white sand. The sand that choked and burned and stung. But there were no guards. For all that Lestrade stood on the edge of the greatest find in the history of archaeology, no one challenged him; no one called 'Who goes?' So down he went.

The walls were white with granite dust, scarred with ancient chisels and the steps threw him inexorably to the left. It came as no surprise to anyone but Lestrade therefore when his forehead collided with the corner of the concrete lintel and he took two paces sideways before his vision cleared again. Ahead of him stretched a bleak corridor, its walls as scarred as those he'd just passed. The glowing light was brighter through an opening at the far end, and that clearly was where the scratchy tune was coming from. It was cold down here, like ice in the dead of night, before the dawn, and Lestrade moved quickly, flapping his arms to keep his circulation going. The thud of his own heart was louder than his feet on the earth floor and try though he might, he could not match the rhythm of the music.

He ducked through an open doorway and found himself in a room, perhaps twelve feet wide and twice as long. There was a small, black doorway diagonally to his left and in the centre, near to where he now stood, a single oil lamp burned on a solitary table and beside it a gramophone, its needle slowing now as the black, spinning record began to reach the end of its momentum.

But it was not these signs of life that gripped Lestrade, but the signs of death. To his right, their white eyes glowing in the oil lamp's flicker, stood two black figures, dressed in gold. Serpents coiled on their heads and they loomed over Lestrade, their legs thrust forward. For a moment, as a draught caught the flame, it looked for all the world as if they were walking towards him. Then he heard a familiar click and felt a cold muzzle nuzzle his left ear.

'One more step towards that door, Mr Lestrade,' a husky voice said, 'and I'll blow your brains all over the wall.'

'Can't we be adult about this?' Lestrade asked, his hands reaching for the ceiling instinctively. Time was he would have risked a lightning swing to his left, deflecting the gun and following through with a fist or his trusty brass knuckles. Now, he was the wrong side of sixty-seven – well, all right, sixty-eight – and his knuckles lay in his jacket pocket. He just didn't have the velocity any more.

'They don't come much more adult than you, do they?' the voice croaked. Lestrade felt powerful hands frisk his pockets, jacket, the trousers. Either this man was good or the ex-Chief Superintendent's luck had changed. 'Well, well,' the frisker had found the knuckles, 'oo-er.' Lestrade heard a click. The frisker had found the secret button that flicked out the switch-blade from the brass grip.

'All right,' the growler said. 'Now you turn very slowly to your left. *Very* slowly, mind you. Excessive speed can cause my trigger finger to tremble.'

Lestrade did what all good coppers are supposed to do – what he was told. In front of him stood a small, wiry man, in the khaki uniform of a British soldier, sergeant's stripes on both sleeves. His shorts reached to his knees and his long socks came thickly up to them from below. Still, with the temperature down here, who could blame him? Lestrade saw his own breath curl out.

'Can I put my hands down?' he asked.

'I don't see why not,' the Sergeant said, but he had not lowered the .38 Webley an iota. 'You will observe a chair to your left front. Would you like to sit on it while you tell me what the bugger you're doin' down here?'

'Thank you, Sergeant . . . er . . .?'

'*Actin'* Sergeant, if you must know,' the Acting Sergeant said. 'Actin' Sergeant Adamson. Didn't the buggers upstairs mention me at all?'

'Er . . . no.' Lestrade eased himself down. 'Perhaps it slipped their minds.'

'Very likely.' Adamson eased back the revolver's hammer. 'On the assumption they've got any. Minds, that is.' Mercifully, he pulled the stylus off the record. 'Vodka?'

'Why not?' Lestrade allowed himself to relax a little.

'There are prob'ly lots of reasons,' Adamson holstered the gun and jerked the cork out of a bottle with uneven teeth. 'For one, it could kill a bloke of your age. Still, we've all got to go some time. No, I'll tell you why them up there didn't mention me. It's because they're all bloody snobs, that's why. That an' the fact that I'm a Communist.'

'A Bolshevik?' Lestrade frowned.

'We comrades prefer the word Communist nowadays.' Adamson poured for both of them. 'Bolshevik is a little par say in the world of international brinkmanship. Now that Comrade Lenin is standin' down, we'll see what this bloke Comrade Stalin is made of.'

'Steel, I understood,' Lestrade said.

'Yeah, well, that's a load o' propaganda bollocks, innit? So, what's an ex-guardian of the Imperialist bourgeoisie doin' down 'ere?'

'I'm beginning to wonder,' Lestrade said. 'I saw your light; heard your music. Couldn't resist it, I suppose.'

'So you're from Scotland Yard, eh?' Adamson's nostrils flared as the first slug of vodka hit his tonsils. 'Knockin' on a bit, aintja?'

'Ah, but I'm cheap,' Lestrade said.

'No, no, comrade. Nyet. Nyet. You don't wanna sell yourself short. If you got nuffink to offer but the labour of your body and the sweat of your brow, make the bastards pay for it, mate. That's what I say. You know my ol' man 'elped to build that place, dontja?'

Adamson was jabbing the chill air with his finger. Surely he couldn't mean the door of the tomb behind Lestrade? Just how mad did you have to be to watch a grave all night? 'The Yard,' the Acting Sergeant went on. ''Course, it was gonna be a wossname, wannit? An opera 'ouse. Yerse, somewhere in the rough granite of its grandiloquent grossness lies the sweat, blood and tears of my ol' dad, Arfur Adamson. 'E 'ad a right go at you blokes on Bloody Sunday, y'know.'

'Did he now?' Lestrade arched an eyebrow. He remembered the day well. And he had only just lived to tell about it. 'And where is he now? Buried in Highgate, next to Comrade Marx?'

'No,' Adamson frowned. ''E's in the Remains of the Day 'Ome for the 'Opelessly Elderly at Stoke Newington. Still gorra mind like a bloody Gillette, of course.'

'Of course. Tell me, Sergeant, what lies beyond that stone door?' Lestrade jerked his thumb behind him.

'What many men would kill for,' Adamson told him, topping up Lestrade's untouched vodka and pouring another for himself. 'The tomb of Tut-Ankh-Amen 'Isself. Next month, ol' Misery Drawers up there's gonna open it up. Only 'e's 'ad a peek in.'

'Haven't you?' Lestrade asked.

'Nah,' Adamson shrugged. 'Bores me rigid, archaeology. I'm only here against the day.'

'The day?'

'The blessed day when we of the Lumpenproletariat, the 'Uddled Masses rise up and overthrow them bourgeois bastards upstairs. You're not of the faith, I suppose, bein' a copper an' all?'

'Liberal, I'm afraid,' Lestrade apologized.

'Waste of a ballot paper,' Adamson assured him.

'What did you make of Lord Carnarvon?' the ex-Chief Superintendent asked.

'Imperialist lackey,' Adamson dismissed him. 'But as a bloke 'e was all right. Always perfectly civil to me. 'E got me this job, as a matter of fact. I was wanderin' around Cairo tryin' to spread the word of the Dialectic, and getting arrested and moved on all the time.'

'No luck with the Dialectic?'

'Wrong dialect, I suppose. Load o' ignorant Wogs just looked at me like I was a bloody Conservative. Well, I ask ya . . .'

'Who killed him, Mr Adamson?' Lestrade's eyes burned into the blank, open face of the Acting Sergeant.

''Oo killed 'oo?' Adamson wanted to know.

'Lord Carnarvon.'

'Nah, mate, you've got it wrong,' the Sergeant chuckled. 'Act of God, was that. Not that we Communists acknowledge such an élitist and autocratic Bein'. Nah, 'e got bit by a mosquito. There's bloody millions of 'em out 'ere. I don't rate your chances o' findin' the one responsible. Not now.'

'You're wrong, Adamson,' Lestrade said. 'I've been sniffing around murders now, man and boy, for more years than your Comrade Lenin has had International Rallies. Carnarvon's death is a cover-up. Why, I don't know. But I know he didn't die of natural causes.'

'Well, stick a whizz bang up my arse!' was the Sergeant's natural rejoinder. 'It's old Surly Bollocks, then. 'Oward Carter.'

'Carter?' Lestrade sipped his vodka and felt the tips fly off his ears. 'Why do you say that?'

'They quarrelled,' Adamson said. 'I've 'eard 'em. Down 'ere of a night. "Go up for a fag, Adamson", "Stretch your legs, Acting Sergeant", and once I've gone, they're at it, 'ammer and sickle. No love lost there, believe you me.'

'What were these rows about?'

'I dunno. The tomb, I suppose. Marvellous, innit? Lord Acton was bloody right when 'e said "Power corrupts". As long as Carter 'n' Carnarvon was findin' bits of crocodile shit, they was mates. Couldn't do enuff for each other. Then, when they find the big one – boom! Not so much as a kiss my arse. Yeah. You take my word for it. If somebody done in ol' Lord C, it was

'Oward Sourpuss Carter. Carter the Martyr, I call 'im. Got more moods than a leper's got spots, 'e 'as. I tell ya,' and he patted his revolver butt, '*I* wouldn't turn my back on 'im.'

'What about Le Clerk, the Frenchman?'

'Nah,' Adamson shook his head, "e wasn't 'ere.'

'No, I mean who killed him?'

"Im too? Bloody 'ell. Wass goin' on? I mean, I'm a ratepayer. What are you blokes doin' about all these murders?'

'Carrying out my enquiries,' Lestrade answered. 'Do you have any theories?'

'Well.' Adamson pursed his lips. 'Frog, wannee? Egyptians don't like 'em, 'cos they ruled over the poor buggers for years, then built the Canal and buggered off. Us British don't like 'em 'cos they was bloody useless in the Great War. Mutinyin' at Verdun all the bloody time. An' anyway, they're foreign. I don't suppose the Yanks are all that crazy about 'em eiver. So, really, it's any bugger's guess, ain't it? Blimey, mate, I don't envy you your job. Could be any one of a million blokes.'

Lestrade left his drink where it was and stood up, sighing. 'Thank you, you've been very helpful. Good-night. And I wish you joy, Adamson.'

And as his footsteps echoed down the corridor that led to the steps and the night, he heard the Acting Sergeant crank up the gramophone to the strains of the Red Flag.

No one was really ready for the apparition that came out of the Eastern Desert a little after breakfast the next day. Lestrade had spent several hours in the tents of the late Lord Carnarvon, painstakingly going over the great man's correspondence, checking his underwear for anything suspicious and so on. Bearing in mind that the late Lord had presumably taken his toiletries with him, first to Luxor, then to Aswan, then to Cairo, the ex-Chief Superintendent was a little surprised to find a monogrammed, ivory-hilted razor among the Earl's effects. Drawing a blank elsewhere, he passed it to Alfred Lucas, with specific instructions to check every nook and cranny of the thing.

Lestrade was just crossing back to the breakfast room when three lorries lurched into the camp, belching sand in all directions. A large man raised his broad-brimmed white fedora to all and sundry. The long-suffering fellahin were used to tourists. The ones who came up-country were not the generous ones of Cairo and Alexandria and Karnak. They kept their hands firmly in their pockets. And anyway, had not Carter Pasha threatened the sack to any fellah asking for baksheesh?

'Hey, buddy,' the big man called, thudding off the lorry's running board. 'Would you be Howard Carter, by any chance?'

'Well, I'd need quite a bit of persuading,' Lestrade said. 'I think you'll find him having breakfast. Over there.'

'Gee, buddy.' The newcomer removed the biggest Havana Lestrade had ever seen from between his lips. Its ash trembled down his immense white waistcoat. 'Is that a tomb?'

'I believe so.'

'Ah, so you're an archaeologist too, huh? Say,' he grabbed Lestrade's arm, 'is that *the* tomb? The resting place of King Tut? Oh, boy, just wait 'til I tell Mildred about this. She wanted to come, you know. But I knew she wouldn't cope with the heat an' all. Man, next to this, downtown Dallas is cool. Oh, I'm Aaron G. String the Third, by the way.' He shook Lestrade's hand warmly. 'Glad to have yuh know me, Mr . . . er . . .?'

'Lestrade. Sholto J. Lestrade – the first, I suspect.'

'Ah,' String patted Lestrade's shallow cheek. 'You ain't just whistling Dixie, bub. Ah jest *love* that cosy accent. See yuh around, Sholto.'

Lestrade had the perfect opportunity to skip breakfast, especially if it meant he had to fight for elbow room with the big Texan. However, he was on the trail of a murderer and men could let things slip at breakfast that they might not when fully awake and on their guard.

'Yessiree,' String assured the team several times over his ham and eggs, carried in special airtight containers on his back-up truck. 'Railways is the name o' the game. Goddam, Howie, ah could build yuh one right here. Man, yuh could clean up tourist-wise. Waddya say?'

Carter scowled at his new and uninvited guest. 'I say I have a lot of work to do. Please keep your fellahin away from the workings, Mr String. This is a dangerous place.'

'Oh, sure, sure. Say, who's in charge of publicity around here?'

'Er . . . that's me,' Hanger said.

'Er . . . Cliff, ain't it?'

Hanger nodded.

'Right. Right. OK Cliff, let's get some pictures with Lindsley here. Harry, boy, you're the photographer, right? Go get your camera, fella. I'll watch the birdie.' He squeezed his fellow American to him. 'Y'know, fer a Yankee, you're a good ol' boy.'

'Thanks,' Hall grimaced. The Massachusetts Institute of Technology had not prepared him for his fellow countrymen like this – whirlwinds in white suits.

'Say, you got a guy from the *Dallas Mouthpiece* here? Only, I figure the folks back home'd drop down dead to see this place!'

The next visitor was all the more anonymous, slipping into camp as the deadly sun sank over the silent guardians of the Valley.

'I am told you are from Scotland Yard,' he said, pulling up a canvas chair alongside Lestrade's. The ex-Chief Superintendent looked at the man by the light of the crackling camp fire. He was thirty or so, with a shock of black hair and dark eyes. He could easily have passed for an Egyptian, but his accent told Lestrade that he was French.

'I am Emil Lamartine,' he said, flashing a warrant card. 'Of ze Sûreté.'

'Sholto Lestrade,' Lestrade said.

'And I am no relation, if you are wondering.'

'Relation?'

'To ze great French poet of ze same name.'

Lestrade didn't know any French poets, called Emil or anything else for that matter. 'I see,' he said.

'I am 'ere to investigate ze death of ze late, great Aegyptologiste, Monsieur le Clerk.'

'So am I,' said Lestrade.

'But 'e was a Frenchman,' Lamartine pointed out, flipping away his warrant card. 'You 'ave no jurisdiction out 'ere. It is a matter for ze Consulat Français.'

'It is a matter for whoever was on the scene first. That was me.'

'I see. I see. Well, perhaps we can . . . er . . .'ow you say, work togezzer, huh?'

'Perhaps,' Lestrade nodded.

'Well, what do you know?'

'The square on the hypoteneuse is equal to the sum of the squares on the other two sides.'

The Frenchman looked blank, then sat bolt upright. 'Monsieur Le Strade. Your name, it is a legend at the Sûreté.'

'It is?'

'To ze detectives of my grandfather's generation, *oui*. But times 'ave changed. I expected better from your 'ands. 'Ave you never 'eard of the Entente Cordiale?'

'I have,' Lestrade assured him, 'and I don't care for it very much. Rather sickly, I find.'

'Well zen,' Lamartine tried a new tack, 'as one professional to anozzer, will you not 'elp me? I 'ave been sent out 'ere by my Consulate. Zis . . .' his dark eyes faltered. 'If you must know, zis is my first murder case.'

'Is it?' Lestrade blew smoke rings to the lapis lazuli of the sky. He couldn't remember the details of his first case. But he remembered that he'd vomited at the sight of the corpse. And he remembered something else. How lonely he'd felt. Uniformed constables. Relatives of the deceased, in deepest mourning. Donegalled superiors at the Yard. They all had one thing in common. They were looking at him – at him for the answers. And at the time, he didn't have any. 'Well, well,' he smiled. 'All right. What little I know, you can have. But not here. There is a saying in my country, Mr Lamartine, that walls have ears.'

'Ah, *oui*, I know it.'

'Well, in this country, you don't need walls. Spoil heaps, oil lamps, even grains of sand listen in to conversations.'

There was a guffaw of laughter from Lindsley Foote Hall's tent, where Aaron G. String was entertaining; or at least, he thought he was.

5

Emil and the detective sat huddled in Lestrade's new quarters. Actually 'quarters' was a rather grandiose term for the no-up, one-down tent Carter had reluctantly lent him. 'Sixteenths' might be more appropriate. It was, however, better than sharing with Jack Holinshed. All right, so the man didn't snore, but the pair of them did spend most of the night wrestling each other for the mosquito net.

'First,' Lestrade said, 'tell me what you know about the late Le Clerk.'

'A first-class brain from ze Sorbonne,' Lamartine told him. 'Following in ze footsteps of ze even later Champoléon, 'e specialized in ze *archéologie* of Egypt. So impassioned was 'e zat 'e only broke off for ze last year of ze war. 'E was something classified in Intelligence.'

'Did he have a family?'

'*Oui*. Several. 'E was – 'ow you say – a bigamist.'

'Isn't that illegal?' Lestrade frowned.

'*Non*, Monsieur,' Lamartine explained, straight-faced. 'It is French. We 'ave 'ad no less than five women at ze Consulate in Cairo over ze last few days, sobbing uncontrollably all over ze Consul.'

'How awkward for him.'

'Not really,' Lamartine shrugged. ''E is, after all, a Frenchman too. Madame Le Consul is used to 'is late 'ours. I need to know 'ow M. Le Clerk died.'

'At first everybody assumed from a fall from a horse. I gather he wasn't much of a rider.'

'I told you,' Lamartine said. ''E was in ze Intelligence, not ze Cavalry. Saumur would never 'ave accepted 'im.'

'He left here, as far as I've been able to gather, quite late on Thursday night.'

'What time?'

'Quite late,' Lestrade repeated, louder this time. 'About ten.'

'Zat is odd.'

'Why?'

''Ow long 'ave you been out 'ere, M. Le Strade?'

'In the Valley of the Kings, two days. In Egypt, about a thousand years.'

'Zen you know zat night is ze Winter of ze Tropics. M. Le Clerk knew it too. Odd zat a man would take off into ze icy darkness by a mode of transport wiz which 'e was less than 'appy.'

Lestrade was impressed. But then, his own contemporary at the Sûreté was the great Goron. The Sûreté invariably impressed.

''Oo did 'e talk to?'

'Virtually everybody,' Lestrade said. 'Obviously, he spent most of his days here with Howard Carter.'

'And what does zis Carter say about ze visit?'

'Not a lot,' Lestrade shrugged. 'They discussed the tomb, of course, and Carter took him down there. Not that there's much to see now. Two reasonably amazing statues and an armed Bolshevik is all you get until they open up the burial chamber itself.'

'Was M. Le Clerk disappointed not to zee inside zat?' Lamartine asked.

'If he was, he didn't say as much to Carter. He does seem to have left rather smartish, though.'

'Zmartische?'

'Er . . . quickly. In a hurry. Perhaps you're right about the horse. Turned into a real night mare, didn't it?'

There was a knock at Lestrade's tent flap – if the sound of a fist on canvas can be called a knock.

'Come in,' the ex-Yard man called.

'Oh, I'm sorry,' Harry Burton's head appeared through the hole. 'I didn't realize you had company.'

'That's all right,' Lestrade beckoned the photographer in. 'Mr Burton, allow me to present Mr Lamartine, of the Sûreté.'

'The Sûreté of Paris, France?' Burton checked. He'd been too long in the company of Aaron String.

'Is zere any ozzer?' Lamartine was appalled, but he stood up to shake the man's hand anyway.

'Mr Burton is the Tut-Ankh-Amen team's photographer,' Lestrade said.

'I'll need one of you come morning, Mr Lamartine,' Burton smiled. 'Light's a bit tricky right now. Talking of which, Lestrade, I came across one I took of Le Clerk. I know you've seen Lindsley's sketches, but, frankly, from the day they invented the camera, painting was dead.'

He passed a photograph to Lestrade. It showed the great Egyptologist standing apart from the group. Carter was there, looking surly, Arthur Mace and Alan Gardiner. There were two men Lestrade did not know and a woman.

'Who are these?' he asked.

Burton craned his neck, 'That's Merton, the *Times* correspondent.' He pointed an elegant, chromium-stained finger. 'At the far side is Weigall, his opposite number from the *Daily Mail*. There's a marriage born in hell.'

'Oh?'

Burton looked at Lestrade. 'Lord Carnarvon was rash enough to give the exclusive of the tomb's excavation to *The Times*. Well, that's all very well, I suppose; unless you work for the *Mail*. I tell you, Lestrade, I didn't know what a bitch was until I met those two.'

'Where are they now?'

'Up-country. At a place called Abu Simbel.'

'They don't get on, yet they travel together?'

'Like a man with a squint,' Burton said. 'One eyeball's constantly watching the other, checking what he's up to. The irony is of course that Arthur Weigall is an archaeologist in his own right. He's no newspaper man, but I suppose the *Mail* thought they'd use a local who knew one end of a sarcophagus from another.'

"Oo is zis woman?' Lamartine asked.

'Yes,' Burton frowned. 'I'm sorry I didn't get a better one of her. That's the only one there is. She came with Le Clerk, or at any rate, I assumed so. She's a Mrs . . .' he checked the back of the print, 'Ralph. English, apparently.'

'Le Clerk doesn't seem to have his hands over her bottom,'

96

Lestrade observed. It was a far cry from all the other photos of the dead man that he'd seen.

'What?'

'Lindsley Hall showed me earlier snaps of Le Clerk – on other digs. He appears to have been in flagrant with a woman in all of them.'

'Oh well,' Burton remembered. 'Le Clerk was all over Mrs Ralph at first. She stuck to him like glue while Howard was showing them round. By nightfall, he was standing apart from her, as in the photo. When we ate, he deliberately moved away; changed seats to avoid her. Perhaps she had a personal problem, but I found her charming.'

'You talked to her?'

'Certainly. She didn't actually go down into the tomb with Howard and Le Clerk. She had an eye infection. Wore dark glasses all the time. I think perhaps . . . well, I don't know.'

'Speculum, then,' Lestrade suggested.

'Pardon?'

'Tell us what you think,' Lestrade made it easy for him.

'Well, perhaps Le Clerk had tried it on. And perhaps Mrs Ralph wasn't having any. He was the type, God knows.'

'Was she?' Lestrade said, almost to himself. 'When did she leave? Not with him, presumably.'

'No. The next morning, I think. Hanger drove her to Luxor.'

'And she didn't find it odd that Le Clerk had gone without her?'

'You must understand, Lestrade,' Burton said, 'that out here, lightning romances are as common – and as short-lived – as desert storms. There's an atmosphere, a madness if you like, that creates a certain chemistry between some men and some women. That chemistry comes and goes. I got the distinct impression that Mrs Ralph was a woman of the world. A lady of great refinement, I'd say.'

There was another knock at the tent flap. It was Alfred Lucas's turn to poke his head around the canvas. 'Oh, I'm sorry,' he said. 'Or shall we make up a foursome for Bridge?'

'I was just going.' Lamartine clambered to his feet. 'It 'as been a long day. *Au revoir*, gentlemen.'

There were mutterings of good-night. Then Lestrade and Lucas stood staring at Burton. 'Ah, right.' The tall photographer sensed when three was a crowd. 'Well, I think I'll turn in. Looks as though I'll be playing host to that String fellow tomorrow morning. I don't think Howard's taken much of a shine to him and I know Lindsley's had enough. See you chaps in the morning.'

Lestrade didn't like the earnest look on Lucas's face. 'Can I offer you a drink?' he asked. 'Jack Holinshed rustled up some brandy from somewhere.'

'Thanks.' Lucas sat down heavily. 'I suppose you have a sixth sense about these things.'

'What? Brandy?'

'Murder.'

Lestrade paused in mid-pour. 'Perhaps you'd better explain, Mr Lucas,' he said.

The chemist did. He pulled an ivory-handled razor from his pocket and opened the business end. 'I ran the tests you wanted,' he said, staring at the Carnarvon crest in the green light of the storm lantern.

'And?'

'Nothing at first,' Lucas said. 'The blade was clean. Carefully wiped, I should imagine.'

'But?'

'Here.' Lucas pointed to the groove in the handle. 'In here I found minute traces of scopalamine.'

Lestrade handed the man his drink. 'That's a new one on me,' he confessed.

'Perhaps you know it better as hyoscine,' Lucas gulped gratefully at the brandy. 'Hyoscyamus Niger, a relative of deadly nightshade.'

'Henbane,' Lestrade said levelly.

'It grows all over the Nile Delta,' Lucas said.

'I know,' Lestrade nodded. 'Dr Smith told me.'

'You've met Sidney?' Lucas brightened. 'He's a stout fellow.'

Lestrade didn't remember Smith being particularly obese, but it *was* darkish in the Cairo mortuary.

'The stuff is absorbed through mucous membranes,' Lucas said, 'but also through the skin. Carnarvon had a mosquito bite;

in Egypt, that's commonplace, and leads to local irritation – no more. But if the blade of his razor was smeared with scopalamine . . . as little as a quarter of a grain could do it.'

'Crippen used a half,' Lestrade murmured.

'Who?'

'Oh, a case of a colleague of mine,' Lestrade said. 'A mousy little man who made two mistakes. He married the wrong woman and he misunderstood the action of quicklime on the body.'

'Easily done,' Lucas nodded grimly, though he perfectly understood the action of quicklime.

'Tell me, Mr Lucas,' Lestrade took the deadly razor from his man, 'did Lord Carnarvon drink?'

'No more than anybody else,' Lucas shrugged. 'Why?'

'What about Le Clerk?'

'I don't know. I believe he had wine with his meal when he visited us. At least, I wasn't aware of his refusing. I don't follow your line of questioning.'

'What about women?' Lestrade probed. 'Was Lord Carnarvon a ladies' man?'

'Lord C?' Lucas was horrified. 'Lord, no. One hundred per cent loyal to Almina as far as I know. What are you getting at, Lestrade?'

'Before you cry "Murder",' Lestrade told the chemist, 'you must eliminate all other possibilities. If my memory serves me correctly – and I have to accede that it doesn't always these days – hyoscine used to be used in cases of alcoholism, to inhibit the craving for drink.'

'Quite right,' Lucas nodded. 'But Carnarvon didn't drink . . .'

'So we can rule that one out,' Lestrade agreed. 'It was also used to dampen a man's ardour – a sort of chemical knee in the vitals.'

'True – although I don't think it was very effective. Bromide now, that may be better.'

'Really?'

'If only because if you overdo the dose, the resultant acne pustules are so offputting to the opposite sex that a chap won't get the chance to exercise his ardour in the first place.'

'It is possible, though,' Lestrade was talking to himself really, 'that Le Clerk was undergoing treatment. We know of his habits

– he of the wandering hands. Perhaps he wanted to control his sex drive – what do they call it, lumbago?'

'I believe that's libido,' Lucas corrected him.

'Only if it's written down,' Lestrade corrected *him*.

There was a shattering of glass somewhere outside. An explosion of gunfire. Then a second. And a third.

'Good God!' Lucas nearly bit through his brandy balloon.

'Stay here,' Lestrade ordered and jerked his head outside the tent flap. A bizarre sight met his gaze. Aaron G. String, in a voluminous white nightgown and tasselled cap, was roaring around in the dust of the camp, circling the tents with a pistol in his hand.

'Is he drunk?' Lucas's head had joined Lestrade's, threatening to give the detective serious canvas burns to the neck.

'What's going on?' Lestrade recognized the voice of Acting-Sergeant Adamson from the darkness beyond the tents.

'Stay where you are, Adamson,' that was Carter calling. 'You leave the tomb and you're fired.'

'Is it the Fascists, sir?' The Acting Sergeant shouted. 'They're all over Germany, you know. And Italy. That bloke Kapp. I wouldn't trust him further than I could throw him.'

String was staring wildly around him, firing at anything that moved.

'How many shots has he got in that thing?' Lucas asked Lestrade.

The ex-Chief Superintendent peered through the murky light. 'Looks like a Colt revolver,' he whispered. 'That'll give him six shots. How many has he fired?' Even as he asked the question he was tumbling out on to the sand, standing legs apart and hands by his sides. He was staring his sixty-eighth birthday in the face. His reactions were slower, his aim less sure. But here he was, in the middle of a cold Egyptian night, his breath smoking out on the air, facing a lunatic with a gun.

'Mr String,' he said softly, reaching out with his right hand, 'is there anything the matter?'

'You Limey bastard,' String blurted, trying to focus. His gun hand came up to the level and he squeezed off a shot.

'Damn!' Lestrade hissed as the bullet ricocheted somewhere behind his head.

'Get down, Lestrade!' He recognized Holinshed's voice off to his right.

'He'll kill you!' That sounded like Carter.

'Hang on!' That was an American voice. 'Wait 'til I get my pencil!' called Lindsley Foote Hall.

'Mr Lestrade, is it?' This was a new voice – one Lestrade didn't recognize. 'Percy Merton, *The Times*. What my readers would like to know is – "What is it like to look Death in the Face?"'

Another shot whistled high over Lestrade's head. At the lines beyond the camp, the camels were shifting, getting restless at the unaccustomed noise. There was a babble of native Egyptian as the fellahin crawled as close to the circle of lamps as they dared.

'Mr Lestrade.' Another new voice. 'Arthur Weigall, *Daily Mail*. *My* readers want to know the answer to that question *and* whether you'll be kind enough to have dinner, should you survive, with our lucky competition winner?'

'You bastards!' String was roaring, saliva dripping from his wobbling lips. 'Where in hell is the John?' And he swung around in an arc, firing wildly with his nickel-plated revolver.

'Six,' Lestrade counted aloud and broke forward at a run. He managed to pull himself up short, however, when String swung back to face him. Now his *left* hand was gleaming with metal. In the Western tradition of his great country, Aaron G. String had *two* pistols. And the muzzle of one of them was now jammed against the right nostril of Sholto J. Lestrade.

'You Limey bastard.' String was trying to focus on his target. 'You sonofabitch, the tip of your goddamn nose is missin'. Did I do that?'

'No, Mr String,' Lestrade said quietly. 'But before you remove the rest of it, I wonder if I might take the gun off you? It must be terribly heavy.'

String's face was crimson in the half-light and his eyes rolled uncontrollably. He was giggling and shaking his head, as though his ears bothered him.

'Are they wearing black shirts?' Adamson wanted to know. 'I can't see a bloody thing down here.'

'Shut up, Acting Sergeant,' Carter ordered.

101

'Nobody move,' Holinshed insisted. 'Mr Lestrade, are you all right?'

'You goddamned sons of bitches,' String growled, his finger flexing on the trigger. 'I know you bastards. You're all a-lookin' down your noses at me 'cos I'm American. Well, let me tell you sumpin'. We sure made you bastards back down at Saratoga – and Yorktown. Yessirree Bob.'

'Fifty pounds, Mr Lestrade,' Merton called, 'for your exclusive.'

'Sixty,'Weigall capped him, with all the backing of Viscount Rothermere.

'Seventy,' Merton would not let 'The Thunderer' be out-done. J. J. Astor and John Walter IV would never have forgiven him.

'Er . . .' Weigall was doing the necessary calculations from his expense account. 'Seventy pounds fourteen and six.'

'Guineas!' roared Merton. 'Seventy guineas!'

'Oh, shit.' Weigall conceded defeat. Then, in a flash of inspiration, 'seventy pounds fourteen and six and a dream cottage.'

'Over here, Aaron,' a wheedling voice called. 'Watch the birdie.'

There was a flash from Burton's camera and for that split second, String's concentration broke. The revolver slipped from Lestrade's nostril and the ex-Yard man used all his training and experience and brought up his right foot crunchingly into the millionaire's crotch. The fat American jack-knifed and Lestrade's right knee came up to catch him a nasty one under his chin. The fat American went down. Lestrade made a deter-mined grab for the gun, but String was faster. Holinshed was racing from behind, Carter and Callender from the left. Lucas batted aside the tent flap and lunged forward. It was all too late. At point-blank range, String fired again and Lestrade hurtled backwards, his hands clawing the air as he sprawled in the desert sands.

String was kneeling now, panting and sniggering in the silence. He saw blood trickling from Lestrade's head and looked at it curiously. Then he looked up to see the ring of astonished faces around him: Holinshed, the blond Englishman; Carter, the archaeologist; Callender, his friend; Lucas, the chemist; Hall, his fellow American. And two or three guys he hadn't met, two of them scribbling furiously on notepads. He sniggered for one last time. The he tucked the muzzle of his Colt neatly under his chin and pulled the trigger. The horrified circle watched as his hair and the top of his head blew up and outwards to spatter the sand with red. Another corpse for the Valley of the Kings.

The words reached him in a jumble, a confused torrent of *non sequiturs* and split infinitives and participles that failed to agree with anybody, least of all themselves. But then, none of this was surprising, because on either side of the bed sat two journalists, one one from *The Times*; the other from the *Mail*.

'Why don't you go home and follow the Bowes Lyons marriage, Weigall?' Merton asked archly. 'Describing yards of tulle is about your *métier*.'

The plump, wavy-haired ex-Inspector of the Antiquities Service scowled back at him. 'Bought any forged diaries recently, Merton? I particularly liked that one that Daniel Defoe typed up during the plague year.'

Percy Merton quivered, his grey eyes flashing. 'A mistake anyone could have made,' he assured his rival.

There was a groan from the man on the bed.

'Look out, he's coming round.' Merton craned forward.

'I got here first.' Weigall sat heavily on the bed.

'I've got Carnarvon's exclusive,' Merton reminded him.

'Ah, but Carnarvon's dead,' Weigall hissed. 'Or had you forgotten to tell your reader that?'

'Mr Lestrade.' Merton poked a pencil under the man's nose. 'Mr Sholto Lestrade, formerly of the Yard, now of Virginia Water?'

Lestrade's eyes narrowed on the flaxen-haired, beetroot-red figure in the camel-coloured suit. 'Who the devil are you?' he croaked.

'His mind's gone,' Weigall muttered. 'Amnesia.'

'I'm Percy Merton of *The Times* newspaper, Mr Lestrade,' 'The Thunderer's' man went on. '*The Times*, you know. Publishes news and so on?'

'Yes,' Weigall sneered. 'Does a good line in obituaries. Mr Merton would like to write yours.'

'Who the devil are you?' Lestrade eased his neck to the right.

'Arthur Weigall,' the heavier man said, his perpetual frown eased for a moment into something akin to a smile. 'I write for the *Daily Mail*.'

Merton snorted. 'Always prone to exaggeration was our Arthur,' he said. '"Write" is a little grandiose for the perfunctory scratchings he actually manages.'

'I may be a novice journalist,' Weigall snapped, 'but at least I'm a trained archaeologist.'

'In a pig's ear,' Merton blurted. It was a phrase he'd picked up from Aaron G. String and he rather liked it.

'What's happening?' Lestrade tried to haul himself up. He was in a bed; he knew that much. And the bed was in a tent. And the tent was in the Valley of the Kings. And the Valley of the Kings . . .

'You've had a blow to the head,' Merton said loudly, as though to a mental defective. 'A bullet grazed your temple.'

Instinctively, Lestrade raised a hand to his forehead. It was swathed in bandages.

'Plucky of you to take on that madman like that.'

'Madam?'

'What did I tell you?' Weigall muttered to Merton. 'Amnesia. That bullet must have creased his brain.'

'String!' Lestrade suddenly shouted and immediately wished he hadn't. The room swam in his vision and he had to steady himself in the bed. 'The last I remember was leaning over him on the ground. What happened next?'

'He shot himself,' Weigall told him.

'Damn you, Weigall,' Merton hissed. 'I wanted to tell him.'

'Well, you're not quick enough, are you?' Weigall preened himself.

'What do you think it was, Mr Lestrade?' Merton asked. 'Touch of the sun, would you say? That drove String to it, I mean?'

'Sun be buggered,' Weigall growled. 'I've been in Egypt for years and I've never seen anybody behave like that. He was obviously as mad as a cobra.'

'Had you ever done him any harm, Mr Lestrade?' Merton

tried a new tack. 'Outmanoeuvred him in a business deal or anything?'

'I only met him yesterday.' Lestrade tried to keep his balance steady. 'Where's the body now?'

'Lucas has rigged up an emergency tent,' Merton told him. 'Won't let anybody near the place.'

'I thought you were up-country,' Lestrade swivelled his eyes to bore into them both, 'at a place called Azu Symnel.'

'Abu Simbel,' Weigall corrected him. 'We were. Fascinating archaeological potential there.'

'Lot of sand was all I saw,' Merton shrugged. 'Reminded me inexorably of Weston-super-Mare with the tide out.'

'Philistine!' Weigall sneered.

'When did you get back?' Lestrade asked.

'Late last night,' Merton said. 'One of the camels threw a shoe or something.'

'Camels don't throw shoes, Merton.' Weigall sighed, convinced anew of the *Times* man's imbecility.

'No,' Merton countered. 'Rather like the *Mail*'s men don't throw tantrums.'

'That Frenchman has already asked us all this, you know,' Weigall said.

'Lamartine the gendarme?'

'That's the chappie. Suspicious cove. 'Course, I haven't forgiven them for Verdun yet.'

'That makes you and Acting Sergeant Adamson. Where is M. Lamartine now?' Lestrade asked.

'In that same bally tent with Lucas,' Merton told him. 'No one's allowed in, not even Howard Carter.'

'Gentlemen,' Lestrade sat upright with a superhuman effort. He felt rivulets of sweat – or was it blood – trickle down from his bandages, 'would you help me up? And get me across this No Man's Land? I must have an urgent word with Mr Lucas . . .'

The tent flap flicked back and let a stream of harsh sunlight flood the darkened room.

'Right. Out of here, you two. Mr Lestrade needs rest.'

'Mr Holinshed,' Lestrade winced.

No one else moved.

'Well?' Holinshed rested his hands on his hips. He was a big man and crusading journalism only went so far in those days. Sheepishly, Merton and Weigall ducked under the flap and saw themselves out.

Holinshed crouched next to the bed, as Lestrade had seen the fellahin do to rest themselves. 'You're looking a bit better than when I saw you last,' he smiled.

'I'm glad to hear you say it,' Lestrade murmured. 'Can you help me over to Lucas's tent?'

'You're in no fit state for a journey of that magnitude,' Holinshed said. 'It's midday, man. *And* you've got no Keating's Powder on. The mosquitoes would make mincemeat out of you.'

'Needs must,' Lestrade told him, 'when the devil drives.'

'The devil, Mr Lestrade?' Holinshed frowned.

The ex-Chief Superintendent gripped his man's lapels. 'Somebody is killing people in this Valley, Mr Holinshed,' he said. 'I've got to find out why.'

The three Ls stood overlooking the last mortal remains of Aaron G. String – Alfred Lucas, bent double, his glasses on his head after the fashion of true pathologists everywhere; Emil Lamartine, sharp-nosed, hawk-eyed, a detective on the climb; and Sholto Lestrade, his head wrapped like a pale Bedouin, his creaking old body in somebody else's galabieh – 'Only', as Jack Holinshed explained while helping him across the burning sand, 'until your bloody shirt is washed and dried.'

'I owe Harry Burton my life, I believe,' Lestrade said. 'If it weren't for his clever camera work, that might be me on the slab.'

'I'm not a doctor,' said Lucas, 'but I'd say you'd better sit down, Mr Lestrade.' The ex-Yard man was grateful to do so.

'What can you tell me?' he asked.

'I'm not a pathologist,' Lucas explained, 'but I think you know the answer before you ask the question.'

'I do?'

'Well,' Lucas sighed, 'I've followed all the rules I normally would for unwrapping a mummy. Lamartine has sat in on a few routine cases in Paris – of sudden death, I mean; not mummy unwrapping.'

106

'You know ze zort of thing, Monsieur Le Strade,' the French-man said. 'Zuicides in ze Zeine, et zetera, et zetera.'

Lestrade nodded. The Seine. The Thames. The Nile. Rivers everywhere just drew some people to their banks. And com-pelled them to jump in.

'Unless I miss my guess,' Lucas held up a slide in the gloom of his makeshift operating theatre, '*this* is the best part of half a grain of scopalamine.'

'Henbane,' said Lestrade, sitting forward in his wicker chair.

'The same,' Lucas frowned. 'And the same thing that killed Carnarvon and Le Clerk. The signs were all there. You saw for yourself.'

'I certainly did,' said Lestrade, nodding carefully.

'The giggling,' Lucas itemized the dead man's symptoms for the benefit of the relatively inexperienced Lamartine. 'Delirium in its "happy" form. Although, I must admit, I've never seen it as bad as that.'

'The flushed face,' Lestrade remembered.

'Dilation of the pupils.'

"Oo was zis John for 'oom 'e was asking?' Lamartine queried. Since discretion was the better part of valour, the French detective had kept his head down on the Night In Question. He'd heard every word, however, from the safety of one of String's trucks.

'Not "John", Mr Lamartine,' Lucas said, '"*the* John". It's a colonial phrase for the toilet.'

'A frequent desire to pass water,' Lestrade observed. 'He also had his head cocked to one side; listening for something.'

'Auditory disturbances. He was probably hearing things. Had a head full of noises.'

'Isn't hyoscine called the truth drug, Mr Lucas?' Lestrade asked. 'That's one symptom we didn't get.'

'Ah, but we did,' Lamartine reminded the Englishman. 'When Mr String remembered 'ow you Engleesh 'ad backed down at zose battles in ze War of . . .'ow you say? Independ-ence, *n'est ce pas*?'

'Now, wait a minute . . .' Lucas began.

Lestrade waved the slur aside. 'Any idea how it was admin-istered?' he asked.

The chemist shook his head. 'None. I haven't had time to check his razor yet, if that's what you're thinking. He seems to have brought his own stuff with him in those lorries of his. Frankly, Lestrade,' Lucas placed his scalpel down on the table next to the huge figure of the dead man, the top of his head on the next table, in bits of red and white, 'I think we ought to send for the Parquet.'

'Really?'

'Look.' The chemist looked at them both. 'Mr Lamartine is . . . well, I don't wish to be rude, but, well, he's young.'

'Napoleon Bonaparte was a general at twenty-five,' the rather hurt Sûreté man reminded him.

'And you, Lestrade, well, you're a little long in the tooth, if I may say so.'

'Methuselah lived nine hundred years,' the ex-Yard man said flatly.

'Ah,' observed Lamartine, 'but 'oo calls zat living, when no girl will give in to no man what is nine 'undred years?'

'You're missing the point, gentlemen.' Lucas found a rag to wipe his bloody hands on. 'The heat won't allow us to keep Mr String above ground for more than another day, or the stench will be unbearable. Three men have died, one in this Valley, one in the desert on the way north and the third in Cairo; all in the space of two weeks. You are both, I'm sure, excellent policemen, but you need help.'

'Lamartine?' Lestrade looked up at the young detective.

'I am working on one murder,' the Frenchman said. 'Zat of Alain Le Clerk. Ze ozzers do not concern me.'

'And I am investigating the death of Lord Carnarvon,' Lestrade said. 'I haven't finished that yet.'

'Stubborn!' Lucas fumed. 'Stupid *and* stubborn! What a disastrous combination. Lestrade, Jack Holinshed has already sent a telegram to your daughter in Cairo. She is no doubt on her way here.'

'I . . .'

But Lucas was in full flight. 'Lindsley Foote Hall has similarly sent one to the American Consulate in Cairo. In two days, the Valley of the Kings will look like Brighton beach. I estimate that you two sleuths have a little over twenty-four hours to interrogate everybody in this camp. Assuming – as of course we cannot – that the three of us are innocent, that only gives you Carter, Hall, Gardiner, Callender, Burton, Merton, Weigall, Holinshed, that maniac Adamson, Cliff Hanger, Arthur Mace and about a hundred and fifty fellahin to go. I wish you joy of it, gentlemen. Now, if you don't mind, I have a body to dispose of.'

Yes, there was the Entente Cordiale. And it was perfectly true that, even at the height of hostilities, William Pitt had sold boots to Napoleon Bonaparte in exchange for corn. French and British troops had fought cheek by jowl at the Alma and Balaclava and Inkermann. And again in the dire desolation of the trenches, Tommy Atkins had walked hand in hand with Jacques Poilou under the arch of the guns. Even so, it wasn't easy to wipe out a thousand years of mistrust and that was why Lestrade and Lamartine carried out their investigations separately. And that was why they had no intention of sharing the results between them. So much for the International Police Commission.

'Pecky' Callender had been saddled with the nauseating Aaron G. String for most of the afternoon. The mad American had insisted on going out in the midday sun, inspecting anything and everything. He had gone down into the tomb with Howard Carter and the archaeologist had re-emerged almost immediately, steam, it seemed, escaping from his ears. Nothing Lestrade or Lamartine could do could induce the great man to divulge the reason for his hasty departure, but Adamson's tongue could be loosened when Lestrade hinted that String had been a confidante of Mussolini and when Lamartine claimed to be a personal friend of Lev Bronstein. Out of the corner of his mouth – the left of course – the Acting Sergeant had given a verbatim account to the two policemen of the conversation he heard in the annexe between the archaeologist and the railroad millionaire. Put quite simply, String offered to buy Carter out. Or Carnarvon. Or the Egyptian government. Or whoever owned the goddamn tomb in the first place. And he named a figure for the tomb of King Tut-Ankh-Amen which made the reparations that Germany was currently failing to pay to the Allies look like small change.

Carter had refused angrily, storming up to the light and

leaving String equally fuming. 'No sonofabitch turns me down like a goddamn eiderdown,' he had roared after Carter. And for the later part of the afternoon, he had bent Lindsley Foote Hall's ear about the Englishman's 'brass neck' and how he intended to 'Get Carter.'

Burton and Gardiner, along with Clifford Hanger, had had the misfortune to eat dinner with the brash American. Everybody else refused, claiming pressing business in their respective tents. The hapless fellah appointed in Cairo to tend to String's every need had made him his nightly cocoa, heavily laced with rye, at about ten thirty. String had read for a while by his specially imported arc lamps – the latest volume of *Railroad Millionaires' Weekly* – before falling into a fitful sleep. He woke about eleven, the valet fellah said, complaining of headaches and a dry throat. The fellah had poured him a refreshing glass of boiled water mixed with a little rye and for the next hour or so, the American had trotted backwards and forwards to the latrine, a handsome portable affair he had brought with him on one of his trucks. The fellah did not see the revolvers until just before one thirty, when they suddenly appeared in the hands of the deceased as he went on what appeared to be a drunken rampage, shooting at everybody in sight.

Jack Holinshed, who had been brought up with guns on his father's estate, confirmed that the weapons were Colts, with rather nicely engraved pearl handles and their calibre was .45.

Clifford Hanger, however, was a changed man. The *bonhomie* of the previous days had vanished and he sat, morose and silent in his tent, a perpetual glass of whisky in his fist. He certainly didn't have the Kruschen feeling and it even looked as though Eno's Fruit Salts would not be of much use to him. Besides, everyone was busy looking very carefully at everyone else, out of the corners of their eyes. And on principle, the newly lacklustre Cliff Hanger would not trust Carter's Little Liver Pills.

'I think the suicide business upset him,' Lestrade told Arthur Weigall that night as the two men sat in Lestrade's tent, huddled around the storm lantern.

The archaeologist-turned-newspaperman looked up sternly, his eyes ablaze in the eerie light. 'It's not that,' he said grimly.

'I've seen this before, Lestrade. You mark my words it'll get us all in the end.'

'It?' Lestrade repeated. There was something in the man's face that made the hair on his scalp crawl. 'What do you mean?'

'Look up there,' Weigall pointed to a small hole in the tent roof. 'See those stars? They've been there for millions of years, Lestrade. When you and I were twinkles in our fathers' eyes; when the Jackal God laid out Tut-Ankh-Amen in those vaults; when the first men crawled up out of the primeval slime; those stars were old then.'

'So?'

Weigall looked at his man. 'Do you believe in fate?' he asked. 'Destiny?'

Lestrade shrugged. 'I take life pretty much as it comes,' he said. His head still hurt and the day had been exhausting. Now he felt all of his sixty-eight years. And he felt cold.

'I want to tell you a story.' Weigall leaned back on the canvas chair. 'It's about my wife. And Osiris.'

'Look, if this is personal', Lestrade said, 'I'd sooner not . . .'

'Oh, I think you should know this, Mr Lestrade,' Weigall said, his eyes boring into Lestrade's. 'I really think you should.'

'All right,' Lestrade nodded. 'I'm in your hands.'

'It started with another wealthy American,' the *Mail* man said. 'Like String, but with a brain and finesse. His name was Theodore Davis. Carter worked for him. So did Joe Linden Smith. And so, for a time, did I. We were working a few miles from here, in the Valley of the Queens and we found a natural amphitheatre – a perfect semicircle half buried in the sand.'

'Amazing.'

'We decided to put on a play there.' The archaeologist's face darkened. 'It was January 1909. The twenty-third to be precise. The first night was to be the twenty-sixth and we were rehearsing on the twenty-third. My wife, Hortense, was playing the wandering spirit of Akhenaten, the father of him whose tomb lies just outside. Joe's wife Corinna was playing Akhenaten's mother, Queen Tiy. She was about to recite the hymn to Aton when . . . I've never seen anything like it, Lestrade, a storm came from nowhere. Oh, I know, desert storms are legendary for their suddeness, but this . . . this was unnatural. Macabre. Sand and stones flying in all directions. The fellahin watching were terrified. And they'd seen storms before, God knows. They ran away, screaming that the gods of Ancient Egypt were stoning them. We managed to get to the shelter of the tomb of Amet-Hu and we spent the night there.'

'What happened?'

'That night, Hortense and Corinna had the same dream. They were standing in the temple of Amon and the statue of the god came to life. It was made of basalt, Lestrade, but it came to life. He raised his flail to Corinna and caught her across the nose, stinging both eyes. Hortense fell before him and he lashed her stomach.'

'Tsk, tsk.' Lestrade shook his hed. 'Well, dreams can be terrifying, can't they?'

'This was no dream, Lestrade,' Weigall whispered. 'By morning, Corinna was in agony. Her eyes were crimson and closed. She couldn't see. Hortense was doubled up with violent stomach cramps. We rushed both of them by river to the hospital in Cairo. The specialist had never seen a worse case of trachoma in his life. My darling Hortense nearly died on the operating table. We've never tried that play since, Lestrade.'

'Er . . . no, well, it's probably just as well.'

Weigall looked at his man and shook his head. 'Scoff if you like,' he said, 'but Clifford Hanger is as much of a victim as Carnarvon or Le Clerk or String. You mark my words. I've seen it. Even Carter goes down with it from time to time.'

'What is it?'

'Who knows?' Weigall shrugged. 'A creeping paralysis, a loss of the will to live, a succumbing to pain and fear. Two of the fellahin have gone mad.'

'Forgive me, Mr Weigall,' Lestrade said, 'but I'm a policeman by training. I have to look for evidence. Hard facts. Truth.'

'Truth?' Weigall echoed, a strange light in his eyes. 'Then take a look at this.'

He rummaged in a brief case by his feet and hauled out a box. Looking carefully from left to right, he unlocked it and placed on Lestrade's lap an object wrapped in sacking.

'What's this?' the ex-Yard man asked.

'Unwrap it and see,' Weigall told him.

Lestrade did. It was an oblong piece of stone, measuring

112

perhaps one foot by two and it was littered with Egyptian hieroglyphs.

'I will assume, Mr Lestrade,' Weigall said, 'that you are unfamiliar with ancient scripts. So let me help you. It says, in the phraseology of the Eighteenth Dynasty – "Death shall come on swift wings to him that toucheth the tomb of the Pharaoh." There,' his stubby fingers pointed to the bottom line, 'there is Horus, the guardian of the tomb, with his hawk head. The fellahin, if they knew of this tablet, would be gone like a shot.'

'Where was it found?'

'In the antechamber,' Weigall said. 'The room that Adamson guards.'

Lestrade's eyes narrowed. It was suddenly icy cold and he wanted to go to sleep. 'Is he . . . is he Horus?' he asked. 'The guardian of the tomb?'

Weigall was shaking his head. 'Horus isn't a man, Lestrade,' he growled. 'He's much more than that. He is Death himself. Carter thinks I've destroyed this. And destroy it I will. But . . . I thought you should see it first. And there's something else.' Weigall rewrapped the stone curse and locked it away in its box. 'On the morning that Carnarvon first went down to the tomb, to the door of the burial chamber, he was laughing. Well, you can understand it, I suppose. This was to be Carter's last dig. After this, Carnarvon was going to withdraw his funds. Then, miraculously, he found the tomb. You can understand why Carnarvon was so happy.'

'Yes, I can. So why . . .?'

'On that morning, I was there. It was before that repugnant freak Merton had arrived. I said to Callender, I said, "If he goes down in that spirit, I give him six weeks to live." Laughing in the House of the Dead! But I was wrong, Lestrade.'

'You were?'

'Oh, yes.' Weigall smiled, like the frozen leer of a corpse. 'You see, Carnarvon lived for another six weeks and three days. You look a little strange. Can I get you a drink?'

6

The fella said the demons came to him that night – the Afreet, the Djinn. By morning, Lestrade was rambling, delirious. He wandered outside his tent a little before breakfast, beckoning to the others. 'Harry,' he called, 'Harry, over here.'

Harry Burton looked at 'Pecky' Callender, then trotted over to him. There was a wildness in the man's eyes, below the white of the bandage and above the grey-brown of the moustache.

'How many of them, Harry?' Lestrade whispered to him. 'I count three.'

'Er . . . yes,' Burton thought it best to humour him, 'that's right. That's what I make it.'

'Look,' Lestrade put an arm around the man's shoulder, 'I know this is bloody silly, but those two over there, by the fountain . . .'

'The . . . er . . . the fountain?' Burton didn't know quite where to look for one in the Valley of the Kings.

'Sorry,' Lestrade said, chuckling. 'I'm not making myself clear, am I? The pink one, the pink fountain.'

'Ah, yes.' Burton began to edge away. 'The pink one.'

'Well, those two blokes standing by it, Harry; who do they remind you of? Particularly the tall one – violin, deerstalker, pipe. Ring any bells for you, eh?'

'Er . . . I'd welcome your opinion, Mr Lestrade.'

Lestrade moved aside, clearly somewhat taken aback. '*Mr* Lestrade?' he echoed, his feet dancing a tired little jig in the red sand. 'Well, *Mr* Bandicoot, I don't think you've called me that in a long time. Well, it's obvious, man. The shifty eyes, the

114

quivering nostrils. It's Sherlock Holmes. Holmes of Baker Street.'

'Oh,' Burton was grinning like a terrified baboon, 'so it is. I couldn't make him out. Sun was in my eyes. Hello!' he called, waving. 'Hello, Mr Holmes.'

'Harry, Harry,' Lestrade hissed, hauling the man's hand down. 'You're making an exhibition of yourself, man,' he said. 'You know as well as I do that Sherlock Holmes has been dead for thirty years. He went over some waterfall on a hiking holiday in Switzerland.'

'Really?' Burton was looking around frantically for assistance. But none was forthcoming. Just in case, like Aaron String, Sholto Lestrade had a brace of pistols tucked away somewhere, the Tut-Ankh-Amen team kept safely in the shadows.

'And that bloke with him is his old chum Dr John Watson. It's not generally known of course that Holmes couldn't stand the fellow. Watson had an IQ of a gnat, apparently, but then, Holmes was prone to hyperbrolly. I always found him reasonably astute.'

'Oh, quite, quite. Is it . . . er . . . is it done to wave at him?'

'Well, that's the damndest thing about it.' Lestrade frowned and stroked his chin. 'You see, he was shot by a German spy, just before the war. There's something not quite right here, Fanny.'

'Fanny?'

Lestrade looked at the photographer. 'Not just now. I've got a bit of a headache.' And he somersaulted neatly backwards over a camp stool and lay motionless in the sand.

It was nearly dark before Emma arrived, by steamer from Luxor. Inspector Macclesfield was with her and Callender and Hall showed the pair into the darkened tent where her father lay.

'Oh, Daddy.' She ran her soft fingers along the bandage that wound like a burial band under his chin. 'In the wars again. Why did you go off like that? Without telling anyone?'

'My fault, I'm afraid.' Jack Holinshed loomed behind them.

'Yours?' Emma was on her feet.

'I brought him here. He wanted to know how Le Clerk, the French Egyptologist, died. So the Valley of the Kings it was.'

'What happened, Jack?'

Holinshed looked at the others. 'Shall we?' he urged, raising the tent flap. 'Your father's sleeping now. There's nothing more you can do.'

She looked at the man on the bed, his face dark and livid on the white of the pillow. The man who gave her life. She remembered all those little things that girls remember about their fathers. The day he first told her who he was. Not Uncle Sholto, who came to Bandicoot Hall sometimes with such a sad face and a pair of handcuffs, but her father. She'd never known her mother, the blonde, life-loving Sarah who had died shortly after the girl's birth. Letitia Bandicoot had been that and Nanny Balsam and Nanny Gote. And it was Harry, handsome, laughing, brave Harry, who had taught her to swim and shoot and ride as he taught his own boys. It all came flooding back. It was the man on the pillow she loved and it was to him she had run, crying and afraid, so many times. So many times. She turned away and felt the wind of the desert chill her soul.

'I don't know,' Holinshed was saying, steadying her shivering arm. 'I don't know whether it's the sun or the head wound. He's lucky to be alive.'

'Can he travel?' she asked him. 'I want to get him home.'

'I think so,' he told her. 'You'll take the river? The desert will be too much.'

'Yes,' she said.

'How's Tilly?'

'She's fine,' Emma said. 'I see her now and then. She showed me round the Native Quarter in Cairo. Fascinating. She had to go away for a few days, to visit friends in Damietta.'

'Ah, yes, the Fahmy Beys. Friends of the family.'

'What happened, Jack?' she said again, drawing her shawl around her.

'It was the damnedest thing.' Holinshed fished in his pocket for his pipe. 'We had an American here, a railroad tycoon. He wanted to buy the tomb. Can you imagine that? The cheek of it!'

'Yes,' Emma nodded. 'Bearing in mind it was a British team who found it.'

'An Egyptian antiquity on Egyptian soil,' Holinshed reminded her.

'Sorry,' she said. 'I'm not really familiar with the politics of this part of the world. There were some ugly scenes in Cairo before we left.'

'It's time we left,' Holinshed said, gazing up at the stars. 'Egypt, I mean. We've outlived our usefulness.'

'You make it sound as if the Empire is a thing of the past,' she smiled.

'Do I?' Holinshed turned to her, pale in the moonlight. 'If you'd asked me ten years ago, how long will Pax Britannica rule the earth, I'd have said "for ever". Now, I'm not so sure.'

'What happened with the American?' Emma's father lay with a shattered head and a shattered mind inside his tent and this man was rambling on about the ifs and buts of world affairs.

'Ah, well . . .' And he told her.

'My God.'

'Emma,' Holinshed suddenly took the girl's hands in his, 'get your father out of here. Tomorrow. While you still can. Three men have died already – Carnarvon, Le Clerk, String. Who's to say who'll be next?' He gazed round at the black hulks of the spoil heaps and the silent hills. 'There's death here, Emma,' he whispered. 'I'm amazed the fellahin have stayed.'

'Accidents,' she said, trying to reassure herself rather than him. 'That's all they are.'

'Is that it?' Holinshed asked. 'Doesn't your father confide in you?'

'Usually,' she frowned. 'Oh, I know you both thought Lord Carnarvon . . .'

'I've spent a fair few years in the East,' he said, 'and believe me, you don't know the half of it in Surrey. There are things here, things you can't even guess at. They're beyond our comprehension.'

'Oh, now, Jack,' she scolded him, 'you've been in the Valley too long. Come back with us to Cairo, tomorrow. Shake the dust of the place for a while. I know Daddy offered to help with Lord Carnarvon, but . . .' she glanced at the faint glow in his tent and the larger-than-life figures moving about the bed, for all the world like embalmers working on the body of a dead king, 'well, it's all gone wrong. I will take him home tomorrow,

117

not because of "things beyond our comprehension", but because an old man has bitten off more than he can chew. I've sent a cable to Fanny on the Riviera, telling her not to worry, but to come home as soon as she can. Norroy and I will sort it all out. And you,' she added sternly at him, 'you get a good night's sleep. You look all in.'

'Yes,' he smiled at her. 'But I'll keep my back to the wall while I'm doing it. If I were you, I'd get Macclesfield to do what the faithful fellahin do and lie across your tent door tonight.'

'Jack!' she chuckled. 'He's an inspector of the Metropolitan Police, not a draught excluder.'

The steamer bore them northwards the next morning. Luckily, the British captain had been at 'V' Beach, Cape Hellas in Gallipoli, so he wasn't at all deterred by the wounded man on the stretcher, apologizing to all and sundry because he'd forgotten his wallet and didn't have the exact fare to Ealing Broadway. Neither did the coffin bother him, although the stars and stripes draped over it was not the usual flag of convenience. The twin Westley-Richardsons coughed into life, churning the brown waters of the Nile and its even browner sons hauled on the cables and she was gone, snorting black smoke to the lapis lazuli that was always the Egyptian sky.

Jack Holinshed walked the upper deck with Merton of *The Times*, Weigall of the *Mail* and Macclesfield of the Met.

'I take it, gentlemen,' Merton was gazing at the left bank, 'that you are not particularly *au fait* with the Sudanese history of some forty years ago.'

'Rather before my time,' Holinshed said.

'Mine too,' confessed Macclesfield.

'The mad Mahdi,' Weigall mumbled. 'Gordon.'

'That's right,' Merton nodded, not a little miffed that his opposition should be so clued up. 'Colonel Stuart, Gordon's Aide, was travelling much as we are now, on a dahabeeyah, and he must have seen tribesmen rather like we are looking at now.'

He was right. Norroy Macclesfield narrowed his eyes against the sun's glare to watch them. In the dust of the Nile bank, the date and palm trees behind them, trotted a line of blue- and black-clad horsemen, rifles bouncing over their shoulders, faces wrapped against the world. 'Dervishes?' he asked.

'Bedouin, certainly,' Weigall commented. 'Painted for war.'

'War?' Macclesfield echoed.

'Storm clouds,' Merton prophesied. 'You mark my words.'

When they reached Cairo, the city seemed strangely silent. Water-carriers and camel castrators went about their business as usual, but the cries of the street Arabs were subdued, their numbers less. One of them half-heartedly offered Norroy Macclesfield the mummified genitals of Rameses VIII on the steamer's gangplank, but the Inspector was not impressed. He'd been on the Force for sixteen years, man and rookie. When you'd seen one, you'd seen 'em all. Everywhere, eyes swivelled; below fezes and above veils. There was an atmosphere you could have cut with a shadoof.

Emil Lamartine had decided to stay in the Valley of the Kings. After all, he had not yet solved the murder of Alain Le Clerk and that rankled with him. What had clinched it, however, was that the captain of the steamer had overheard his accent at the bank and said in a very loud voice that he'd carried enough Belgian detectives for a lifetime. Lamartine didn't know what he was talking about, but the slur was enough. He turned on his heel in the dust and walked away.

Blue-jacketed Ghaffirs, the Irregulars attached to the police, met the steamer at the landing and they weren't waiting for the cotton to load. Their grim-faced sergeant muttered something to Jack Holinshed and the ashen-faced Englishman turned to his companions.

'They're here to protect us,' he said. 'There's been some trouble. Four of them will get String to the mortuary. We'd better get to Shepheard's Hotel and stay there.'

'What's going on?' Emma asked him.

'Zagloul,' growled Weigall.

'Zagloul,' Merton nodded, unwilling to let his rival have the last editorial word.

'What's Zagloul?' Emma surveyed the naked docklands, isolated pairs of fellahin whispering and scurrying through dingy alleyways. 'A sort of Ramadan?'

'A sort of bastard,' Merton said grimly. 'Oh, I'm sorry, Emma, I forgot myself.'

'Said Zagloul Pasha', Weigall enlightened her, 'is likely to become the next Prime Minister of this country.'

'The British protectorate ended last year, Miss Lestrade,' Merton said, lifting out his battered briefcase in the unaccountable absence of any porters, 'but the British don't seem to know that. We still control antiquities, foreign policy, the police, trade, the army of course . . .'

'In fact, it's difficult to know what we don't still control.' Weigall began to descend the gangplank. 'That's what Zagloul can't stomach.'

'He's the local nationalist ruler,' Merton said. 'Weigall, you were here in '19, weren't you? Cowering under tables and so on?'

'There was trouble, yes,' the *Mail* man said. 'But where I was is absolutely no concern of yours. Zagloul's followers overturned trams, broke street lamps, looted shops and stoned Europeans.'

'Phew,' they heard Lindsley Foote Hall call from the bank. 'At least I'll be all right.' He'd come to Cairo to get some lead in his pencils.

'They hit railway and telegraph lines in rural areas,' Weigall went on, watching the shadows carefully. 'At Luxor, they took British officers on leave off a train and butchered them.'

'Assassination is an old Egyptian practice, Miss Lestrade,' Merton said. 'You and I play whist; Egyptians knife each other.'

'Or poison,' Hanger said.

The others looked at him. The excavation team's publicity man had said virtually nothing on the way up-river. His voice sounded odd. His face looked peculiar. It was Howard Carter, of all people, who patted his shoulder and helped him down the wobbling planks. Last of all, they brought Lestrade, bounced on his stretcher by the dynamics of the wood and the angle of the plank.

'For God's sake, Fifi,' he chuckled, 'slow down. I've just had my ribs broken.'

Shepheard's Hotel was an oasis of British in a sea of Egyptian. It resembled the Alamo, manned against the Mexicans or the

British legation at Peking, boarded to withstand the fists of the righteous Boxers. All that was missing was rifles at the windows.

No one slept that night. Only Lestrade. And Aaron G. String, safe in the arms of Jesus.

Breakfast was certainly different from that in the narrow, dark entrance to the tomb where most of the company had become used to eating. There were silver tureens, gleaming porcelain and squeaky glasses, but not a lot, unfortunately, to put in any of them. The Major Domo apologized, first in English, then in French, then in German and finally in Egyptian, for the fact that two thirds of the kitchen staff had deserted and taken with them most of the hotel's supplies.

What had they left, a German guest demanded to know, having got the best seats in the dining-room. The answer, apparently, was coffee. And, given the situation, it was on the house.

It was a little after nine that Clifford Hanger skipped into the dining-room, the smell of Turkish beans filling his nostrils.

'Howard!' he beamed, pulling up a chair next to the archaeologist.

'Clifford,' the surly man with the chin and the broken nose responded.

'You seem a little better, Mr Hanger,' Jack Holinshed said. 'More yourself.'

'Absolutely,' the ad man thumped the table. 'Vomited buckets last night. Right as rain now. Now, Howard, about those Tut-Ankh-Amen propelling pencils . . .'

'Euphoria.' Burton leaned across to the bandaged figure of Lestrade. The photographer had run out of developing fluid and Cairo was his only hope. He just prayed that 'Kemal's Cameras' was still loyal to the British.

'You what?' The ex-Chief Superintendent loosened the linen to hear. 'Is that a country or something? God, this tea tastes terrible!'

Burton turned away. 'Miss Lestrade, I'm really worried about your father,' he whispered. 'I fear we're looking at the onset of gagadom. Sans eyes, sans teeth, sans everything.'

She looked beyond Burton to her dad. She'd seen him in bandages before, seen him not follow a conversation before, but the vacancy in the eyes was new and it frightened her.

'But, then,' Burton helped himself to more coffee, 'that doesn't explain Hanger. Morose one minute, euphoric the next.'

'Could it be the sun, do you think, Mr Burton?' Macclesfield leaned across Emma Lestrade. Their hands touched briefly and he moved back, blushing.

The photographer shook his head. 'The sort of hallucinations Mr Lestrade was having earlier, in the Valley of the Kings, yes – that could be heatstroke. But it doesn't usually last this long.'

'Mr Lestrade?' the Major Domo was a worried-looking man the wrong side of fifty. But then, in Cairo in the spring of 1923, who wasn't?

'Er . . . yes,' Emma said, in view of the fact that her father wasn't responding.

'A note has just been delivered,' the Major Domo said.

'Thank you.' Emma took it.

'I am instructed to wait for a reply.'

'I see.' She tore open the envelope. 'My God!' she gasped.

'What is it?' Macclesfield and Holinshed chorused.

All eyes round the table were fixed on the lovely girl from Virginia Water.

'Not bad news, I hope?' Hanger beamed. 'Bottom fallen out of camiknickers?'

'Norroy,' she turned to the big Inspector, 'it's Walter Hambrook and Bob Fabian. They've been kidnapped.'

'Kidnapped?' The cry was taken up along the English table. A few Frenchmen looked up in alarm. The Germans kept on drinking coffee.

'Another old Egyptian practice,' Merton of *The Times* said, leaving his place and joining Emma. 'May I?' He reached for the letter.

'No,' Macclesfield snapped. 'Don't touch it.' He tweezed it out of Emma's grasp with a pair of sugar tongs.

'What does it say?' Weigall asked.

'"We have the Englishmen Hambrook and Fabian",' Macclesfield read *sotto voce*. '"You, Mr Lestrade, are to come to the Mosque El-Muayyad at midnight tonight and bring with you the archaeologist Howard Carter, despoiler of tombs."'

'Good God!' Weigall sat down heavily.

'Do they mean business?' Macclesfield asked the company.

'Is it signed?' Merton asked.

'"Zagloul Pasha",' Macclesfield read.

'They mean business,' the *Times* man nodded grimly. 'Carter, what about it?'

'What about it?' Carter echoed. 'You expect me to give myself up voluntarily to an unruly mob? Are you out of your mind?'

'If anybody's out of his mind,' Lestrade chimed in, 'it's going to be me. Norroy, get the lads. We'll need "Crusher" Wainwright, "The Hulk" Harrington . . . oh, and Bruce Partington, unless he's got any other plans.'

'Er . . .' Macclesfield didn't know what to say to the old guv'nor.

'Daddy,' Emma smiled at him, squeezing his hand, 'they're not here at the moment. They're back at the Yard. We're in Cairo, Daddy. Egypt.'

He chuckled, patting her hand in return. 'I know Cairo's in Egypt, my dear.' He winked at her. 'That was one of the few things I learnt from old Mercator, my geography teacher. Still, if they're not available, I'll have to go alone.'

'Don't be silly,' she scolded softly. 'We couldn't let you go, even if you were . . .'

'. . . Not senile as a goat,' Hanger always had a word for it.

'Gentlemen,' Macclesfield said. 'You appear to know this Zagloul. Is it likely he's really got my colleagues?'

'By the short and curlies, I'd say,' was Merton's opinion. 'Holinshed? You've been out here on and off all your life, haven't you? What do you think?'

'I think Zagloul is not the kind of man to bluff. If he says he's got them, he's got them.'

'My view . . .' Weigall began.

'. . . Is always obscured by a colossal inferiority,' Merton cut in. 'Don't try anything, Macclesfield, Zagloul will have you for breakfast.'

'Well, that would be better than this tea,' Lestrade commented helpfully, pushing the cup away from him.

'It's simple,' Hanger suddenly said, lolling back in his chair. 'Carter has to be jettisoned.'

'What?' The archaeologist couldn't believe his ears.

'I'm sorry, Howard,' the ad-man shrugged. 'One thing you learn in my line of work is – cut your losses. Quit while you're ahead. We've no proof that this Zagloul wants you dead.'

'We've every proof he wants *all* Englishmen dead,' Merton corrected him. 'Take my word for it, Macclesfield, stay here.'

'He's right, Norroy,' Lestrade nodded. 'I'll go alone.'

'Don't be ridiculous, Lestrade,' Holinshed said. 'You couldn't even find the Mosque El-Muayyad, never mind negotiate with Zagloul.'

'Now, look . . .' Lestrade wobbled to his feet. Suddenly there was a whistle and whine and a shattering of glass. A woman screamed. Come to think of it, it might have been the Major Domo. The window sash flew wide, the curtains and blinds jerking with the thump of bullets.

'Everybody on the floor!' Macclesfield roared and dived on to Emma Lestrade, perhaps to cushion his landing.

'Rifles,' Weigall hissed. 'They've got rifles.'

'Well, well,' Merton tutted beside him. 'It's really comforting to have a *Mail* man with one in a crisis.'

'Golly, this is exciting,' they heard Hanger shout.

'Hello!' a distant native voice rang out.

A number of European heads popped up over the window-sills.

'Lestrade Pasha!' it went on.

The ex-Yard man stood up, only to be yanked down again by Macclesfield and Emma.

'Will you come', the voice wanted to know, 'to the Mosque El-Muayyad at midnight?'

'Yes!' Lestrade called back.

'On the word of an Englishman?'

Macclesfield and Holinshed were squinting into the sun-baked square to see where the rifle fire – and the voice – had come from. There was no one visible at all. Only a solitary donkey grazing on the palm leaves in the piazza, under the huge, white statue of Lord Kitchener, a former Sirdar.

'On the word of an ex-officer of Scotland Yard,' Lestrade called.

'And you will have with you the Englishman who is called Carter Pasha?'

'I will!' Lestrade promised.

'Over my dead body,' Carter growled from his position behind the table cloth.

They all peered at him from under chairs. It had not been a wise choice of words.

Midnight. One more hour 'til morning. All day, the guests of Shepheard's Hotel had huddled in their solidarity in the games room, drinking coffee. Then the French accused the Germans of cheating at *vingt-et-un* and an unholy row had broken out. In vain had the Major Domo reminded them that they'd already had the War to End All Wars and the two parties retired, screaming insults at each other about Alsace and Lorraine, whoever they were, to the opposite ends of the hotel.

'Where are our reparations?' the French wanted to know.

'Get your soldiers out of our Ruhr!' the Germans demanded. It was all very unseemly.

In vain too had Emma Lestrade argued with her father. It wasn't as if he was on home turf, threading the labyrinthine alleyways of Whitechapel. It wasn't as if he had the resources of the Yard behind him. And it wasn't as if he was any longer a young . . . and that was as far as she had got. She'd taken the wrong turn and she knew it. From now on, she'd just have to hope that Norroy Macclesfield could handle it.

'It' was Emma's idea. Unwrap Lestrade's head wound, put him in leather gaiters and a pith hat and in the darkness of the Old Native Quarter, he might *just* pass for Howard Carter. Come to think of it, in the darkness of the Old Native Quarter, he *might* pass for Lord Kitchener – hundreds had. As for Norroy Macclesfield, Emma assumed that Said Zagloul Pasha didn't have a clue what her old man looked like. Who was to say he wasn't black-haired, with shoulders like pyramids? He might well pass for Lestrade. Lestrade might well pass out. She crossed everything she had, sitting in the Ladies' Room with Tilly Holinshed, and she prayed.

'You mustn't worry, Emma, darling,' the blonder girl said. 'God, I'm tired of drinking coffee. I must say it's rather beastly of the natives to have taken the Moët et Chandon – especially since they don't drink it. Rather beastly of Howard Carter not to have offered himself, don't you think?'

'You make him sound like a sacrifice, Tilly,' Emma said. For safety's sake, the Major Domo and the hotel's management had decided not to put on any lights. There was an eerie stillness throughout the hotel. There had been no palm court orchestra all day. Everyone from the leading fiddle down had gone, abandoning their instruments in the shadow of Zagloul. There was no clash and carry at dinner time – only coffee for those who could stomach it, yet again; followed by coffee in the dining-room.

'But your father and a perfectly innocent man are out there risking their lives,' the girl went on.

'I'm not sure Norroy Macclesfield is as innocent as all that,' Emma still had the sang-froid to observe, 'for all he blushes at the flash of a garter.'

'Well,' Tilly sniffed, 'that's men for you.'

'Is there no one in your life?' Emma asked her.

Even in the darkness, Tilly Holinshed was a striking woman, her face lit by the street lights in the square, filtering through the windows.

'Only one,' she said softly.

'Look.' Emma moved closer to her. 'It's none of my business, I know . . . I shouldn't pry, but . . . well, I've got to talk about something or I'll start climbing the walls.'

'Not that then.' Tilly suddenly tossed her head. 'It's something . . . you wouldn't understand. Do you think they'll start shooting again?'

Emma twisted her wrist to try and read the time in the pale light. 'Nothing for three hours,' she said. 'But they *are* still out there. They saw Daddy and Norroy go.'

'How do you know?'

'Haha,' Emma tapped the side of her nose knowingly. 'Copper's daughter. It's in the blood.' She craned her neck. 'That alleyway,' she said. 'To the left of the palm tree.'

Tilly craned too. 'What about it?'

'There's a man there, a fellah. He's carrying what looks like a Lee-Enfield.'

'Gosh, Emma,' Tilly laughed, 'that's quite amazing. All I can see is alleyway.'

They sat in silence for a moment. Deep. Impenetrable.

'What did you mean, by the way, a minute ago?'

'I told you,' she sensed Tilly stiffen, 'I don't want to talk about it.'

'No,' Emma explained. 'I mean when you said my father and "a perfectly innocent man". Isn't Howard Carter an innocent man?'

'Is he?' Tilly looked at the copper's daughter. 'I wonder.'

'I'm not surprised you can't see,' Emma said, after another silence. 'Still wearing your dark glasses. It must seem like pitch to you.'

'I had a bit too much sun,' she said. 'While I was visiting the Fahmy Beys. I've always had weak eyes. Whenever I've come to Egypt, I've had to keep my glasses on all the time.'

'But now, surely, in the dark . . .'

'Very well,' Tilly nodded, her hands in her lap. 'It shouldn't hurt for a while, you're right.' And she took them off.

Emma saw the woman's eyes flash in the street light. How lovely, she thought. Then, even in that half-light, she saw the scars at their outer edges, where the lids drooped to the cheeks. Poor thing, she thought, poor thing.

'What dreadful sunburn, darling,' she said.

'What?' Tilly seemed not to understand. 'Oh, yes, yes. You see why the glasses are so essential.'

And Emma gazed across the pale domes and minarets of Cairo, where her other two poor things were out under the stars.

A blind beggar had hobbled towards them as they reached the Mosque El-Muayyad. The pink of the Cairo sky was black here, for no electricity had permeated through to the Old Native Quarter; only the occasional flaring bracket, guttering in wrought iron on street corners.

'Baksheesh, baksheesh,' the old beggar mumbled in a tooth-less sort of way, but Macclesfield had brushed him aside, watching intently both the black, seething lanes ahead, across which acrid smoke perpetually drifted, and the demeanour of his old guv'nor, stooping a little now. Poor old bugger. What a time for his mind to go.

'Get a shufty at his belt, Norroy?' Lestrade suddenly whispered.

'Guv'nor?' Macclesfield stopped. The sound of his own voice frightened him.

'That's Mr Carter to you,' Lestrade hissed out of the corner of his mouth.

'Are you . . . all right? Yourself, I mean.'

'No,' Lestrade insisted. 'I'm Howard Carter. Really, Norroy, we've just had this conversation. Do try to stay with it, man.'

'No, I mean . . . for a while there . . .' Macclesfield stopped again. 'Back at the hotel . . . Were you just faking? When you came back from the desert?'

Lestrade winked. 'Like that Hammett bloke? Mad Sou' by Sou' West, you mean?'

'Er . . . something like that,' Macclesfield frowned.

'No. Whatever it was, I came over decidedly queer for a while. Such dreams . . .' Lestrade had stopped too. 'But earlier this afternoon I . . . what do they say in polite circles? Purged myself. Felt better right away.'

'What did you mean?' Macclesfield asked. 'About chummy's belt?'

'An ugly knife lay buried in it,' Lestrade whispered. 'Sheep-skinning job, but very fancy. Now, what's a beggar doing with a chiv like that, eh?'

'What indeed, guv. Christ Almighty.'

'What?'

'There!' Macclesfield had suddenly crouched, his buttocks on his heels. 'Third alley on the left. I count four.'

'Plus the three on my side,' muttered Lestrade.

'That's seven.' Macclesfield swallowed hard.

'Very good, Norroy,' Lestrade humoured him, 'but I'm afraid our little sum isn't over yet. There are . . . four more to my left.' He turned slowly to face them.

'Fifteen,' Macclesfield whispered.

'Er . . . no, Norroy.' Lestrade, even when staring death in the face, couldn't help correcting his man. 'I think you'll find that's eleven.'

'And if you turn to your right, guv, you'll see the other four you haven't taken into account yet.'

'Fifteen,' Lestrade nodded. 'Isn't that the number of blokes in a rugby team?' His back was to Macclesfield's now.

'I believe it is,' Macclesfield said.

'Ever played?'

'Nah.' Macclesfield shook his head. It was as well, the rest of him was already doing it. 'Soccer man, myself. Played inside left for G Division.'

'No!' Lestrade, even when staring death in the face, was impressed.

'Straight up,' Macclesfield asserted. 'Is that, by the way, how you intend to tackle this lot? Straight up?'

'Is there any other way?' Lestrade felt the warm brass knuckles in his pocket. The Englishmen had got themselves cornered in a meeting of four streets – a crossroads of fear. There were, of course, in theory, four avenues of escape, but each of them was blocked by a silent, menacing mob of black-clad fellahin, their faces swathed, their eyes watchful. Lestrade clicked the catch on his weapon and the four-inch blade snapped out, ripping a hole in his serge pocket. Norroy Macclesfield had left his gun at home. Now his hand lighted on the ebony life preserver in his pocket. He cradled it lovingly.

'Lestrade Pasha!' one of the voices from the blackness called.

Nothing. Lestrade nudged Macclesfield. 'Er . . . yes,' the burly Yard man said. 'Er . . . who wants to know?'

'Allah already knows.' A cultured voice behind them made them turn.

It was the old blind beggar, the rags over his eyes uplifted, his grimy face leering in the half-light. 'Mr Lestrade,' he beamed, waving his fingers under his nose as though wafting a smell away. 'Appearances can be deceptive, can they not?'

Macclesfield cleared his throat, wishing he'd been able to grey up his hair a little to make this subterfuge more convincing. Wishing he was in hell with the gates shut.

'They can indeed, Mr . . . er . . .?'

'Said Zagloul Pasha.' The beggar saluted again. 'May my tribe increase. Ah, I see you've brought Mr Carter Pasha. Excellent, excellent.'

Lestrade moved forward so that most of his face was lost under the all-embracing brim of his Panama. 'Why do you want to talk to me?' he asked.

'Oh, I don't want to talk to you, Mr Carter. I want to kill you.'

Macclesfield filled the space at Lestrade's shoulder. As he did so, he sensed the ground lessening between him and the men at his back.

'Why?' Lestrade asked levelly. 'What have I ever done to you?'

'You have . . .' Zagloul stopped, his crooked smile frozen. They saw his eyes narrow, even in the darkness. 'You have impersonated an archaeologist.' His voice was like the scrape of steel from a desert scabbard – Lestrade supposed – though he'd never actually heard such a thing.

'And you.' Zagloul jabbed a bandaged finger at Macclesfield. 'I presume you are impersonating a police officer.'

'Oh, no,' Macclesfield assured him. 'I *am* a police officer.'

Lestrade may never have heard the scrape of steel from a scabbard in the desert, but he heard it now in a Cairo alley. Several times. It wasn't a noise he cared for at all. He sensed Macclesfield ease the cosh into his fist. His own knuckles nuzzled the brass.

'I should have recognized your silhouette, Mr Lestrade.'

Lestrade squinted at his man. 'Mustapha?'

'Last week, yes. Today, I am feeling myself. Where is Carter Pasha?'

'Where are my men, Hambrook and Fabian?' Lestrade countered.

'And is this not also your man?'

Lestrade said: 'This gentleman beside me . . .' he glanced at the firm jaw, the quiet eyes, '. . . has nothing to do with any of this. In fact, I've only just met him. Let him go.'

'Come off it, guv'nor,' Macclesfield mumbled. 'I'm Norroy Macclesfield,' he called. 'Scotland Yard.'

'Ah, yes.' Zagloul grinned a gappy smile, then peeled off the liquorice stuck to his teeth. 'The Parquet of London. We have heard of your Scotland Yard. You doubtless have heard of how we deal with liars and traitors.'

'Doubtless,' Lestrade nodded. 'But I don't see how Mr Macclesfield and I fit that bill.'

'You are not Carter Pasha,' Zagloul shrieked, pointing at Lestrade. 'And you are not Lestrade Pasha.'

'Tsk, tsk.' Lestrade clicked his tongue and shook his head.

'Yes, that was a bit of a fib, wasn't it? Well, it won't happen again. Now, tell me, Mr Zagloul, while your boys are fetching Mr Hambrook and Mr Fabian for us, why is it you want Howard Carter dead?'

'He is a despoiler of tombs.' Zagloul had done exactly what Lestrade hoped he would do. He had come within stabbing distance.

'An archaeologist, surely,' Lestrade insisted. 'Have you seen the care he takes with his artefacts? I've watched the man at work; believe me, he has great respect.'

'Respect for the artefacts as ancient things, I have no doubt. But not as sacred objects from the tombs of our ancient kings. It is as though someone – an Egyptian perhaps – had come across your King Arthur's Excalibur or your King John's treasure – that which he lost in the Wash.'

'I think you must have misunderstood English history, sir,' Macclesfield said. 'We don't send our jewellery to the laundry. Only our clothes.'

'Quiet, Norroy,' Lestrade hissed. 'The grown-ups are talking.'

'You are not Egyptians,' Zagloul growled. 'Neither is Carter. You cannot understand. He will plunder the tomb of Tutankhamun as grave robbers have plundered other tombs in antiquity. Worse – he will take its priceless treasure home to England.'

'No, no.' Lestrade shook his head. 'I happen to know that various objects are already in the Museum here in Cairo. Others will follow.'

'Follow, yes,' Zagloul nodded sagely. 'Much after the manner of the Greek marbles – stuffed down the trousers of Lord Elgin.'

'All I want', Lestrade said, 'is my men, Hambrook and Fabian. I am not in the least interested in the Greeks losing their marbles.'

'And if I do not give them to you?' Zagloul's right eyebrow lifted in the darkness.

'Well then, we'll just have to take them,' Lestrade shrugged.

Zagloul gabbled something in Egyptian to his fellahin. There was a giggle. 'I have just translated your little joke for the benefit of my men,' he smiled. 'They enjoyed it very much.'

'I don't know very much about international law,' Lestrade confessed. 'But I do know that grabbing two British policemen in broad daylight is called kidnapping.'

'Kidnapping?' Zagloul looked around his growling, shuffling mob with hands outspread. 'It is well known that Allah made the English mad. Messrs Fabian and Hambrook are merely enjoying my hospitality in the Souk El Khasher. You had your chance to have them returned to you intact. All you had to do was give me Howard Carter. As it is, you will have them returned to you in pieces.' He flashed a commanding hand in the shadows and two of the fellahin spun on their heels.

'Wait!' Lestrade shouted.

Zagloul snarled in his native tongue and the fellahin swung back to join the others. 'I do hope this is not another of your subterfuges, Mr Lestrade,' he sighed. 'Because my patience is wearing a little thin.'

'What if I bring Howard Carter to you? Here. Now. Say . . . in half an hour.'

'Are you suggesting that I should let you go?'

'You'll never get Carter any other way.'

'We can storm the Shepheard's Hotel,' Zagloul assured him.

'With the twin Brownings?' Lestrade frowned.

'The twin . . .?' Zagloul cocked his head, unsure of what he'd heard.

'Brownings,' Lestrade nodded.

Zagloul hesitated, then he clicked his fingers. 'That is nothing,' he said and introduced two henchmen with a flourish. 'These are the Hussain brothers.'

The henchmen blocked out the street lamp with their bulk.

'No, no,' smiled Lestrade. 'You misunderstand. The twin Brownings in the hotel are not brothers; they are guns. You try to cross that space, Zagloul, and the manager has orders to open fire. That'll put a vent in your galabieh. Do you really think we English conquered a quarter of the world by walking into unlit alleyways in unsatisfactory disguises?'

Zagloul stood with his hands on his hips, less at home here than he had seemed as the happy-go-lucky Mustapha with his ships of the desert. 'Are you telling me that the only way I will have Carter Pasha is to send you back for him?'

'The only way,' nodded Lestrade.

The people's leader hesitated, glancing up and down the dingy alleyways, reading his men's faces, the way their fingers danced on their dagger hilts.

'I'll take my chances with the Brownings,' he mumbled. Then he clicked his fingers and the pack closed in.

'How many fingers am I holding up?' the voice asked.

'Whose are they?' Lestrade asked.

'They're mine, Daddy. Emma, your daughter. Fruit of your loins.'

'That's enough of that kind of talk, young lady,' he scolded her. 'This may be 1923, but there *are* limits. What's the question I'm supposed to ask?'

'"Where am I?"' she prompted him.

'Ah, yes,' he nodded. It hurt like hell. 'Three.'

'What?'

'Fingers. You're holding up three fingers. And I am lying – I think; am I? Yes, I'm definitely lying in the Shepheard's Hotel. Norroy?' He suddenly jerked forward, regretting it instantly.

'He's fine. Apart from the dislocated shoulder,' she said. 'And the wry neck.'

Lestrade frowned. 'I never saw anything particularly amusing in it. Er . . . is it me or is my lip forming a balcony outside the window?' He tried to look down at it, but the bristles of his moustache were in the way.

He felt her hand on his cheek. 'You've got concussion, Daddy. Dr Smith says a possible fracture of the skull. I'm taking you home.'

'Dr Smith? He deals with dead people, for God's sake.'

'Exactly,' she said, tucking him up under the eiderdown. 'And if you stay here much longer, he'll be dealing with you. He took his chance to nip into the hotel while you were out. Now he's taken his chance to nip out again. Incidentally, he confirmed Mr Lucas's findings on Aaron G. String. He was poisoned. Except he doesn't know by what. Hyoscine and something, he says.'

'Well, that's something,' Lestrade sighed. 'Any news of Hambrook and Fabian?'

'Well, they're a little over-exposed to Turkish delight and Walter says he never wants to see another fig again in his life, but apart from that . . .'

Lestrade frowned. It was like cycling up Everest. 'But surely', he said, 'they were kidnapped. The depreciation. The flies. Chained to the wall like animals . . . How did they get out?'

'Through the door,' she told him.

'Of the Souk El Khasher? Isn't it some sort of fortress? Dungeon?'

'It's a brothel, Daddy,' she raised both eyebrows, 'whatever that is.' She fluttered her eyelashes at him.

'Never you mind what that is, my girl.' He wagged a finger at her. Or was it three? 'They just walked out?'

She twisted her lips. 'Once Bob had found his trousers, yes. The poor lambs had existed on nothing but rice wine, figs and Turkish delight for nearly two days. You could tell how much they'd suffered by the way Wally Hambrook went back to give some girl a tip.'

'Yes,' Lestrade nodded. 'I can imagine what that was.'

There was a tap on the door. British hotel this may have been, but the plumbing was decidedly Egyptian. Norroy Macclesfield's bruised face swam into Lestrade's vision.

'Norroy.' He extended a hand that may have been his own. 'How'd we do?'

'Three of 'em down, guv, before your lights probably went out. Then the Parquet arrived.'

'Ah,' Lestrade smiled. 'Just like the Met, eh? Always around when you need us.'

'Not exactly, guv.' The Yard man shifted uneasily. 'Emma . . . Miss Lestrade here gave them a ring . . .'

'A ring?'

Emma poured the men a stiff brandy each. 'I bribed a kitchen porter, about the only one who hadn't abandoned ship as it were, and gave him my ring to fetch the Parquet. They followed you into the Old Native Quarter.'

Lestrade's face fell. 'Not Paul's ring?' he asked her. Even through his pain, he saw hers. The memories etched on her face of the man she'd loved and lost twice. 'No,' she lied. 'Not Paul's ring.' And she hid her hand quickly.

'Three blokes called Guest, Keen and Nettlefold,' Macclesfield told him. 'Thankfully each one built like a brick privy. They balanced the odds a bit. Unfortunately, Zagloul was hit.'

'Hit?'

'The Cairo papers this morning are saying it was an assassination attempt. The Major Domo managed to get hold of one,' Emma told him.

'Actually,' Macclesfield explained, 'it was a result of a nudge by the Hussain brothers on Pomeroy Nettlefold's right arm. Blew a bit of a hole in Zagloul's leg.'

'Well, I never.' Lestrade shook his head slowly and waited for his eyes to catch up. 'Police brutality again. Where is Zagloul now?'

'Here in the hotel,' Emma said. 'Room 203.'

'What?' Lestrade sat upright in his pillows and instantly regretted it. 'Why?'

'He's catching the plane with us tomorrow.'

'The plane?' Lestrade frowned. 'Where are we all going?'

'Home,' Emma said emphatically. 'Where an elderly gent of more years than he has had any right to can potter in his garden without the chance of a stray bullet or a poisoned cup of coffee.'

'"Elderly gent"?' Lestrade scowled. 'How dare you? You've obviously forgotten just how bad Fanny's coffee can be. Don't you see, Emma, there's work to be done? Carnarvon, Le Clerk, String. I don't know who killed them yet.'

'Well, you won't find out if you join their number,' his daughter told him.

'Miss Lestrade,' Macclesfield shifted awkwardly in his bedside chair, 'I think you ought to tell him.'

'Tell him what?' There was a roaring in Lestrade's head that dulled all sound. Macclesfield seemed to be coming and going behind the opaque veil of the mosquito nets.

'Zagloul is here under house arrest,' Emma said.

'For kidnapping and grievous bodily harm?' Lestrade asked.

'No.' She shook her head and stood up. 'For murder, Daddy. While Guest, Keen and Nettlefold were carrying you back here last night, a shot was fired, apparently by Zagloul's men.'

'It was a damned good shot, too,' Macclesfield nodded, always a man to give credit where it was due.

'How good?' Lestrade asked. 'Who did it hit?'

Emma and Macclesfield looked at each other.

'Hanger,' she said. 'Clifford Hanger. He's dead.'

7

'The shot came from where?' Lestrade peered under the window sash.

'We presumed', Holinshed told him, 'that alleyway there, next to the statue of Lord Kitchener.'

The ex-detective nodded with difficulty. There was no shattered glass, no rip in the green-striped awning.

'Has anything been touched?' he asked.

'Nothing,' Holinshed assured him.

'Whose idea was that?'

'Mine,' Holinshed said. 'Isn't that what you police chappies insist upon? Nothing to be disturbed?'

'Indeed,' smiled Lestrade. It was rare for anyone to be *that* informed. Jack Holinshed was one in a million. The mortal remains of Clifford Hanger lay sprawled on the bed, his head lying in a dark pillow of brown blood. The heavy flies of Cairo droned in the room, buzzing off every now and then, only to reland on their grisly banquet when Lestrade's back was turned.

'God,' Holinshed hissed.

'Not exactly sweetness and light, is it?' Lestrade peered at the dead man's face. 'Norroy, light that lamp, will you? How long has it been? Since he died, I mean?'

'Er . . . let's see.' Holinshed was glad of a chance to move away to check his wrist-watch by the corridor light. 'Nearly twenty hours. They brought you back at twelve thirty. That's when we heard the shot.'

Macclesfield blew out the match and the oil lamp's flare lit the room.

'Is this wise, guv?' he asked. 'If there's a sniper out there . . .'

'Get the blind,' Lestrade ordered. He could barely see the alleyway now, beyond the alabaster bulk of Kitchener. The tropic night was falling fast. 'Though with Zagloul in the building, I doubt we'll have any more of it. They'll be afraid of retaliation if they fire again. Why was his window open?'

'What?' Holinshed asked.

Lestrade glanced back and forth. 'From the angle he's lying on the bed, he must have been standing by it, facing the window, looking out. If the bullet came from out there, it would have had to have smashed the glass. Unless it was open.'

'Fresh air?' Holinshed suggested.

'Would you risk that, knowing there was an untold number of natives out there with rifles trained on you?'

'No,' Holinshed conceded. 'But then, I'm not in advertising. You must admit, Hanger was a little strange towards the end.'

'He was a little strange towards the beginning,' Lestrade observed. He crouched over the body. It was only a minute before the blasted head began to blur and swim in his vision and Norroy Macclesfield only just caught him before he slumped forward.

'Better sit yourself down, guv,' he said, although, what with his sling, it was rather a case of the blind leading the blind. 'He really shouldn't wander the streets of Cairo at night, you know,' he whispered to Holinshed. 'Not at his age.'

'I heard that,' Lestrade snapped. 'Besides, it was nothing to an afternoon stroll in the Jago or the Nichol when I was your age. Hoxton would make Zagloul's lads look like a Sunday School outing any day of the week.' His eyes focused again on the dead man. One of his braces had slipped off his shoulder and his tie was at half mast. Lestrade noticed a pair of cuff-links lay on the bedside table, along with a glass of water.

'Pass me that, Norroy,' he said.

'Of course, guv,' the Inspector said. 'Sorry, I should have thought of that myself.'

'We're all of us slipping a bit.' Lestrade took the proffered glass. 'It's probably the heat.' And he dipped his nose towards the contents.

'Aren't you going to drink it, guv?' Macclesfield asked. 'I'm sure it's been well passed by the management. This *is* Shepheard's Hotel.'

'I don't want to drink it, Norroy,' Lestrade frowned. 'I just want to smell it.'

Macclesfield looked at Holinshed. 'Perhaps you're right,' the latter said.

'Look at the wound,' Lestrade ordered. 'Tell me how he died, Norroy.'

The Inspector pulled the lamp a little closer. 'Gunshot,' he said.

'Go on.'

'Entry wound just above the left eyebrow. Exit wound . . .' he rolled his man over, '. . . behind the left ear.'

'Angle of shot?'

'Lower right.' Macclesfield was confident.

'So where was our marksman?' Lestrade badgered him.

'That would depend on where Hanger was standing.'

'Assuming he just fell back where he was.'

'Can we assume that?' Macclesfield wondered aloud.

'There's no blood anywhere else to tell us otherwise,' Lestrade shrugged.

Macclesfield crossed to the window, gingerly lifting a corner of the blind. 'Mr Holinshed's right, then; that alleyway has my vote. Behind Kitchener's statue.'

'Mr Holinshed, did you see us come in last night?'

'Heard, rather than saw.'

'Where were you?'

'In my room. Number 181.'

'The floor above this one?'

'That's right. But it's on the far side of the building. I heard a babble of native voices and police whistles. By the time I got to the foyer you and Macclesfield were on stretchers on the floor, together with the Parquet.'

'Did you hear a shot?'

'No, but I came down in the lift. That's in the centre of the hotel and quite lushly padded. I don't remember a shot after I reached the foyer, though I was intent on checking you and Macclesfield. I was also intrigued to find Zagloul with you. Then there was the rebarricading of the doors to see to.'

'What else do you make of the wound, Norroy?'

The Yard man turned back to the corpse. He looked stumped. 'If you're asking me what sort of bullet, guv, I don't know.'

'Neither do I,' confessed Lestrade. 'But I know a man who does. When we get back to the Yard, look up Bob Churchill. He'll tell you just by sniffing it.'

'We'll have to get a doctor in here pretty soon, guv,' Macclesfield said. 'People will be starting to talk about Cliff Hanger before too long. Especially those downwind of him. I suppose we should have asked Dr Smith to have a look at him, but he wasn't here five minutes, just long enough to patch you up. Still, we can at least dig the bullet out.'

'It's too late for that,' Lestrade said.

'Forensically, you mean?' Macclesfield asked, peering at the shattered skull again. 'Too mangled for recognition?'

'No, Norroy,' Lestrade said. 'You're a good copper, but a spotty young lad named Simpson I met at St Bart's a few weeks ago can run rings round you. Squat down there by the window-sill.'

'What? Here?'

'That's right.'

Holinshed looked on bemused.

'Now look up, in a line from where your head is. Imagine you're following the path of a bullet.'

'My God.' Macclesfield's finger snaked out.

All eyes except Hanger's followed it. There was a pale mark on the wooden panel of the far wall, a little to the right of a painting of the death of Gordon, hung there no doubt to make the British guest feel at home in a native country that really belonged to somebody else.

'What is it?' Holinshed asked.

'It's a bullet mark,' Macclesfield told him, standing round the bed, a penknife in his good hand.

'You won't need that,' Lestrade said. 'The bullet's long gone.'

'How do you know, guv?' the Inspector asked.

'Look *again* at the wound,' the ex-Yard man said patiently. 'The entry wound. See anything?'

There was a pause. 'Jesus,' Macclesfield said softly.

'What?' Holinshed squinted too, but didn't know what he was looking for.

'Powder burns,' said Lestrade.

'What does that mean?' Holinshed asked.

'Tell him, Norroy.'

'It means', it was the Inspector's turn to twist his head this way and that along the line of shot, 'that no one fired from that alleyway behind Kitchener . . .'

'Or if they did, they didn't hit Hanger.'

'Powder burns are only left around a gunshot wound if the gun in question is fired at close range.'

'Inches,' confirmed Lestrade. 'Not feet.'

'So . . . Hanger . . .' Holinshed was trying to reason it out.

'Was standing facing the window, yes. He had his back to the bed. His killer stood there, slightly to one side where Macclesfield is now,' Lestrade told him. 'Then he fired – a revolver or an automatic – from his hip. Hanger was leaning forward – perhaps to watch the scene as the Parquet covered our retreat into the hotel. The bullet entered the front of his skull, peppering his skin with powder burns. On its way out, it blew out the back of his head and buried itself into the woodwork over there.'

'But what makes you think the bullet isn't still lodged in the wall?' Holinshed asked.

'Because whoever our killer is, he – or she – had to lose that bullet. It doesn't take much of a forensic expert to tell an automatic or pistol bullet from that of a rifle – it's only about one third the size. He also knew that a pistol shot would be unlikely to do such lethal damage from all the way across the Square. So to make the alley-shot theory plausible, he'd have to dig the bullet out and hide it.'

'I see.' Holinshed shook his head. 'Ingenious.'

'Except', Macclesfield said, 'he hadn't reckoned on Mr Lestrade here. The powder burns gave it away. If the fatal shot *had* been fired by a rifle from across the square, there'd be no burns at all.'

'And I nearly missed it in this half-light,' Lestrade admitted. 'Gentlemen, we must keep our wits about us. Whoever killed Clifford Hanger is here in the hotel. And what's more, he's changed tack.'

'Tack?' Holinshed was lost.

Lestrade nodded grimly. 'So far he's killed carefully, with a

141

poison like henbane that the experts can't quite put their finger on. Now he's rattled. Using firearms he's not familiar with. Now he's making mistakes.'

'Well, that's good,' Holinshed grinned. 'Isn't it?'

The current – and ex – Yard men were shaking their heads. 'No, Mr Holinshed,' Macclesfield said. 'That's bad. It makes him scared. And that in turn makes him dangerous.'

The man in the fez sensed he was fighting a losing battle. All morning he had stood his ground. A hostile mob had gathered shortly before dawn chanting, in English: 'Death to the British!' Most of them carried clubs, a few of them swords, a couple had rifles.

'Zagloul for Prime Minister!' they roared, the women with them ullulating, several paces behind their menfolk, of course.

'I tell you, it is impossible,' the man in the fez persisted. 'They have told us that any aircraft attempting to take off from this airport today will be shot down.'.

'Shot down?' Howard Carter repeated. 'Good God, man, they've got rifles, not Howitzers!'

'Anti-aircraft guns,' Captain Mainwaring corrected him. 'Howitzers are rather *passé* nowadays. Look, Ahmed, Flight Controller you may be, but Olivia is out there on the runway, ticking over nicely. Veronica's got all the tea, coffee and G and Ts on board, haven't you, Veronica?'

'All tickety boo, Captain.' She flashed her best air-hostess smile at him.

'But I cannot be held responsible,' Ahmed insisted. 'What if they fire at you while you are crossing the tarmacadamized surface? They, fellow countrymen that they are, are an ugly looking bunch.'

'Look . . . er . . . Ahmed, isn't it?' Merton of *The Times* waded in. 'No one's held an Egyptian responsible for anything for four thousand years.'

'Quite,' Mainwaring concurred. 'And anyway, some of us have been fired on before. I don't think a few Egyptian fellahin are going to measure up to Boelcke's Circus, do you?'

Lestrade had once spent several weeks with George Sanger's Circus. He didn't remember it as being *quite* that bad. But then, ex-Chief Superintendent Lestrade was between a rock and a hard place. Behind him lay Zagloul's snipers, fanatical patriots who had already had a damn good attempt to sever his head from his body; and in front the prospect of another flight into hell in the wicker death chairs of the de Havilland Hercules.

Macclesfield and Mainwaring got their heads together in a corner of the departure lounge. The senior inspector beckoned over his two juniors.

'Captain,' Macclesfield whispered. 'How far to your plane, would you say?'

Mainwaring squinted across the sun-baked flat. 'Four, perhaps five hundred yards.'

'That's a bloody long way.' Hambrook shook his head.

'Once we're all on board, how long 'til take-off?'

'Five minutes,' Mainwaring said. 'Less than three in a Sopwith, but the Hercules is a big job and Olivia's a bit of a bitch to get up in the morning. Rather like my wife, actually.'

'How many of us are going, Norroy?' Fabian asked.

'Well, if we've got any sense, all of us. But I think the Holinsheds have just come to see us off.'

'I'm not overjoyed at the prospect of taking that Zagloul chappie home with us,' Hambrook said. 'Some sort of dissident, isn't he?'

'Or some sort of national hero, whichever side you happen to be on,' Macclesfield countered. 'Anyway, we're not taking him. He's coming with us.'

'Er . . . the subtlety of that remark has got a little away from me, Norroy,' said Fabian.

'Well, he's not any longer our prisoner as I understand it. We can't hold him for the death of Hanger. He wants to go to London to talk to the Prime Minister, whoever that is at the moment, and yours, Captain, is the next available flight. The Parquet would rather he was out of the way.'

'He's also our insurance policy,' Hambrook said. 'With him in tow we stand less chance of being hit.'

'Right,' said Mainwaring. 'So you chappies are the experts. How do we play it?'

Macclesfield mused a little space. God, he had a worried face. 'Women in the centre. Emma . . . Miss Lestrade and your Veronica.'

'Ah, but she's an employee of Imperial Airways,' Mainwaring said. 'Her first duty is the safety of the passengers.'

'Even so,' Macclesfield said, 'I'm going to have to insist.'

Mainwaring shrugged. 'All right. Then what?'

'Hambrook, you lead.'

'Ah, a sort of Policeman's Excuse Me.'

'You might say that,' Macclesfield scowled.

'Shouldn't that be me?' Mainwaring asked. 'As the only one who understands the mechanical gubbins out there?'

'Yes, it should.' Macclesfield nodded. 'But that's precisely it. You're too precious to lose. Chances are the first man on the tarmac will be a target . . .'

'Ah,' Fabian beamed. 'Let me guess – something like "chances are the last man on the tarmac will be a target".'

'Something like that,' Macclesfield said. He saw the crests collapse from his colleagues. 'Look, lads,' he said, 'I'm not one to carp, but there *is* a little matter of two inspectors of Scotland Yard getting themselves incarcerated – if that's the right word – in a Cairo bordello for two days. If a little thing like that were to reach the reasonably enormous ears of Chief Constable Wensley . . .'

'Whereas a nice bit of heroism at Cairo airport . . .' Hambrook had caught Macclesfield's drift.

'. . . Would go down said ears a treat,' Bob Fabian finished his sentence.

'I can see why you boys are in the Flying Squad,' Macclesfield beamed at them. 'You make a chap proud to be a policeman.'

'Where are we going to put the civilians?' Mainwaring asked.

'I want Zagloul near the back. Fabian, you take one arm, I'll take the other. I want him walking backwards.'

'Backwards?' the pilot and two of the Yard men chorused.

'Yes,' Macclesfield confirmed. 'I want those herberts at the perimeter fence to see his face at all times. Just in case one of them gets trigger happy and forgets who he is.'

'I thought they wanted Carter,' Hambrook said. 'Isn't that what this bit of nonsense is all about?'

'So they do,' Macclesfield nodded. 'So he's Merton's and Weigall's problem. They'll have to hedge him round as best they can. They'll be tucked in behind you, Captain, just ahead of the ladies.'

'That leaves the old guv'nor.' Fabian nodded in his direction. 'Sunstroke, senility, concussion. He won't make twenty yards.'

'He will,' Macclesfield nodded. 'But he'll be on his own. We'll tuck him in behind Zagloul, Fabian, just ahead of you.'

'But that . . . that makes *him* the last man on the tarmac,' Hambrook noted.

'I can't help that. Zagloul's been hit in the groin. He's not going to break any Olympic records and there's no stretcher and no wheelchair. The Ghaffirs have already said we can't have theirs. After all, they *are* Egyptians. Loyalty only goes so far you know. And Lestrade doesn't have the strength to hold the Wog up.'

'Well,' Hambrook twisted his immense moustache, 'I can't say I like it.'

'Oh, you don't have to *like* it,' Macclesfield told him. 'But there's got to be a certain amount of lumping along the way.'

And he formed his motley crew up in the departure lounge, Ahmed, the Flight Controller complaining bitterly throughout.

'Tooled up?' Macclesfield asked Hambrook, checking his line like a general.

The Inspector waved a chair leg at him. Best not to enquire where that came from.

Macclesfield clapped the man's shoulder. 'Captain Mainwaring?'

'My trusty Webley.' The pilot patted his trouser pocket.

'Standard issue for Imperial Airways?' Macclesfield frowned.

'Standard issue for Guy Mainwaring,' he smiled.

'Gentlemen of the Press,' Macclesfield invited them into line. Weigall and Merton stood loosely around. 'Mr Carter in the middle.' He leaned to whisper in the archaeologist's ear. 'Can't have those two side by side, can we?'

The archaeologist scowled. 'You know we're all going to die, don't you?' he said, loudly. 'What difference does it make where we stand, for God's sake?'

'Ladies?'

Veronica and Emma came next. 'There, there, Mr Carter,' the hostess said. 'Once you're on board, I'll make you a nice cup of tea. *And* you can go forward and look in the cockpit.'

'Madam,' he turned to the girl in her trim powder blue, 'I have gazed on the Eighth Wonder of the World. Looking at

145

a few dials and a steering-wheel can hold no pleasures for me.'

'Joystick,' Veronica corrected him.

Emma squeezed Macclesfield's hand. He blushed a deep crimson. 'Tooled up,' she nodded, and bent to remove her shoes. 'Lotus and Delta Daintyheels,' she smiled. 'Death at twenty feet. I'll get two of them before I go down.'

He smiled.

'Norroy,' she held his sleeve, 'look after Daddy.'

He nodded. 'Mr Zagloul, you will turn round.'

'Why?' the wounded man asked.

'I want you to walk like an Egytian,' Macclesfield told him. 'I shall be on one side of you, Inspector Fabian on the other. At any movement from a rifleman among your people you will call upon him to desist. And you will do it in English so that I know what you are talking about. Captain Mainwaring is armed. One signal from me and he will put a bullet in your brain.' He waited until Fabian had linked his left arm through Zagloul's. The junior inspector raised his right fist. It held a bicycle chain.

'What are you doing with my bicycle chain?' Ahmed, the Flight Controller wanted to know. 'I will lodge an official complaint,' he shrieked.

'You do that,' Macclesfield said. 'In triplicate, please. Care of Chief Constable Wensley, Scotland Yard. Guv?'

Sholto Lestrade had jammed his Panama hat on to his newly bandaged head. His face was the colour of the desert sand, but his eyes still flashed fire. 'Tooled up,' he said softly and his brass knuckles glinted in the early morning light.

'You'll be the last man on the tarmac, sir,' Macclesfield said.

'Story of my life, Norroy,' Lestrade shrugged.

'Mr Lestrade,' Jack Holinshed extended a hand, 'it's been an experience. Give my love to dear old Blighty.'

'Who?'

Tilly Holinshed leaned forward and pecked him on the cheek. Her perfume wafted over the ex-Chief Superintendent and his bandage collided briefly with her dark glasses. 'Take care of yourself,' she said.

'You're sure you won't come with us?' Macclesfield asked. 'I've got a feeling Cairo isn't going to be very safe for us British for a while.'

146

'We have business to tie up here,' Holinshed said. 'I'm not armed, I'm afraid, but we'll keep a look-out for you and shout a warning at the first sign of trouble.'

'Thanks.' Macclesfield looped his arm through Zagloul's. 'Up your tower, Flight Controller. Hambrook, you've got the column.'

'Actually,' hissed Merton, '*I've* got the column.'

Hambrook clicked back the door and they began their walk in the sun.

'Dashed annoying, Captain,' the Inspector said, 'having no porters. This suitcase isn't exactly light.'

'No dashing!' Macclesfield growled. 'Parade ground formation, Hambrook. Think yourself back to S Division.'

'It was cutlass drill in my day,' Lestrade muttered.

As Hambrook reached the edge of the building's shadow, a great howl erupted from the perimeter fence and the mob began rattling the wire like enraged monkeys in a cage, jostling each other to get at the cursed Englishmen.

'Tell them, Zagloul,' Macclesfield nudged the Egyptian in the ribs with his good arm.

'No shooting,' Zagloul bellowed above the hubbub. '"Now lettest thou thy servant depart in peace."'

'That's very good, Mr Zagloul,' Fabian said. 'St Luke, Chapter 2, Verse 29, if my old Sunday School teacher wasn't having me on. Mind you, he had a lot of us on – his knee, mostly, but that's another story.'

'I am gratified', Zagloul said, 'that you are impressed by my grasp of your Scriptures. Unfortunately, that lot aren't. You see, it's not in the Koran.'

'Allahu Akbhar!' they screamed at the perimeter fence and rifles came up to the ready.

'Daddy!' Emma bit her lip, but it was too late. She'd cried out.

'Steady,' his calm, soft voice reassured her. 'Look at the plane, Emma. Just look at the plane.'

'I feel like one of those ducks in a fairground shooting gallery.' She tried to laugh.

'Why do you always want the impossible at times like these?' he chided her. Nobody was listening to them.

Suddenly there was a rattle of gunfire and the shattering of

147

glass. Instinctively, the whole group out on the tarmac turned; even Zagloul, who was now facing the plane. The Holinsheds, brother and sister, came hurtling out of the double doors of the airport lounge, a machete-waving mob at their heels.

'They rushed the building,' Jack shouted, 'as we tried to get a better vantage point. I don't believe it. I just don't believe it.'

'They let us get out of the hotel,' Lestrade said, swerving awkwardly as Tilly Holinshed hurtled past him. 'I thought that was too easy.'

A bullet kicked dust spots off the ground feet from them. 'I think about now, Norroy,' Lestrade shouted and the tight little formation scattered. Only Zagloul still staggered, wedged as he was between the policemen, his feet slithering on the tarmac. Mainwaring crouched, crooked his arm and aimed his Webley.

'Oh, bugger,' Carter heard him say as his bullet found the shoulder of Ahmed, the Flight Controller. 'The only Egyptian out there marginally on our side and I have to shoot him. Oh bugger, oh bugger.'

'You've got to watch those,' Lestrade said as he wobbled past the crouching Captain. 'They have a tendency to kick to the left.'

'Imperial Airways announce the immediate departure of their Flight 401 from Cairo,' Veronica was shouting, lying prone at the top of the steps beside the plane. Stray bullets were thudding into the silver fuselage, an almost painful blur in the sun.

Hambrook hauled Carter up the steps and threw him inside, then Weigall, then Merton. Both pressmen reappeared within seconds, their noses pressed against the glass of the windows, scribbling notes furiously as the scene unfolded before them.

'Can you use one of these?' Mainwaring threw his pistol to Lestrade. 'I've got to start the bus up.' And he leapt up to the propellor, swinging one of its blades down with all his body weight. 'Veronica', he shouted, 'the red button. On the left. Just above my lucky St Christopher.'

'What about it, sir?' he heard the girl scream back.

'Push the bally thing, dear!'

And she scurried inside the aircraft.

Tilly and Emma had reached the steps, and the ex-Chief Superintendent's daughter whirled to face the running foe. Her father was crouching on the steps below her, his good hand held steady, his fist full of Mainwaring's revolver. There was a whine as a rifle bullet ricocheted off the handrail and there was a blast from Lestrade's gun. A running Egyptian jack-knifed and went down. A second later, another fell, victim of a masterly lob of a Lotus and Delta Daintyheel.

'I see they kick to the left too,' Lestrade grinned at his girl.

Macclesfield and Fabian threw the wounded Egyptian into the aircraft and turned back to drag Emma, her blood up, inside. The roar of the de Havilland's engines announced to a tense and waiting world that Veronica had found Mainwaring's red button and Mainwaring in turn had leapt again for the propellor blade and kicked the engines into action. Even allowing for the pressure he was under, the sudden rattle of the steps and the heat and the flies, it was not Lestrade's best shot. The luckless Ahmed was just dragging himself off the forecourt when the ex-policeman's second bullet found the Flight Controller's other arm and he nose-dived to the tarmac.

'I think we'd better make our excuses, Mr Lestrade,' Mainwaring said, bounding up the steps. Together, he and Holinshed made for the door and momentarily wedged themselves there.

'After you, Mr Holinshed,' Mainwaring insisted. 'The passenger comes first every time. Mr Lestrade,' the Captain called back, 'I really am going to have to more or less insist now.' And he grabbed the kneeling ex-Yard man by the collar and dragged him inside.

As Veronica slid the steel door shut, a barrage of sticks and stones clattered against it. Lestrade rolled over and lay still. 'Well,' Mainwaring said, 'we don't appear to have a Flight Controller, so we'll just have to hope the runway's clear for take-off.'

'Could you fasten your seat belts, ladies and gentlemen?' Veronica shouted as trays and glasses slid the length of the aisle. But the interior of the Hercules looked like a battlefield; men and women, fighting for breath, bandages unravelling as she spoke. The only one sitting in a chair was the Captain and he kicked the de Havilland to the left.

*

It was over the Delta that things began to go wrong. For a man with a bullet in his groin, Said Zagloul Pasha was good behaviour itself. But then, an ounce of lead where your wedding tackle is usually housed does tend to slow a man up. He had not only himself but his four wives to think of. And a future Prime Minister of Egypt could not afford the scandal of a divorce, a Decree Isis as it was known in those days. Weigall and Merton sat at opposite ends of the passenger lounge, each of them writing an article that was going to win them the Adie Prize For Reporting From Dangerous Places. The three serving policemen sat together, swapping notes on the incident they'd left behind at the airport. Sholto Lestrade sat hunched over his knees, trying not to have a stomach. One or two more bits of turbulence and he wouldn't have.

Veronica was just serving cocktails to the ladies when the Hercules coughed and jerked upwards.

'Bloody Hell!' Carter was sketching something like a hippopotamus, except that now it had the tail of a kangaroo.

'Veronica!' a strangely strangled Captain Mainwaring was summoning his Johanna Factotum.

'Feels a bit rough, Wally,' Fabian frowned, watching the piece of lemon dancing on the surface of his G and T.

'Bit like that old Crossley old Wensley tried to palm us off with in the Squad.'

'Er . . . should the sky be that way up, Norroy?' Fabian asked. 'I only ask because you're normally nearer to it than we are.'

Macclesfield jammed his nose against the window, not by choice, but because the lurching of the aircraft gave him no alternative.

'I don't think there's much in it,' he said. 'Not when we seem to be falling out of it rather after the manner of a stone.'

Zagloul raised an eyebrow. It was the only fear he'd ever show, in front of the cursed English, that is. Allah was good, he kept telling himself. And Mohammed was his Prophet.

Merton of *The Times* was on his feet, striding manfully for the blunt end, where the driver was. 'Mainwaring,' he called. 'Mainwaring, what's going on?'

A rather oddly coloured Veronica blocked the gangway, the green of her face clashing slightly with the powder blue of her

150

dress. 'There's no cause for alarm.' She smiled, but her teeth were gritted and the dimples in her cheeks were like bullet holes.

'Good God!' Arthur Weigall was the first passenger to notice it. 'The port engine's cut out! The blades aren't working!'

'It's perfectly safe,' Veronica assured him. 'Routine, in fact. Captain Mainwaring does that every so often. It's called feathering.'

'Feathering be buggered!' Percy Merton was peering out of a starboard window. 'This one isn't working either.'

'Ah, no.' The Imperial Airways girl knew panic when she smelt it. 'That's important for balance, you see. Feathering has to be done in pairs, or it . . . doesn't work. A plane like the de Havilland can easily function on one engine.'

'What happens if that one stops?' Carter asked.

'Well,' Veronica giggled a little hysterically. 'Then we really *would* be in trouble.' And, as if on cue, the Hercules's growling died away. All they heard now was the moan of the wind through the fuselage and a staccato rattle that turned out to be Zagloul's false teeth. Veronica didn't hear either of those things, because she'd slid to the gangway floor in a dead faint.

'If my Elementary Physics serves me aright,' Merton told the assembled company, rather gratuituously, 'we're going to hit the ground in . . .' he checked his watch for good measure, 'one minute, eighteen seconds. Seventeen. Sixteen . . .'

'For God's sake, shut up, Merton!' Arthur Weigall waddled forward and stepped over the fallen hostess, batting aside the powder-blue curtain. Guy Mainwaring was wrestling with the controls.

'If I can just keep her nose up', he barked, 'we might make the sea.'

'Will that help?' Holinshed was at Weigall's elbow.

'I may be able to pancake,' the Captain told him.

'I couldn't touch a thing,' Hambrook muttered.

Everybody fell silent. It was strangely eerie, gliding at six . . . no . . . five . . . no, four thousand feet, at the mercy of the Mediterranean winds.

'Our Father,' Carter began and Tilly Holinshed seemed to be mumbling something alongside him.

'I don't think we need that just yet,' her brother snapped.

151

'Mainwaring, I know a bit about engines. If we can get one prop going, will that pull her round?'

'It would get us to Palermo,' the Captain said. 'I hadn't really envisaged returning to Cairo.'

'Right. Help me out.'

'What?' almost everybody chorused.

'You can't be serious!' Merton shouted at him. 'Holinshed. Snap out of it, man. I didn't think you would be the one to crack.'

'He might have something.' Mainwaring leapt out of his seat, but the Hercules yawed to starboard and the blue-grey horizon swivelled in the windshield. 'One of us can't do it alone. The force of the wind will rip you off the wings in seconds. Besides, I'm the only one with the skill – not to mention the insurance cover – to free a de Havilland engine. Holinshed, take my hand.'

The big man did so. 'A human chain,' he shouted. 'Come on, Merton!'

'Somebody will have to stay at the helm,' Mainwaring shouted, throwing his hat on to his seat. 'Keep pushing that red button. And keep the joystick back. If her nose goes down, we've all had it.'

'I'm sorry,' Weigall sniffed, 'but *nothing* will induce me to hold hands with *him*.' And he sneered at Merton, folding his arms for good measure. Carter plugged the gap as Mainwaring slid open the little port window and clambered out. The wind whipped his tie up his nose and blew his trousers against his legs. Immediately he dropped on to his chest and lay on the silvered wing. The women rushed to the side but the wing was above them and only the good Captain's legs were visible, flailing about as he edged himself along the struts towards the far engine nacelle.

'I'll have to sit this one out,' Macclesfield apologized, his left arm useless in this situation. Hambrook grabbed Weigall's left hand and Fabian Hambrook's. 'I hope this isn't going to get back to the boys in the Squad,' he said pointedly to Macclesfield. One by one, the humans of the chain emerged on to the rocking aircraft's wing. Holinshed's hair was blasted backwards but he buried his nose on to the metal skin and flexed both his arms.

152

Merton tried to say something, but the rush of air knocked the breath out of him.

Lestrade was on his feet, but only just, and he glanced down at the seated Zagloul. 'I will have to decline,' the Egyptian said. 'What with my trouble . . .' and he waved in the general direction of his groin.

'Hmm,' Lestrade nodded. 'I guessed there'd be some Moslem reason why you couldn't lend a hand.' And he snatched the wriggling fingers of Walter Hambrook and held on.

'Daddy,' Emma was alongside him. 'You're in no fit state.'

'Macclesfield,' Lestrade ignored her, 'can you fly this bloody thing?'

'Er . . . no,' the Inspector told him, staring in disbelief at the rows of dials in front of him.

Emma elbowed him aside. 'Men!' she snorted and whipped off her cloche, hoisted up her skirt and gripped the joystick firmly in both hands. By now, Lestrade was perched half in and half out of the lounge, the devilling wind blowing his moustache hairs up his nostrils.

Macclesfield snatched the guv'nor's flapping hand and jammed his shoulder, the painful one, against the fuselage. Emma stared ahead, ramming her finger again and again against the red button. The Hercules coughed as Mainwaring's right hand hit the upright propellor. They were losing height fast now, plummeting towards the grey-green of the Nile Delta, criss-crossed with the river's brown.

In the lounge, Tilly was bringing Veronica round; slapping the girl's face – anything to keep herself busy, to fight the panic she felt inside. It might have been kinder, she suddenly realized, to keep the hostess out of it. 'Fasten your seat belts, ladies and gentlemen,' the girl slurred, as she came to. 'We'll be coming in to land shortly.'

'How often do these planes crash?' Tilly asked her, trying not to sound hysterical.

Veronica's eyes flickered upwards. 'Only once,' she said and her head lolled back again.

Tilly looked up. Beyond the flapping blue curtain, she saw Emma Lestrade wrestling with the controls, the biggest of the policemen reaching out of the fuselage and up to where

153

the bandaged ex-Chief Superintendent was dangling like a puppet on the struts, buffeted mercilessly by the air currents. Then, there was a roar, and the Hercules barked back into life.

'Keep her nose up,' Mainwaring yelled, but no one heard him, not even Holinshed who was at full stretch, holding grimly on to the pilot's left hand.

Emma had the joystick jammed back under her breasts and the ground was hurtling beneath them now.

'Undercart down! Undercart down!' Mainwaring was screaming. It was all to no avail of course. Emma couldn't even catch his orders, still less did she know which lever to push. Or was it pull? She saw the sparkling sluggish waters of the Delta as they gushed their way to the sea, the clumps of palm trees and the dusty roads. She saw the little sand-blown homes and the fellahin dashing for cover in all directions. She even saw the nodding yellow heads of the henbane flower, flattening in the rush of the aircraft's downpull. Lestrade felt something hit him in the left foot, the one that was dangling below the wing. Only Zagloul, from his position in the lounge, realized that it was the top of a fig tree. Then the Hercules soared upwards, the chain gang on its port wing sliding backwards with a concerted scream. Merton, for his part, was glad he'd worn the brown trousers that morning.

With his free hand, Mainwaring jabbed towards the fuselage and slowly, as if afraid to believe their luck, they crawled back inside. Macclesfield hauled his old guv'nor down to safety and so it went on until Mainwaring jumped on to the carpet and stood there, grinning widely.

'I believe we have you to thank for our lives, Mr Holinshed,' the Captain said. 'Frankly, if we hadn't just done it, I wouldn't have believed it possible.'

There was a clearing of a throat behind him.

'Ah, Miss Lestrade,' the Captain retrieved his cap, 'I think you'd better wear this from now on.' And he planted it on her head, along with a kiss. 'If you don't mind, Mr Lestrade.'

Hambrook and Fabian minded greatly. So did Norroy Macclesfield but he wasn't going to show it.

'Any chance of waking your girl up?' Zagloul asked. 'All you

154

people had to do was risk your lives on the wing. I had to watch it. I'd kill for a G and T.'

So they came back, on a wing and a prayer. As the Pope himself was to do two generations later, when the Hercules touched down at Palermo, Zagloul kissed the tarmacadam. Well, it was a nice gesture and a useful one for a future Prime Minister in search of allies.

Three days later, the battered little company, Olivia's engines fixed, roared into Croydon. Said Zagloul Pasha was escorted by officials of his own Embassy to the Savoy. Unfortunately, he'd have to wait to see the Prime Minister because Mr Bonar Law had resigned with a throat problem, and His Majesty was dithering as to the choice of successor. It was likely to be Lord Curzon, currently at the Foreign Office, but you could never rule out the Chancellor of the Exchequer, Stanley Baldwin. Of course, the unimaginable *could* happen and somebody might think of Neville Chamberlain, the new Minister of Health. No, come to think of it, nobody would think of him. Ever.

Sholto and Emma Lestrade wrapped themselves in the arms of Fanny in the arrivals lounge at Croydon and all was right with the world.

'Emma,' her father scolded her, 'you shouldn't have sent Fanny that telegram. She's cut her holiday short now.'

'Now you leave her alone, Sholto Lestrade.' His wife thumped his good arm. Not, after hanging on to the Hercules's wing, that he had one, really. 'She was concerned, that's all. I didn't know whether to get to Egypt or come home. Anyway, Cousin Val was just about driving me up the wall by then. And France seemed to have come to a full stop because of the death of Sarah Bernhardt. Just as well you've retired, dear. What would you do in the Police Revue now?'

'Ah,' smiled Lestrade. 'Her voice was liquid gold.'

Fanny looked at him. 'That's very lyrical for you, dear.'

'Yes, isn't it?' he said and neglected to tell her that it was something he'd read in one of Percy Merton's columns.

'What now?' Fanny asked him as the three of them bundled into a cab and the April rain began to bounce on the windows.

155

'Well,' Lestrade sighed, looking from right to left at the two loves of his life, 'first, a bath, a brandy and a good cigar, not necessarily in that order. Then a visit to Lady Carnarvon, I think.'

'Was it the sun, dear,' Fanny said, stroking the nut-brown of her husband's face, 'that Emma spoke of in her telegram?'

He looked wryly at her, then into the middle distance as the car taxied off the runway. 'Oh, no,' he said. 'That was the poison. A mixture, I fancy, of henbane and something else. I think we've all come nearer to death in the last few weeks than we know.'

'And then, there were the engines,' Emma said.

'Yes,' Lestrade chuckled. 'Rather ironic, that. Escaping poison and nationalist bullets to end up in some Egyptian mud flats because of engine failure.'

'But they didn't fail, Daddy,' his daughter said.

'What?' He turned to her.

'I had a long chat with Guy Mainwaring in Paris yesterday, while he was waiting for the plane to be double-checked. All three engines had been tampered with. It was sabotage. We were all supposed to die.'

8

The lights burned late in Virginia Water that night. The large Victorian house of which Sir Edwin Lutyens once said 'Good isn't the word' was a far cry from Lestrade's old office at the Yard. But his study had the same green-baize wall festooned with bits of paper, the same shoe boxes stuffed with a filing system of sorts and the same carefully preserved layers of dust. Madison, Lestrade's wife's man, was only allowed in here on alternate Thursdays – the day Lestrade was wont to pop into the Yard for a chat with old Walter Dew to familiarize himself with the latest developments of police work and explain them to Walter.

Fanny had gone to bed a little after midnight. For all she was a copper's daughter herself and years younger than her husband, the hectic pace of the Riviera had taken its toll. She had also worried herself sick about Lestrade and had not slept. She sat with Sholto and Emma in the study, liaising with Madison on the tripe sandwiches and cocoa, which came in a seemingly endless stream from the kitchen. She offered her comments on the current case where she could, but her dad had been a uniformed man. He'd risen to Chief Constable of the County, but he'd be the first to admit he wasn't a natural detective. She was out of her depth. One minute she was wrestling with the complexities of poison, the next Emma was taking her cocoa out of her hand and Sholto was kissing her good-night.

'Don't be long,' she said to them both and patted their smiling cheeks.

'Well, then,' Lestrade stretched out on the settee, folding his arms and letting his tired head loll back, 'let's do it one more time, Sergeant Lestrade, and then I'll let you go off duty. Have you ever thought of going in for the Force, Emma?'

She looked at him, her mouth hanging open. 'There was a time, Daddy dearest, when I thought of nothing else. From the time I was eight until I was twenty-two. You put me off.'

'I did?' Lestrade was outraged.

'Every time you came to Bandicoot Hall or I came up to London we'd have the same conversation. You said it was no job for a woman.'

'It's isn't. It's the last thing on earth I'd want a daughter of mine to do.'

'Well, then . . .'

'It's just that you're good at it,' he told her, beaming with pride. 'You'd make Inspector any day if you were a bloke.'

'Ah,' she raised a finger. 'If I were a bloke, I'd be voting by now too. No, those policewomen's uniforms are so ghastly, I'll settle for being a policeman's wife.'

Lestrade's eyebrows rose imperceptibly. 'Oh?' he growled. 'Anyone in particular?'

'No,' she said innocently. 'Just speaking metaphorically. Murder one.'

'You're changing the subject,' he told her.

'No, I'm not. Murder One.'

'Go on then.'

'Fifth Earl of Carnarvon. Nice old boy. Friend to Antiquities. Bags of loot. Financed Howard Carter's current expedition.'

'Cause of death?'

'Death certificate says pneumonia. The whisper is malaria. The reality is hyoscine poisoning. And that means it had to be somebody who was with Carnarvon in the Valley of the Kings. There's your list,' Emma said, lolling back in the armchair. 'Who's your money on?'

'Nobody at the moment. Cigar?'

Emma's eyes widened. Not long ago, the old man was muttering about her smoking at all. The merest sight of a Will's Capstan or a Cavander's Army Club would have had him frothing at the mouth. Now he was passing round the Havanas. A sure sign that she'd arrived. Well, it had been a long time coming. 'Thanks,' she said, and took one. He lit up for them both as if she were Harry Bandicoot or Walter Dew or any of the other men he'd whiled away many a midnight hour with, wrestling with the imponderables of life; and with them, the imponderables of death.

'Murder Two.' She blew, as he did, smoke rings to the panelled ceiling.

'Alain Le Clerk, French Egyptologist. Bit of a boy in the fol-de-rols department. Seemed to like mummies of all sorts. Apparently found thrown from his horse, but the actual cause of death, poisoning, by hyoscine.'

'Makes Dr Crippen look rather feeble, doesn't it?' Emma said, staring at the overlapping pieces of paper.

'There was one woman, though, he seems not to have taken to – the mysterious Mrs Ralph.'

'Ah, yes. You saw the photograph, Daddy. What did she look like?'

Daddy shrugged. 'What with the sun-hat and the sun-glasses, who knows? Curvy enough for our late *ami* I should've thought, but according to Burton they didn't hit it off.'

'Perhaps he made a pass', she was talking to herself really, 'and got a rebuff.'

'Perhaps. But something made him leave that Valley, in a hurry, in the dark of a freezing night, on a horse he knew he couldn't control. Something frightened him.'

'Mrs Ralph?' Emma frowned. 'Surely not. Perhaps she'd brought a paternity suit.'

'Give me Murder Three.' He drew deeply on the cheroot.

'Aaron G. String, the American railway magnate. Wide in every sense of the word. Loud. Boorish. Even other Americans like Lindsley Foote Hall were embarrassed by him. Went berserk one night in the Valley of the Kings. Hallucinating. Blew his brains out having had a damn good go at yours. How is the head, by the way?'

'Glad to be in England', Lestrade told her, 'now that April's here.'

'April was here when you left, Daddy,' Emma chuckled. 'It's only been three weeks.'

'I know,' he sighed. 'It seems like millennia. Cause of death?'

'Gunshot wound.' She frowned. She wasn't at all sure about her father's summation on the state of his head.

'Yes, but before that. Had he not blown his brains out, as

you so colourfully put it, what *would* have been the cause of death?'

'Hyoscine poisoning,' Emma said. 'Although . . .'

'Yes?'

'Well, didn't Doctor Smith, the Cairo Practor, say there was something else, but he didn't know what?'

'That's right. I got the distinct impression that Smith was a good man. Nobody's fool sort of bloke. Why wouldn't he know what else was in String's bloodstream? What other sort of poison?'

'Perhaps it's a new one,' Emma suggested. 'Some new chemical on the market. When I was in school in Switzerland, Monsieur Le Petomane told us that the Periodic Table was by no means absolute.'

Lestrade wasn't listening to the end of that. The only thing he'd learned at school that was absolute was the Ablative and he'd never known for sure what that was. 'Or old,' he said suddenly and he felt the hairs crawl on the back of his neck.

'What?' Emma looked at him. 'Daddy, a strange inscrutable glint has come into your eye. What are you thinking?'

'You said,' he said, '"perhaps it's a new one". A new poison. Well, yes, that's possible. But equally, what if it's an old one? A poison that the ancients knew but which has been lost to time?'

'You mean, a poison from the time of the Pharaohs?'

'From the Eighteenth Dynasty,' Lestrade nodded. 'From the time of Tut-Ankh-Amen himself.'

'The curse,' Emma whispered, suddenly, inexplicably afraid. 'The curse of the Pharaoh's tomb that Arthur Weigall told you about. Oh, Daddy, is it possible?'

He was on his feet now, pacing the carpet, puffing frenetically, turning every now and then to scan the board. She watched him closely, proud, awed slightly. She was watching the world's second greatest detective in action, deducting with the best of them.

'Tell me', he almost shouted, 'what Carnarvon was doing in Egypt in the first place?'

'Looking for evidence of the ancient world,' she answered him.

'Evidence, be buggered!' Lestrade roared. 'What was he really after?'

'Er . . . treasure.'

He snapped his fingers. 'Got it in two. The Frenchman Le Clerk, what was he after?'

'Treasure.' She sat upright, the light dawning in her eyes.

'Aaron G. String.'

'Treasure,' she whooped. 'He even offered to buy the tomb outright, didn't he?'

'He did.' Lestrade prowled to his desk, rummaged in the papers strewn there and prowled back again to the board. 'He did indeed. Lindsley Hall told me and I wasn't listening. He said they'd all come to Egypt for the same thing. To rob the dead. To steal the very heart of Egypt itself. *That's* why they died.'

'So the curse is true?' Emma felt her own heart thumping in the lamplight.

'In a way, yes. Oh, there's nothing supernatural about it. Nothing magic. Somebody wants to protect the tomb. And that somebody is prepared to kill to do it.'

'Zagloul!' Emma clapped her hands.

Lestrade was shaking his head. 'He'd do it by bullet and ballot,' he said. 'Besides, he was on the plane.'

'The plane? I don't follow.'

'You told me, Emma,' he said, looking round vaguely for an ashtray. 'The plane was sabotaged.'

'Yes,' she said. 'By Zagloul's men, trying to stop us from taking off.'

'Really?' He raised an eyebrow. 'You think about that for a moment.'

She did. She had. 'It doesn't make sense,' she said.

'That's right,' he nodded behind his own smoke. 'Why not?'

'Because they knew that Zagloul would be on board. If they couldn't stop us at the airport, they'd lost.'

Lestrade nodded again. 'Zagloul's a wily old bird. He'll turn an apparent abduction to his own advantage. *And* he'll keep the treasures of the tomb in Egypt. No, whoever got at that plane's engines wasn't on board. They expected us to fall out of the sky somewhere over the Delta or over the sea. Either way, there'd be little left.'

'So that takes us back to Egypt,' Emma said. 'One of the fellahin, perhaps?'

'The fellahin use poison, yes. Apparently, it's quite common. And henbane is the most common of all. But this takes an expert. Tell me, what did Mainwaring say about the plane? The sabotage, I mean?'

'He said that somebody had filed down some bolts, I think. The vibration of the aircraft made them seize up. It was a simple matter to replace them once we'd landed, but in the air . . . well . . .'

'Did he say the plane was under guard before take-off, bearing in mind the disturbances in Cairo?'

'Yes, it was.'

'British guards? Or Egyptians?'

'Er . . . British, I think. Yes, the Sirdar's troops.'

'I thought so, though where they were when we needed them, I can't imagine.'

'Why?'

'They wouldn't have allowed an Egyptian near the plane,' Lestrade explained. 'But a white man, an Englishman like themselves? That's different. Especially if he knew all the right words, the people involved.'

'But . . . an Englishman, Daddy? Howard Carter, Lord Carnarvon, two thirds of the expedition team, they're all Englishmen. Why should one of them want to kill to protect an *Egyptian* tomb? It just doesn't make sense.'

'We're forgetting one thing in all this.' Lestrade's eyes narrowed over his cigar.

'What?'

'Clifford Hanger, our fourth victim.'

'Gunshot,' Emma volunteered. 'Like Aaron String.'

'But not like him,' her father countered. 'The shot was not self-administered. But he was killed by someone in the hotel.'

'How far did you get with that?'

He looked wryly at her. 'Before someone insisted that I come home, you mean? Not very far.'

'Daddy.' She crossed to him, knelt at his feet and rested her chin on his knee. 'You nearly died out there. You were poisoned, weren't you? Shot at? Beaten up? If I don't say this, nobody else will – you're too old to be . . .' But he'd clamped a hand over her lips.

'Why was I poisoned?' he asked. 'Why did I nearly go the same way as Aaron String?'

Emma frowned. 'I don't know,' she said.

'Because I came too close,' Lestrade told her. 'I was in danger of stumbling on to something. So was Cliff Hanger. That's why he had to die. And in a hurry. There was no time for the random effects of hyoscine and something else. The Curse of the Pharaohs is too damned slow when push comes to shove. At that point, a little Smith and Wesson or a Parabellum comes in pretty handy.'

'Who wasn't on the plane with us?' Emma said. She was asking herself really. 'Arthur Mace,' she read them off the wall, 'Alfred Lucas, Pecky Callender, Harry Burton, Alan Gardiner, Lindsley Foote Hall and Acting Sergeant Adamson. Who's your money on now, Dad?'

Lestrade sighed, giving up the ghost and stubbing out the cigar in one of Fanny's hyacinth pots. 'I don't know,' he said. 'But I know a man who does. Or, to be precise, a man and a woman.'

'Oh?'

'In the scheme of things,' he said, 'assuming I'm right about the grave robbers, who's the biggest thief of all?'

'Er . . . Lord Carnarvon,' Emma said, 'because without him, there'd be no expedition.'

'Exactly. But he's dead. So who's next?'

'Carter,' she clicked her fingers. 'Carter's the expert. The front man as they say these days.'

'Precisely. So he's our man. The next sitting target.'

'*That* was what the plane was all about,' Emma shouted. 'It was to get Carter.'

Lestrade nodded. 'But now the target's widened,' he said. 'Who has Carter come to see?'

'Almina,' Emma told him. 'Lady Carnarvon.'

'. . . Whose money he still needs to continue to finance the whole operation. So Lady C becomes a sitting target too.'

'What are you saying, Daddy?' Emma frowned, looking up at him.

'There's an old saying', he smiled, 'in the land we left three days ago. It goes something like "If the mountain will not come to Mohammed, then Mohammed must go to the mountain".'

163

'So . . . we are Mohammed.'

'*I* am Mohammed,' he corrected her. 'And Carter and Lady C are the mountains. The twin peaks. Don't worry, I'll get Fred Wensley on to them. Round-the-clock protection. With just a *teeny* gap left in the high security. Just big enough for a murderer to think he can squeeze through.'

'Daddy,' she was his little girl again, all ringlets and taffeta, looking up into that dark, sad face, 'will it be all right?'

'Of course.' He kissed her on the forehead. 'It will always be all right.'

'Round-the-clock protection?' Chief Constable Fred Wensley looked as though Lestrade had just made an indecent proposal.

'It's only for a while,' his old oppo urged.

'Sholto, Sholto,' Wensley sighed, shaking his head. 'I've got racecourse gangs, Indians protesting over the salt tax, the possibility of a spread of the Norfolk farmhands strike; front desks all over the Divisions are being besieged by wives petitioning against their husbands' adultery. Riots over Baldwin putting a penny on a pint; the Duke of York is marrying Elizabeth Bowes Lyon tomorrow, and to cap it all, there's a new marathon-dance craze about to hit.'

'Is there?'

'The police in Baltimore stopped one after fifty-three hours non-stop. Good God, after a couple of minutes on the floor, Mrs Wensley always tells me to sit down. In Cleveland, the girl who won had worn out five male partners – which reminds me, Kate Meyrick is up to her old tricks again. Night-clubs! I'd ban 'em out of hand. Her ankles had swollen to twice their normal size, you know.'

'Kate Meyrick's . . .?' Lestrade frowned. 'You did say ankles?'

'No, no.' Wensley ran his hands through what little hair he had left. 'Not her. The winning girl in Cleveland. Then of course, there's the Old Fogey Murders and the little-mentioned fact that you've had three of my inspectors off on a little jolly for the past three weeks!'

'Jolly?' Lestrade exploded. 'I've just finished telling you . . .'

'. . . How you nearly died; yes, I know. All the papers said was "Some Unpleasantness In The Streets Of Cairo".'

'You didn't read that in the *Daily Mail*, did you?' Lestrade was horrified.

'I don't read *anything* in the *Daily Mail*,' Wensley assured him. 'I'm sorry, Sholto. Even if your assumption about Howard Carter is correct – and I'm by no means certain that it is – I can't spare you so much as a copper at the moment. Stretched isn't the word for it.'

'What *is* the word for it on the Old Fogey business?' Lestrade asked.

'No breaks. No leads. No collar,' Wensley shrugged. 'I'd have been a damned sight happier if there'd been another one while those three wise monkeys of yours were away. That would have eliminated them entirely.'

'Well, there it is,' Lestrade said. 'Mind how you go, Fred.' And he made for the door.

'By the way,' Wensley stopped him, 'didn't have any trouble with the man at the desk, did you?'

'No,' Lestrade said. 'Why?'

'Oh, usual thing,' the Chief Constable told him. 'Spate of racism in the Met again. In America, half the police force are supposed to be associate members of the Ku Klux Klan and you do look rather dark this morning.'

'What's this obsession of yours with America, Fred?' Lestrade leaned on the glass-panelled door. 'Dance crazes? Policemen in the Klu Kucks Kan? When I left three weeks ago, this place was England.'

'Ah, you mark my words,' Wensley wagged a finger at him, 'the world's turning, Sholto. I fear the days of the Empire are numbered. Don't fancy a Coca Cola do you?' And he held up a bottle of dark liquid.

'Next time I have fish and chips, I'll come to you to sprinkle some,' Lestrade said and saw himself out.

Howard Carter was a particularly difficult man to find. Without his Panama, his jodhpurs and his cravat, and without the awe-inspiring splendour of Karnak or the Valley of the Kings, he was really very ordinary indeed. He was not at the Strand Palace, where he said he'd be. Nor had they seen him at the

Indiana Club, Mecca of archaeologists the world o'er. His mother, Mrs Carter, hadn't seen the boy for years.

'That's it!' she'd snapped at Lestrade. 'He's got time to gallivant all over these heathen countries, but as for visiting his dear old mum, oh dear, no. Well, that's bloody typical, that is. Always poking about in other people's business. It's macabre, that's what it is. Macabre. And tell him when you see him, he still owes me three and six from 1909. Mothers are like elephants, they never forget, and they don't bloody well fade away either.'

So it was that Emma telephoned her old school chum, Lady Evelyn Herbert.

'Darling, how lovely to hear from you.'

'Darling, I was so sorry about poor Lord C.'

'Yes, it was rather a blow.'

'How's Lady C taking it?'

'Mumsy? On the chin, as always.'

'We've been there, you know. To Egypt.'

'No. What a coincidence.'

'Coincidence? I thought you'd asked for Daddy's services?'

'Lord, no . . . um . . . I mean, I wish I'd thought of it.'

'Jack Holinshed said you had.'

'Jack? Oh, he's such a *darling* isn't he? And *so* good looking. I hear he's broken it orff with that ghastly Pamela de Vere Hinchinbrook.'

'Wasn't she in the Ladies' Tug Of War Team at the Antwerp Olympics?'

'That's right. Anchor woman.'

'Well, no wonder Jack broke it off.'

'Oh, you are a one, Emma. No, it's typical of Jack to say what he did. Hates to poke about in other people's business. I would have engaged your daddy, of course, but well, it all came as such a shock. How is Tilly?'

'Fine. We had a bit of a rough ride getting out.'

'Really? Nothing about that in the *Tatler*. But the natives can be so revolting, can't they?'

'You haven't seen Howard Carter, I suppose?'

'Little man? Broken nose? Bally huge chin?'

'That's him.'

'Not for a while, no. But Mumsy has. In fact, she's seeing him now.'

'What, as we speak?'

'As our resonance reverberates on the wires, yes.'

'Where are they?'

'Well, let's see. The wedding? No, that was Westminster Abbey a couple of days ago. Didn't Lizzie Bowes Lyon look an absolute fright in that dress? After all the fuss about it, I thought it would have been something other than her mother's.'

'So, Howard and Mumsy . . .?'

'Wait a minute. What day is it?'

'Saturday.'

'Saturday. Saturday. Yes, I'm just checking Mumsy's social calendar. It's just here by the phone. Yes, I thought so. Wembley.'

'Wembley?'

'The football thingie. Mumsy's an absolute fanatic. She wanders all over the place to watch Bolton.'

'Does she?'

'Bizarre, isn't it? But as she says: "Life has to go on." That's where they'll be. The VIP enclosure. Byee.'

And she was gone.

'Wembley,' Emma told Lestrade. 'The football thingie.'

'Are you sure?' he asked.

'Has the Pope's Encyclical called for World Peace?'

'I'll get the Lanchester.'

'Daddy,' she snatched up a set of keys, 'that jalopy of yours is twenty years old if it's a day. We'll take my Austin.'

The Baby Seven died just yards from the ground at Wembley. The Empire Stadium was a magnificent sight, every bit as imposing as Karnak, Lestrade thought. But in fact, his view of it was rather impeded. He spent most of his time with his face jammed against the canvas roof of his daughter's motor, pushing for all he was worth. But the heat of the Tropics, the after-effects of poisoning and the clubs of Zagloul Pasha's fellahin had taken their toll. He got the vehicle off the roadway with the help of Emma and two patrolling constables who looked rather askance at this coloured gentleman in the company of so young a girl. While Lestrade whistled 'You made me shove you' to the car, 'She should have bought a Buick, She should have bought a Buick', the two coppers wandered off, whispering together about white slavery and muttering embrocations.

'Police.' Lestrade flashed an old tram ticket to the bloke on the turnstile and jostled his way through the host of flat caps, holding on grimly to Emma's hand. He'd never seen so many people in his life, all of them swaying in time to hymns and ragtime tunes, chanting 'Here we go, here we go, here we go'.

The Lestrades of two generations cut below the edge of the crowd, seeping now beyond the congested terraces, and made for the VIP enclosure where they'd built a large, striped awning to keep off the rain. Of Howard Carter and Lady Almina Carnarvon, there was no sign.

'God,' Lestrade heard a worried official mutter, 'this is disastrous. Disastrous.'

The official was talking to a uniformed Chief Superintendent, resplendent in blue and silver.

'I'm looking for Lady Carnarvon,' Lestrade said.

'What's the matter?' the Chief Superintendent ignored the ex-Chief Superintendent, turning instead to the official.

'What's the matter? What's the matter?' For all it was a cool end of April, the official was sweating, mopping his brow with an outsize handkerchief. 'Look at that bloody crowd, that's what's the matter. Do you know how many this stadium holds? Do you? Do you?'

'A hundred thousand, isn't it?' the Chief Superintendent was calm itself. He'd worked his way up through the ranks, man and boy; from Horse Troughs to high office. He knew how many beans made nine. Nine of them did.

'Well, I'll tell you how many,' the official shrieked, hysteria etched in every wrinkle. 'A hundred thousand, that's how many. But that's not the point. That's not the point,' the official swept on, eyes swivelling wildly from left to right. 'There seems to have been a miscalculation. According to the turnstile returns,' he waved a wad of paper under the policemen's noses, 'according to these, no less than a hundred and twenty-six thousand persons have been let in. And that's not all . . .'

'I knew it wouldn't be,' the Chief Superintendent sighed.

'I'm trying to find Lady Carnarvon,' Lestrade tried again.

'And I'm trying to find some peace of mind,' the Chief Superintendent snapped, looking the nut-brown man up and down. 'You'll find the Indian contingent over there.'

'Thanks to your lax security,' the official railed, 'an estimated seventy-five thousand more have climbed in over the walls. That means, apart from the huge loss of profit – a *huge* loss of profit – there are . . .'

'Two hundred and one thousand.' The Chief Superintendent's mental arithmetic was calmer than the official's.

'No, no,' the official was shouting. 'You see, that's just where you're wrong. There's two hundred and one thousand people in a stadium designed to hold one hundred thousand. That's . . . that's . . .'

'Twice the capacity,' the Chief Superintendent told him.

'That's twice the amount this place will hold. Look at 'em,' he screamed, pointing a trembling finger. 'They're spilling over on to the pitch. Thousands will die. Thousands!'

He suddenly reeled backwards from a stinging slap from the Chief Superintendent, never one to suffer officials gladly. 'No one's going to die, you horrible little man. Get a grip on yourself.' He flicked a loudhailer up to his lips. 'Gentlemen, I'm afraid we're going to have to ask you to show your ticket receipts. Some of you crafty buggers haven't paid. We've all got your number. Of course, the match will be delayed a little . . .'

'Yes, till week next Thursday,' Lestrade growled.

'Look,' the Chief Superintendent bellowed at him through his loudhailer, then realized his error when Lestrade went an even funnier colour. 'Look,' he let it fall to his side, 'I thought I told you, the Indian contingent . . .'

'I don't want the Indian contingent,' Lestrade snapped. 'Are you supposed to be in charge here?'

'I *am* in charge here.' The Chief Superintendent stood his ground. 'You men,' he pointed to a knot of constabulary eyeing the crowd nervously, 'get out there and start collecting. Nine-pence a head. And make sure you give receipts.'

'How many men have you got?' Lestrade asked.

'Thirty-six,' the Chief Superintendent told him. 'Look, who the bloody hell are you?'

'Sholto Lestrade,' Lestrade answered. 'Formerly of Scotland Yard.

'Oh, yeah,' the Chief Constable looked him up and down again, 'and I'm the Angel of Mons.'

'Got any horses?'

'Why doesn't that bloody band shut up?' the Chief Superintendent muttered.

In the centre of the pitch, the Coldstream Guards, in scarlet and gold, were playing all the tunes of glory, but the space between them and the flat-capped crowd was lessening all the time as they still trickled in over the walls and through the turnstiles.

At their ragged edges, where the hapless policemen were now asking to see ticket stubs, scuffles were breaking out, helmets flying.

'Answer him!' Emma shrieked, grabbing the man's lapels.

'Four,' he snapped. 'Four horses.'

'Where?' Lestrade couldn't see any.

'In the tunnel,' the Chief Superintendent said. 'Where the teams come out.'

'Emma,' Lestrade gripped the girl's hand. 'you wait here. Lady C should be somewhere in this lot. Find her. Carter too. And for God's sake, keep your head down.' And he kissed her.

'Daddy . . .' But he was gone, unravelling the bandage from his head, flinging the Panama to the winds. She spun on her heels from the Chief Superintendent, still looking authoritative with his loudhailer, but paralysed by inexperience.

The tunnel was full of more anxious officials, men in ludicrous long shorts and the smell of liniment. Four coppers lounged there too, their horses tethered to the space at the rear.

'Whose is the grey?' Lestrade asked.

'Mine.' A curly-headed constable straightened. 'Why?'

'Message from the Chief Superintendent. You're to lend him to me.'

'Her,' the constable corrected him. 'Him is a her. Gertie.'

'Fine,' Lestrade said. 'I've ridden mares before.'

'Who are you?'

'Lestrade of the Yard,' Lestrade said, glancing at the Divisonal silver letters on the constable's collar. 'How's old Bill Cooper? Still sucking his thumb?'

170

'Well . . . yes, sir, as a matter of fact . . .'

'Get your tunic off, lad, and your helmet.'

'Look, Mr . . . Lestrade, I don't really think . . .'

'I know, son.' Lestrade winked at him. 'That's what they pay us Chief Supers to do. What's your name by the way?'

The lad straightened. 'Storey, sir. George Storey.'

'Righto, George.' He snatched the dangling tunic. 'Blimey, I must have put on a few pounds since last season.'

'Are you sure the Chief Superintendent . . .' Storey handed him his helmet.

'As sure as I'm standing here.' Lestrade breathed in to hook up the bottom three buttons. He rammed the helmet on his head. 'I haven't got time for the boots. You lads,' he called to the others, standing open-mouthed, 'give me five minutes. If I'm still in the saddle by then, come out – slowly, mind. No cantering. Softly, softly preventee crushee.'

And he crossed to the waiting animal.

'Er . . . excuse me, sir . . .'

'Yes, George?'

'You get on the other side, sir,' Storey told him.

Lestrade turned and winked. 'Well spotted, Storey. You'll go far. Somebody give me a bunk-up.'

Four policemen found the stirrup for him and pushed so hard he almost sailed right over the top. Luckily, Gertie was parked nearest the wall, so Lestrade merely hit it with his shoulder and bounced back again into the saddle. He took up the reins and pulled the animal back. Nothing.

'Heyup, Gertie.' Storey clicked his tongue and the grey whirled with a splaying tail and walked placidly up the tunnel. A man with a centre parting and long shorts hailed him. 'Can we start, officer?' he asked in a Northern twang.

'How many men have you got?' Lestrade asked, unable to stop his horse.

'Eleven.' The Bolton Wanderers captain seemed a little surprised by the question.

'Well,' Lestrade called back, 'there are two hundred and one thousand people out there. I'd think you'd find yourselves under a bit of pressure.'

'Good gate, Albert,' his vice captain said to him. 'Must be very nearly a full house.'

171

Now, Lestrade thought, the basics. He was pointing the right way – he knew that because the animal's ears were twitching *ahead* of him; always a good sign. His knees were tight against the saddle leather and his heels were down approximately where his heart was. It was as well he couldn't see Gertie's face from where he was – the flared nostrils, the rolling eyes. All horse and rider could see was a jammed mass of people, pressing ever wider across the pitch, rolling up the scattered policemen disappearing at the crowd's edges. Not many sugar lumps there, Gertie told herself.

The band of the Coldstream Guards had stopped playing and were packing up their instruments. There were roars from the crowd, indignant now at the delay and incensed by the pressure from the boys in blue.

Emma's eyes narrowed on her prey. *There* was Lady Carnarvon, radiant as ever in a rather fetching little black number by Coco Chanel. And hangdog as ever, the mournful face of Howard Carter loomed at her shoulder.

'Lady C, Mr Carter, what a lovely surprise!' She bounded over to them.

'Emma, my dear.' Lady Carnarvon unwrapped her face from her Bolton Wanderers scarf and kissed the girl. 'I didn't know you were in town.'

'Miss Lestrade.' Carter tipped his hat.

'Quite beastly, this delay, isn't it?' the old girl said.

'I was very sorry to hear about Lord C,' Emma said.

'Thank you, my dear,' she nodded. 'But he's at rest now, overlooking his beloved Highclere. My, you've got a tan. Been somewhere nice?'

'Egypt,' she said. 'Didn't you mention it, Mr Carter?'

'Slipped my mind,' the surly archaeologist said.

'Oh, my God, no.'

'What is it, dear?' Lady Carnarvon sensed the girl stiffen at her side. She seemed to be staring at the policeman, the one on the white horse. 'Oh, he'll be all right. I have heard it said,' Lady Carnarvon whispered in her ear, 'and only a few moments ago, not a million miles from this enclosure, that the riff-raff are intent on causing trouble. Violence on the terraces, indeed! Stuff and nonsense. Why, those fellows are simply like our servants at home or the fellahin in Egypt – rather whiter, of course. Give them plenty of largesse at Christmas and the vote or two and they're happy enough. And I have yet to see a howling mob of vermin that was the equal of a lone policeman on a white horse.'

The lone policeman on the white horse was feeling very much alone at that moment. Gertie couldn't push her way any further and with the instinct of a police horse, swung herself sideways to roll the crowd back. Admirably trained, Lestrade thought, but he also knew that the animal now presented a greater target. One broken bottle in the wrong hands could rip the old girl's belly wide open. He kept up the same banter, level, steady, keeping the reins tight and the long-handled truncheon firmly scabbarded at the saddlebow.

'Come along now, gentlemen,' he cooed, as though to nervous pigeons. 'We can't start the match until you move back, can we? Now, you don't need that brick, sir, do you? Put it back in your pocket, there's a good gentleman. That's it, now. Move along there. Move along.'

Five minutes had passed. The same five minutes that to Emma Bandicoot-Lestrade felt like years. Turning as far as he dared, Lestrade saw three other coppers walking their horses across the pitch.

'All together now!' He raised a hand, wobbling in the saddle as he did so. 'The king's just arrived. Those blokes behind me, that's the signal. Let's hear it for His Majesty.' And he broke, albeit flatly, into 'God Save The King'. One by one, the flat caps came off and the bricks and bats disappeared. One by one, the crowd melted away, as Bolton Wanderer supporter sat side by side with West Hammer and peace was restored to Wembley Stadium.

Emma breathed an audible sigh of relief as the singing reached a crescendo and top hats all round her were swept off.

'I don't see him,' Lady Carnarvon said. 'I don't see the king. Where is His Majesty?'

'British Honduras,' someone nearby told her, between lines. 'Deuc'd peculiar, isn't it?'

Emma saw the man on the white horse wheel and canter back across the pitch. She saw him reel at the tunnel entrance. Then a great roar went up and huge applause burst from the massive crowd.

'Come on you Wanderers!' Lady Carnarvon bellowed, whirling a wooden rattle for all she was worth. 'Up Bolton!'

Emma was still watching the figure on the white horse, struggling to stay in the saddle as the teams jogged out in keyed-up lines. She was standing on tiptoe, hoping her father was all right when she felt it. A thump in the centre of her back. From an over-exuberant fan no doubt. Even so, it hurt and for a moment, it knocked the breath out of her. She slumped forward, the feathered cloches in front of her a blur.

There was a scream. The girl was falling. As she went down, Lady Carnarvon's black dress was daubed with red.

There was no doubt about it. The man on the white horse had saved the day. Stories about more casualties than the Somme were grossly exaggerated. There was only one. A young woman stabbed and in the VIP enclosure too. A number of the brick-carrying vermin read all about it next day in the *News of the World* and shook their heads. Nobs stabbing each other! What was the world coming to?

Sholto Lestrade had had gravity to help him dismount and he rapidly exchanged clothes again with a bewildered George Storey who had the presence of mind to remount, keep his mouth shut and earn himself a place in history.

'You ought to be in hospital,' Lestrade looked into the face of his only daughter, lying on her soft white pillows back at home.

'You see.' Fanny held her hand. 'We can't *both* be wrong.'

'Hello, hello, hello,' Emma whispered. 'What's all this, then?' She ran her fingers across her father's cheek. It was wet with tears.

'I'm sorry,' he managed. 'I should have been there.'

'You were,' she told him, easing herself back on the pillow as best she could. 'Saving hundreds, perhaps thousands of lives. I was so proud of you.'

'And I of you,' he smiled through the tears, 'but . . .'

'Let's have nothing said', she wagged a finger at him, 'about sending a girl to do a man's job.'

'Not a bit of it,' he promised. 'The fact is, Sergeant Lestrade – by the way, I'm promoting you to Honorary Inspector from today – the fact is, you saved the life of Lady Carnarvon or Howard Carter or both.'

'I did? How?'

He leaned back. 'I've made my enquiries,' he said. 'It wasn't easy. I'd forgotten what an unobservant, tight-lipped lot the nobs of old England are.'

'Sholto,' Fanny tutted, 'you sound more like a Bolshevik every day.'

'Communist, dear,' he corrected her. 'They're calling themselves Communists now, apparently.'

'And?' Emma was all ears. She had her father's ears. Mercifully, the haute couture of 1923 hid them from view.

'Chummy was a woman.'

'A woman?' Emma frowned. Even that much movement cost her a lot.

'For a trained archaeologist, Howard Carter has the observational skills of a gnat. As for Lady C, she was able to give me a blow-by-blow account of the game and the midfield accuracy of Bolton, but an attack by a maniac on a young girl known personally to her that happened only inches away seems to have left her strangely unmoved. Luckily, a little kid called Algie came up trumps. He noticed a woman, swathed in black, not dressed at all like the other females in the enclosure and he asked his mother who she was. The reply was, if my memory serves, "Don't stare dear. She's foreign. They can't help having no dress sense."'

'Foreign?' Emma queried.

'You and I, Emma, have seen quite a few examples of the get-up recently. At least, if little Algie's description is anything to go by.'

'Egyptian?' Emma asked.

'Egyptian,' Lestrade nodded. 'But that's not all. She was wearing a veil.'

'So?'

'So nosy little Algie – and thank God he was – couldn't help noticing the woman's eyes.'

'Her eyes? What about them?'

'She had nicks on her eyelids, at the outer corners.'

'What does that mean?'

'I asked friend Carter about that.'

'And?'

'It's an old Egyptian custom,' her father told her, 'especially among high-born Egyptians. They tattoo themselves to ward off afreets, evil spirits. Devils.'

'I see. I don't suppose we know who this woman was?'

'Oh, yes,' Lestrade said. 'We know exactly who she was. She was Mrs Ralph. The question I can't answer – yet – is who Mrs Ralph is.'

'Now, come on.' Fanny stood up. 'The doctor's explicit instructions were to let Emma sleep. You need a bit of kip too, Sholto, after all that nonsense on the white horse.' And she pushed him out of the room.

'Fanny,' Emma called to her and she doubled back.

'Yes, darling.' She smoothed the girl's soft cheek.

'He doesn't know, does he?' she whispered. 'How bad it is, I mean?'

Fanny Lestrade felt the tears starting again, as she'd felt them in the morning when the doctor had told the women that Emma might never walk again. 'No.' She tried to smile. 'He doesn't know.'

She felt Emma relax and the girl who was everything in the world to them both turned her face to the wall.

9

'Are you all right, guv?' The earnest face of Norroy Macclesfield peered out from under his trilby.

'Just a touch of dejar-view, that's all,' Lestrade said. He was squatting beside the body of William Pargetter, in front of the very cabinet they'd all stood in front of only a month ago. The only difference was that one of them was lying down, his head smashed to a pulp, his glasses shattered nearby.

'I know what you mean,' Macclesfield said. 'Uncanny, isn't it?'

'I don't suppose that lad Simpson's around, is he?' Lestrade straightened as best he could. His thighs hadn't been right since the Cup Final and he still felt decidedly wembley. 'He's a useful little adjunctive.'

'It's exactly the same spot that Albert Weez was killed – except the murderer dragged him into the underground tunnels.'

'Are we looking for the same man, Norroy?' Lestrade asked.

There was a flash as the police photographer went to work. 'Very nice, Bailey,' Lestrade said. 'Now take a few of the body, will you, and stop playing silly buggers.'

'Could be a copycat,' Macclesfield said.

'What did the papers say when Albert Weez died? How much detail was there?'

The Inspector shrugged. 'Can't remember. I'll get one of my lads on that. It's not likely, though, that they'd mention this room and this cabinet, is it?'

'No,' Lestrade said. 'Which is why I think your copycat idea isn't likely either. What have we got here? Three, four blows to the head?'

Macclesfield nodded. 'Blunt instrument. Killer struck from behind. Right-handed, I'd say.'

'So would I,' Lestrade mumbled. 'That cuts the odds down.'

'How's Emma?'

'Since you called yesterday, you mean?' Lestrade raised an eyebrow. 'She's fine, Norroy. It'd take more than a chiv to put my girl down.'

'Look, guv.' Macclesfield fidgeted. 'Can't I work on that one?'

'Don't ask me, Macclesfield,' Lestrade laughed. 'I don't work for the Yard any more. You'd have to have a word with Fred Wensley. Besides, "that one" as you put it, is only part of the whole bloody mess. Emma wasn't a target. Howard Carter and Lady Carnarvon were. Emma just got in the way.'

'You asked Wensley for men?' Macclesfield checked.

'Now, don't go getting your combs in a bunch over that,' Lestrade warned him. 'Other side, Bailey. Get that arc of blood over the cabinet. If Fred Wensley says he's got no manpower, he's got no manpower. It's that simple.'

'I know,' Macclesfield muttered. 'I know.'

'There's a man in the house now,' Lestrade reassured him. 'Built like a wardrobe. She'll be fine. Now, let's get back to these Old Fogeys.'

'I just don't see how you can bother about this case when the other's still hanging over everybody's head like the truncheon of Damocles.'

'I promised Fred Wensley,' Lestrade almost apologized. He saw the light in Norroy Macclesfield's eye. 'We go back a long way,' he said. 'When he was a rookie in the Ripper case.'

'What of Carter and Lady C? Won't chummie of the knife try again?'

'Probably,' Lestrade nodded. 'But I was canny there. After the match, I persuaded them both to attend the Police Charity Fête at Thames Ditton today. If they're not safe in the company of nearly four hundred policemen, we might as well all hang up our truncheons. Who found the body?'

'Nightwatchman,' Macclesfield sat on the edge of a laboratory bench. 'Weez's successor.'

'You've talked to him?'

'Briefly. He's in the canteen, giving one of the lads a statement.'

'The canteen,' said Lestrade. 'You interest me strangely. Come on, Norroy. These things in these jars are giving me the willies. Bailey, Mr Macclesfield will be in the canteen when you've finished, buying me a cup of tea.'

'Very good, sir.'

Macclesfield led the way. 'Fill me in, then,' said Lestrade.

'The nightwatchman's name is Davies. He came on duty at two o'clock this morning.'

'When did he find the body?'

'Just before seven. He noticed a light burning in Pargetter's little office, back there, next to the cabinet.'

'Did he touch anything?'

'He says not,' Macclesfield shrugged, 'but you know how it is, guv. There's one sort of finder who brings up his breakfast and the other sort who has to interfere. Just can't keep his hands off.'

'And you think this Davies is one of the latter?'

'Well, we haven't lifted any prints, yet.'

'You won't,' Lestrade prophesied. 'Not apart from Pargetter's and Davies's anyway. Our boy's too clever.'

They reached the lift and a uniformed operator growled, 'Goin' down.'

The policemen got on, wedged between a fat lady and a wheelchair.

'What's known about Pargetter?' Lestrade asked.

'Single bloke. Loner. Nobody seems to have liked him much. Busybody. You know the type.'

Lestrade did. He hadn't exactly cottoned to the man when they'd met.

'But he did have a visitor last night.'

'That's a blinding glimpse of the obvious, Norroy.' Lestrade tipped his hat to the fat lady who had just trodden on him.

'No, I mean somebody we know about. Linklater saw him.'

'Who the hell's Linklater?'

The fat lady turned to scowl at the rather obnoxious man with the appalling skin colour. She didn't care for his battered Panama and she didn't care for his raised voice.

'The other nightwatchman,' Macclesfield told him. 'The one who links with Davies.'

'Who in turn links with Linklater?'

179

'Right. Linklater does the six-to-two shift.'

'Who does the day shift?'

'There isn't one, guv. They're nightwatchmen.'

'Right,' said Lestrade. 'I just like to get these things straight.'

'Excuse me,' the fat lady wobbled. 'Are you by any chance a Time-and-Motion person?'

'Liberal,' Lestrade beamed, tipping his hat.

'Ground floor,' the lift operator growled. 'Paediatrics, Obstetrics.'

'Wash your mouth out!' The fat lady spun round on him and pushed past the policemen, treading firmly on Lestrade again.

'Where were we, Norroy?'

'That was Paediatrics and Obstetrics, sir,' the lift operator offered. 'We're now on our way to Canteen and Maintenance.'

'Thank you,' Lestrade said. 'What about this visitor, Norroy?'

'Linklater said Pargetter had a visitor at just before nine.'

'You've talked to Linklater?'

'I've got a man on that now. I got it from Davies who got it from Linklater.'

'And?'

'Canteen, Maintenance.' The lift operator jerked with his contrivance.

'Never a dull moment for you, is there?' Lestrade said to him, before colliding briefly with the wheelchair on his way out. 'So what did this visitor look like?'

'Don't know, guv,' Macclesfield said.

'But you said Linklater saw him.'

'Saw a silhouette, yes. But that was all.'

'Well . . .' Lestrade batted his way through the yellowish opaque door. 'Male? Female? Big? Small? Come on, Norroy, I had high hopes of you, man.'

'Male,' Macclesfield said. 'Definitely male. Other than that, nothing.'

'Yes,' the floozy at the canteen counter shrilled.

'Er . . . two teas, dear, please,' Lestrade ordered. 'My dad's buying. Oh, and one of those squidgy things – what are they called?'

'I dunno, mate, I'm only Queen Mary's Volunteer Reserve. I don't get paid for this, y'know. Just do it out the goodness of me 'eart, that's all. It's a squidgy thing, ain't it? D'you wannit or not?'

'No, thanks,' said Lestrade. 'I just went off it.'

The policemen found a table in the corner, away from distraught patients' visitors, clergymen come to administer the last rites and Salvation Army bandsmen. One of the last badgered the Yard men to buy a *War Cry*. Macclesfield stumped up but Lestrade told the sister that he paid by weekly subscription and May's edition had landed on his mat only that morning.

'Bit unusual, isn't it?' he muttered to Macclesfield, stirring his tea.

'What? The Sallies selling the *War Cry*?' The Inspector wondered anew where the old boy had been living since 1869.

'No, Pargetter getting a visitor on a Sunday night.'

'Very. Linklater was suspicious.'

Lestrade snorted. 'So suspicious he didn't notice anything about the visitor except that he was a bloke. Marvellous! What would we do without the great British public, eh, Norroy? I assume, by the by, that you had no interference from the City lads on this one?'

'McNulty's gone down with a nasty case of shingles,' Macclesfield told him. 'Everybody else is too stretched; what with the dance craze from America and the new adultery laws . . .'

'Yes, yes.' Lestrade raised his hands. He'd been this way before. 'Refresh my memory as to what we know about Pargetter.'

'Relatively short-sighted, I'd say,' Macclesfield said, 'judging by the thickness of his glasses. Ill-fitting dentures.'

'That's right,' Lestrade remembered. 'Sounded like an Olivetti as he spoke. Did you find his teeth, by the way?'

Macclesfield checked his notebook. 'Sixteen feet to his right. Against a bin that said "No Waste Products". Under all that blood, he was a pasty-faced individual. "Who would have thought the old man had so much blood in him?"'

'Nine pints, Norroy,' Lestrade gave Macclesfield the benefit of his vast experience, 'like the rest of us. Anyway, he wasn't so old, was he?'

'Fifty-two.'

'Ha,' Lestrade scoffed, 'a mere stripling. Is it me or does this tea taste of formaldehyde? How long had Pargetter been the pharmacist at Bart's?'

'Eight years. Before that at St Thomas's. Another eight.'

'Bachelor, wasn't he?'

'Lived with his sister,' Macclesfield nodded. 'Eighty-three, Splendesham Villas, Norwood. One of my lads is on to it.'

'Tell me', Lestrade had given up on the tea and nudged the cup away from him, 'about the cabinet.'

'The poisons cupboard, you mean? Or that bunch of no-hopers who hang around Stanley Baldwin?'

Lestrade nodded. 'The former, Norroy.'

'It hadn't been smashed, if that's what you mean.'

'And the key?' Lestrade asked. 'The one that Pargetter carried at all times?'

'Still around his neck,' Macclesfield told him.

'God knows how we'd know now if anything had been taken . . .'

'I checked his books.'

'And?'

'Everything's there that's supposed to be there. We're not looking at robbery for a motive.'

Lestrade slumped back in his chair, watching somebody else decline the squidgy thing on the plate at the canteen counter. 'It doesn't add up, Norroy,' he said. 'Either Pargetter isn't a victim of the Old Fogey murderer or . . .'

'Or?' Macclesfield's face lit up. He'd seen that expression on Lestrade's face before.

'When we were here earlier,' the guv'nor said, 'looking into the death of "Whizzo" Weez, what was taken; from the cabinet, I mean?'

'Er . . .' Macclesfield had to flick back through his notes. The sand of the Nile dropped like sifted sugar into his tea. It would probably improve its taste. 'Potassium cyanide. One bottle.'

'Hmm. Tell me about potassium cyanide.'

'Er . . .' there was a pause long enough to turn Macclesfield crimson with embarrassment.

'Well, thank you, Norroy,' Lestrade tutted. 'We won't make Chief Inspector if our chemistry is in *quite* such disarray, will we? Potassium cyanide or KCN is found in flat crystalline masses which are delinquent. Batmen in the army use it for cleaning regimental lace – not that there's much of that about now in these drab days, I don't suppose. Photographers use it too . . .'

'Cecilia Beaton!' Macclesfield clicked his fingers. 'The mad photographer of Hemel Hempstead.'

'That's the one,' Lestrade nodded. 'Took blokes' likenesses, then gave them a complimentary glass of potassium cyanide. She lost a lot of custom that way. Two and a half grains can cause death. Symptoms include headache, vertigo, bad breath – oh, and death of course.'

'Does this help?' Macclesfield was wondering.

'Probably not.'

'Hang on, though.' Macclesfield had just remembered something.

'Norroy,' Lestrade narrowed his eyes at the younger man, 'you look like you've just remembered something.'

'Well, when was this? When Weez died?'

'End of March,' Lestrade said.

'That's right. And if I remember Pargetter aright, he said he'd checked his register. And there was a bottle of potassium cyanide missing.'

'Norroy,' Lestrade said softly, 'we've just had this conversation.'

'Yes, yes.' Macclesfield was tapping his pencil end on the table, thinking. 'But there's no mention of potassium cyanide in the order book, I'd stake my reputation on it.'

'Steady, Norroy.' Lestrade held the man's sleeve. 'Let's not be *too* rash, now. What are you talking about, order book?'

'Well,' Macclesfield said, 'anything ordered by the pharmacy is logged in an order book.'

'By Pargetter?'

'Well, perhaps initially, but the book itself is typed up and kept in Hospital Records.'

'Er . . . I'm sorry, Norroy . . .'

'Don't you see, guv, William Pargetter is claiming that a bottle of potassium cyanide had been half inched, mysteriously, from a locked cabinet, but the order book says there was no potassium cyanide *in* the cabinet. Why should there be? What does a hospital want with stuff used by photographers and batmen?'

'Then why should Pargetter . . .? Norroy,' Lestrade was on his feet, 'where are these Hospital Records? Show me this order book. If this means what I think it means . . .' And they dashed from the canteen.

'Hyoscine.' Lestrade tapped the page several times. 'Get up to that cabinet in the pharmacy, Norroy. I'll lay you any odds you like that *that's* what's missing from the cabinet. And that's why William Pargetter died. He's not an Old Fogey victim and neither was Albert Weez. Why wasn't the cabinet broken into when we found Weez's body? Because there was no need for that. Pargetter had opened it with his own key. He took out of it a bottle of hyoscine and gave it to person or persons unknown. Unfortunately for Albert Weez, he witnessed this little illegal transaction going on and the recipient of the poison caved in his head for it. To draw us off the scent he dragged him into the catacombs below. But a sharp-eyed young medical student sussed him.'

'But why not fake a break-in?' Macclesfield asked. 'If Pargetter was in on it?'

'Because he was an arrogant bastard, that's why not,' Lestrade said. 'Remember how proud he was? Hadn't had a day off in sixteen and a half years? Even doctors would have to wait while he was at lunch, et cetera? No, he expected us to be overawed by his superior science. He assumed we wouldn't know potassium cyanide from hyoscine. In any case, the window in the laboratory *had* been tampered with. Perhaps Weez just caught them in flagrant before they could complete the business.'

'We nearly didn't,' Macclesfield muttered. 'Know potassium cyanide from hyoscine, I mean.'

'You know what I think?' Lestrade slammed shut the order book.

'No, guv, what?'

'I don't think our friend in the Valley of the Kings got his hyoscine from the henbane growing wild in the Nile Delta. I think he got it right here, upstairs, from Pargetter's poison

184

cabinet. And Pargetter knew he had. *That's* why he died. Come on, Norroy. We'll check that cabinet and then we'll pay a call on Mr Davies, the nightwatchman. If we have to hypnotize the bugger, I want more from him than the fact that Pargetter's visitor was a bloke, I want much more.'

Lestrade may have wanted more, but he didn't get it. What he got, as spring blossomed into summer, was a series of brick walls. Nightwatchman Davies turned out to have the shortest sight south of Watford. Yes, he'd found it odd that the pharmacist should be in on a Sunday evening and even odder that some bloke had come to see him. But then, that probably wasn't so much of a coincidence, was it? On account of how Mr Pargetter was there, he'd obviously arranged for his visitor to come, didn't the police think? *That* was a question that was occurring to many in the spring and summer of 1923. Didn't the police think? What Davies didn't know, and the police did, was that William Pargetter had no phone. How, then, if Davies's assumption was correct, had his visitor contacted him?

Miss Pargetter had been of very little help. No, she knew of no one who wished her brother ill. He was a very clever man who knew all about science and things. His only hobby, it turned out, other than science and things, was Egyptology and Norroy Macclesfield found a vast number of newspaper clippings, most of them showing Howard Carter and Lord Carnarvon posed by variously sized heaps of spoil. One thing Miss Pargetter did remember, as she got the tea things ready for her brother's return, was something odd he had said when he left home that Sunday. 'Who'd have thought it,' he'd said to his sister. 'A descendent of Horemheb after all these centuries.'

'Horem Who, dear?' she'd asked.

'Horemheb,' he'd repeated. 'General and Pharaoh of the Eighteenth Dynasty.'

Miss Pargetter admitted, as she buttered the bread, that she didn't really know what he'd been talking about. She hardly ever knew what William was talking about. But if that rather nice Inspector Macclesfield cared to wait a little longer, William would be home and he could ask him himself. Regrettably,

Inspector Macclesfield was pushed for time, but he left a lady policeman at Eighty-three, Splendesham Villas. That way, just in case William was late, she could help Miss Pargetter with the washing up.

In the meantime, Fred Wensley had been able to spare a copper or two after all and there was a night-and-day surveillance on Lady Carnarvon and Howard Carter. The two of them burned a great deal of midnight oil together. Carter was anxious to get back to the Valley of the Kings and into that most holy of places, the tomb of Tut-Ankh-Amen, the greatest archaeological discovery the world had ever known. Lady C was very supportive. It was what Lord C would have wanted.

And there, the case seemed to hang, suspended like a felon below the trap. In the dark and silent watches of the night, Lestrade fancied he heard the creak of the taut rope, swaying with its grisly weight.

But the world, thanks to *The Times* and the *Daily Mail*, had now come to know of the Pharaoh's curse. 'Death In The Valley', thundered 'The Thunderer', 'and our man, Percy Merton, was there.' 'Slaughter Round the Sarcophagus', trumpeted the *Mail*, 'and our man, Arthur Weigall, was there.' It was as a result of this that Sir Arthur Conan Doyle went into print with his usual half-baked theories. But then, only three years before, he'd found fairies at the bottom of somebody's garden at Cottingley and no one took him seriously any more. This was the twenties, daring, roaring. Arthur Conan Doyle – like Sholto Lestrade – was a dinosaur. The stories in *The Times* and the *Mail*, complete with Dream Cottage, also caused an elderly woman to ring the Yard several times, insisting on being put through to Mr Lestrade. Her name was Marie Corelli.

'Oh, yes,; the man on the Yard switchboard had humoured her. 'Aren't you a novelist?'

'No!' she had bellowed. 'I am *the* novelist.'

Even so, the man on the Yard switchboard couldn't give out Mr Lestrade's telephone number. But he did promise to leave a message. Lestrade himself, wandering between Emma's bedroom where his girl had lain now for over a month, and his study, where the pieces of paper flapped and overlapped, was increasingly coming to believe that the answer lay back there, in that dead desert, where the mosquitoes buzzed around the sleeping Pharaohs and the ghosts of dead kings roamed the night.

And in the world at large? Jack Hobbs, the Surrey and England opening batsman, completed his hundredth century against Somerset at Bath. Lady C, as inveterate a supporter of Surrey Cricket Club as she was of Bolton Wanderers, insisted on being there, along with Howard Carter, bored to death, and two even more bored policemen, wearing straw hats and trying to look incognito.

In America, John Macready and Oakley Kelley flew non-stop across the United States in a monoplane, flying 2700 miles in twenty-seven hours. Lestrade shuddered when he read it and asked aloud 'Why?'.

'Because it's there, sir,' Madison had told him while dusting the ormolu. That had to suffice.

'*Do* be quiet, Sholto,' Fanny snapped, fiddling with her Cat's Whisker. 'I'm trying to listen to this new "Woman's Hour" programme. Princess Alice is talking about adoption.'

'God,' growled Lestrade. 'Who'd want to adopt her?' Anyway, when's "Man's Hour" on, that's what I'd like to know.'

And Stanley Baldwin moved to Number Ten after Mr What-ever-His-Name-Was retired with cancer of the throat. The first thing he did was to change Whatsisname's wallpaper, the first prerogative of Prime Ministers. And Labour Party members everywhere despaired when they heard Mr Ramsay MacDonald declare that Mr Baldwin's outlook was very close to his. They'd all been rather worried about Ramsay Mac for some time.

Emma gave a cheer early in June when the actress Mrs Hilton Philipson became the third woman MP. She gave a louder one two days later when Benito Mussolini approved a bill to allow women to vote in Italian municipal elections.

'Things are pretty grim in Germany, Sholto,' Fanny had said one morning, having read Mr Weigall's latest exciting instal-ment. 'Do you know a pound of tea costs anything between 27,250 and 43,600 marks?'

'Good Lord,' Lestrade had muttered. 'That's what you get for losing a war, I suppose. Haven't seen my spats anywhere, have you?'

And three weeks after that, Lady C, Howard Carter and their two policemen were looking right, looking left, looking right again at Wimbledon, where the ravishing, if big-footed, Suzanne Lenglen beat the corsets off Kathleen McKane for the Ladies' Singles title.

And then, a little after six in the morning, on Tuesday, 10 July, Inspector Norroy Macclesfield turned up at Lestrade's house in Virginia Water. Madison let him in. Lestrade was all for throwing him out. 'Good God, Norroy, I know you're concerned for Emma; we all are, but it's only . . .' he floundered for his ancient half hunter, but he wasn't carrying it in his pyjamas and had to resort to the grandmother in the hall, . . . a little after six.'

'This isn't about Miss Lestrade, guv,' the big man said, ashen faced. 'It's about Prince Ali Kemal Fahmy Bey.'

'Who?'

'Fahmy Bey – friends of the Holinsheds.'

'Oh, yes,' said Lestrade. 'I remember. She went to visit them in Cairo, didn't she?'

'According to your notes, sir, Damietta. Well, they're in London now. At least, one of them is. The other one's dead. I think I'd like you in on this one.'

The Savoy Hotel, in the Strand, had been opened in 1889, the year in which half the Metropolitan Police Force, it seemed, had been concentrating its efforts on monitoring the comings and goings of nobs and errand boys at a homosexual brothel in Cleveland Street. So famous was this hotel that they'd named a part of Sardinia and a cabbage after it.

Macclesfield's station wagon lurched on to the pavement outside its 250-foot frontage shortly before seven. He and Lestrade hurried past the huge bronze statue of Peter of Savoy, who once owned the place, and on past a row of liveried flunkeys to the lifts. The fourth floor was sealed off, much to the consternation of the *maître d'* who was doing his best to keep all the policemen to the tradesmen's entrances at the back. If only they'd been exponents of sensitive policing, they'd have come up-river in their launches and scuttled in through the arches. As it was, their great unwelcome boots had been tramping all over his Axminster. Peter of Savoy would have turned in his grave.

A dark-haired, beautiful woman sat smoking nervously on a divan in the lounge of the opulent suite. Around her stood a number of policemen, in and out of uniform and a face Lestrade knew all too well.

'Sir Edward Marshall Hall,' he nodded.

'Lestrade.' The King's Counsel bowed with all the theatricality that only he could muster at that hour. 'Who is in charge of this case?'

'I am,' Macclesfield admitted.

'You are . . .?'

'Inspector Macclesfield, sir, of Scotland Yard.'

'Never heard of you, but since you seem to be lead truncheon at the moment, I feel I must protest the presence of an interested outsider, viz and to wit ex-Chief Superintendent Lestrade.'

'Mr Lestrade is here at my request, sir,' Macclesfield told him. 'Now, if I may have your name?'

Good for you, thought Lestrade, though he was too wily a warrior to voice it aloud.

'I am Sir Edward Marshall Hall, KC, probably the most popular and sought-after defence lawyer in the country today. I am representing Madame Fahmy Bey.'

'And you are . . .?' Lestrade turned to the beautiful woman.

The beautiful woman looked at him blankly.

'Gentlemen,' Lestrade summoned the barrister and Macclesfield to him, 'could we have a chat please? Perhaps in the adjoining room?'

'If you wish.' Marshall Hall led the way as he usually did in such matters.

Lestrade found himself in the bedroom of the Fahmy Beys. The aristocratic features of Marshall Hall had got lumpier over the years and it had to be said he looked better in a wig than a Homburg.

'This is highly irregular,' Lestrade told them. 'I may even go so far as to compute that you are in danger of obstructing the police in their enquiries.'

'Stuff and nonsense, Lestrade,' Marshall Hall said, perching on Madame Fahmy's dressing-table chair and checking his cravat in the mirror. He and the former Chief Superintendent had crossed swords before. He was known to snore loudly during prosecuting counsel's summings-up, and the giving of police evidence. 'I was briefed by Freke Palmer this morning and happened to be taking breakfast at the Savoy. While I was here, I thought I might as well present my card to Madame Fahmy.'

'Ah yes.' Lestrade recognized the solicitor's card which Marshall Hall now handed to him. 'Freke by name and freak by nature. My point is that you are a little premature, Mr Marshall Hall.'

Marshall Hall ignored the senior policeman and began rifling through Madame Fahmy's make-up. He caught sight of Lestrade in the dressing-table mirror. 'If you're waiting for me to go, Lestrade,' he smiled acidly, 'I'm afraid you'll have rather a long wait.'

'Indeed?'

'Indeed. You see, there's a problem.'

'Oh? What might that be?'

'Parlez-vous français?'

'What?' Lestrade blinked.

'I thought not.' Marshall Hall allowed the merest hint of a smile to flicker across his tight lips. 'I asked if you spoke French. You clearly don't.'

'Why is that a problem?' Lestrade asked.

'Because Madame Fahmy does not speak anything else *but*,' Marshall Hall said. 'Luckily, I speak it like a native. Shall we?'

Sir Edward Marshall Hall spoke it like a native to the distraught woman in the dazzling white ball gown, streaked with her husband's blood, for several minutes. Then Macclesfield arranged for her to be sent to Holloway Prison in the company of himself and a woman policeman. He could manage *'ici'* and *'la'* and *'Après vous'* so he didn't feel too rudderless.

One by one, Lestrade questioned the hotel staff. First, Arthur Mariani, the Night Manager, who told the ex-Yard man that he had been summoned by one of his porters at shortly after two o'clock. The storm was subsiding by then and the livid lightning flashes were illuminating the Strand less often. Apparently, the porter – Cabin – had been moving luggage when Prince Fahmy Bey had come hurtling out of his suite, screaming 'Look what she's done to me' and pointing to a reddened cheek. Cabin had offered him his usual 'tsk, tsk', having been in the night-portering business for a long time, and was then confronted with Madame Fahmy, her throat as red as her husband's cheek. She was babbling incoherently in something foreign and Cabin asked the squabbling pair if they'd mind keeping it down only there was a party in for the Noise Abatement Society's AGM and it probably wouldn't go down too well, all this hullabaloo. Madame Fahmy obeyed and vanished inside. With that, a little Yorkshire terrier had come scuttling out and proceeded to prolong its active life against the night porter's left leg. Prince Fahmy whistled to the animal as Cabin dragged his way along the corridor, shaking his leg as unobtrusively as he could. Suddenly, he heard three explosions, definitely not thunder, and spun back to see the Prince staggering against the wall, half in, half out of his front door. The speed of Cabin's turn had shaken the dog off and it bounced, yelping against the wall. Cabin had dashed back to the fallen guest and saw his wife in the doorway, a smoking gun in her hand. Then she'd dropped it to the ground as though it was red hot. Cabin had gone to fetch Mariani who in turn had called the police.

Costa, the Prince's negro servant, was built like a brick pyramid, his muscles rippling under his expensive, hand-made suit. Lestrade didn't get very far with him. His English wasn't of the best, but the negro could handle that. All he seemed to remember of his time in the Beys' service was that he owed the Prince his life and that Madame Fahmy was sent shopping for dresses in Costa's company. He had orders to watch the woman very closely and he took his job very seriously, although he did get some funny looks from the salespersons in Harrod's and Liberty's when they'd both squeeze into the changing cubicles together.

The French maid spoke no English at all and spent her entire five minutes with Lestrade sobbing hysterically.

The anxious-looking Egyptian was rather more articulate. His name was Said Ernani and he was the dead man's secretary.

'How long', Lestrade asked him, 'were the Prince and Madame Fahmy married?'

'It was a whirlwind romance,' Ernani said. 'Truly a marriage made in heaven. They met in Paris in May of last year.'

'Did the Prince *do* anything, apart from rule, I mean?'

Ernani gave him a strange, Oriental look. 'He was a diplomat, attaché to the Egyptian Legation in Paris.'

'I see. And what brought the couple to England?'

'A ship.'

'No, no.' Lestrade had clearly not made himself clear. 'I mean, why did they come?'

Ernani's already dark face darkened further. 'Madame Fahmy needed an operation.'

'Really – what on?'

'An operating table in your St Bartholomew's Hospital.'

'No, I mean, what part of her body?'

Ernani shuddered. 'I am a Moslem,' he said. 'We do not speak of the parts of a woman's body.'

'I see.' Lestrade watched his man closely. 'What was the relationship between the Prince and Madame Fahmy?'

'They were husband and wife,' Ernani told him, wondering faintly why Scotland Yard was so famed. The Parquet in his native land were infinitely more incisive than this, especially when they were pulling out your fingernails.

'No, I meant, did they get on?'

It was Ernani's turn to smile. 'You must realize, former Detective Chief Superintendent, Madame is a foreigner. She is not as other wives. A Moslem by decree, yes, but she wore no veil. Constantly disporting herself, showing those unmentionable parts of her body to men other than her husband.'

'You mean she was something of a flirt?'

'She had the volatile nature of all her race.'

'There were rows?'

'Disputations,' Ernani preferred.

'Violence?'

'There was violence last night,' the secretary said, 'in which she killed her master.'

'No, before that,' Lestrade badgered him. 'Did he use violence against her?'

'He may have spoken sharply to her on occasion.'

'And in doing so, clasped his hand around her throat?'

'A playful Moslem custom,' Ernani assured him.

'Did Madame Fahmy own the gun?'

'She did. A .32 Browning automatic of Belgian manufacture. She carried it to protect her jewels. The jewels my magnanimous master lavished upon her.'

'What did they quarrel about last night?'

'It was the storm,' Ernani said. 'A storm of unparalleled ferocity. It would make the most placid of men snappy.'

'And Prince Fahmy snapped?'

'He ruptured a little.'

'What did he rupture about?' In all his three weeks in Egypt, Lestrade had not met an Egyptian so tight-lipped.

'The delicate operation of which we spoke.' Ernani placed the tips of his index fingers together. 'Madame Fahmy wished to have it performed in Paris.'

'Why?'

'Because she is French.'

'And Prince Fahmy did not approve?'

'No. Dr Gordon had made all the arrangements. For today, in fact. That is why he is here.'

'Here, in the hotel?'

Ernani nodded.

'Why wasn't I told?'

'Because you did not ask, former Chief Superintendent.'

Lestrade felt his knuckles whiten and his moustache curl. 'You were with the couple earlier in the day?'

'At dinner, yes.'

'And they argued then?'

'There were words.'

'What about?'

'I cannot remember – except that Madame Fahmy refused to dance with the Prince.'

'Why?'

'She could not shimmy like her sister Kate. In the event I danced with Madame.'

'And you shimmied?'

Ernani shook his head. 'I trotted as the fox.'

'I see. Can you think of any reason why Madame Fahmy should have shot her husband?'

Ernani looked into the middle distance. 'Who can know the cunning of the jackal, the wisdom of the stars, the caprice of a woman? She was full of Western decadence,' he sneered. 'It is all around us.'

'You don't like the Savoy, Mr Ernani?'

'I go where my master dictates,' the secretary told him. 'It has always been so.'

'Where will I find this Dr Gordon?' Lestrade asked.

The secretary checked his watch. 'It is after twelve. He will be in the cocktail lounge.'

'Another pink gin, Lestrade?'

'Thank you, Doctor,' the ex-Yard man said. 'But I'm finding it difficult enough to balance on this damned stool as it is. Can we go over to the window, to a proper seat?'

'Yes, of course. Deuc'd hot, isn't it, again? Eddie.' He beckoned to the barman. 'Hair of the dog, please. And a little more dog next time. Last one was almost pure hair.'

'Comin' up, sir,' Eddie chirped, throwing a Manhattan to the ceiling.

'Madame Fahmy's operation.' Lestrade sat by the open window, watching behind the nets the rich world of the sun-baked Strand go by.

'Ah, now that's confidential,' Gordon said. 'As the family physician . . .'

'As the family physician, you've already told me, in the strictest confidence of course, that he knocked her about, had sworn on the Koran to kill her, locked her in her cabin on board his luxury yacht and so on. What can be left?'

'Well, her piles, of course . . . oh, damn! There, I've blurted it!'

'Piles, doctor?'

At that moment, Eddie the Barman arrived with Gordon's gin. ''Ave you, Doc? That's a bugger, ain't it? Napoleon 'ad them, you know. Still, you bein' a medical bloke an' all, you'll know what to do about it.'

Eddie scuttled away to polish his glasses.

'Piles?' Lestrade closed to his man, left eyebrow reaching his hairline.

'Haemorrhoids, to be technical. Swollen blood vessels of the back passage. Need I be more graphic?'

'No, indeed.' Lestrade leaned back on the plush of the Savoy chairs. 'I was just wondering why Madame Fahmy should be so insistent that she should have the operation in France.'

'To get away from him,' Gordon said, sipping the pink liquid.

'But so would she in London, while she was in hospital anyway.'

'No.' Gordon shook his head. 'You don't understand, Lestrade. Prince Fahmy Bey was . . . well, let's just say abnormal. He had peculiar inclinations.'

'Er . . . I'm not sure I'm following this conversation, Doctor,' the detective confessed.

'Hunnish practices, Lestrade, of the Bulgarian variety . . . Good God, man, how can you have reached your advanced years and still be so coy? It's very common in Egypt, I understand, as a means of birth control. Me, I prefer Marie Stopes, myself.'

Lestrade had seen a photograph of the woman once. There was no accounting for taste.

'Contraceptive or not,' Gordon went on, 'you can imagine the agony of the procedure for Madame Fahmy. Naturally, none of this can come out in court . . .'

'It might save her life,' Lestrade pointed out.

'It might also shock the great British public, Lestrade. We can't have that. Bedroom peccadilloes are personal to man and wife. They're not to be bandied about by the newspapers. If the judge is over twenty-three he won't admit it into evidence. Nor would Marshall Hall ask him to. There are proprieties.'

Lestrade shrugged.

'Just because Prince Fahmy goes around buggering his secretary . . .' the doctor muttered.

'Ernani?' Lestrade blinked.

'Lord, yes. Reptilian sort of cove, isn't he? Look at this.' The family GP whisked out of his inside pocket a cartoon from an Egyptian newspaper.

'What's this?' Lestrade asked him.

'It's a cartoon from an Egyptian newspaper,' Gordon explained. 'Three silhouettes. This is the Light – in other words,

Prince Fahmy. This,' he pointed to the second, 'the Shadow of the Light – Ernani. And this,' his finger tapped the third silhouette, 'the Shadow of the Shadow of the Light.'

'Who's that?'

It was Gordon's turn to shrug. 'Ernani's secretary? I don't know. But Fahmy was known to lead a somewhat dissolute life-style in Cairo with Ernani and that man. I don't know if the Koran says anything explicit about it. *Gray's Anatomy* certainly does. Not to mention Leviticus, if my strict Methodist upbringing serves me – another gin, Eddie,' he shouted – 'Thou shalt not lie with mankind as with womankind; it is abomination.'

'Hmm,' Lestrade nodded. 'But presumably, if it's a matter of standing up . . .'

Lestrade was going to have lunch at the Savoy, but it was all written in French and then he saw the price, which was written in English, so in the event he nipped out to his old haunt at the Coal Hole for a saveloy and a pint. By three he was back on the fourth floor, pacing the corridor as Cabin the night porter had done in the wee small hours, with thunder and lightning crashing around him. Norroy Macclesfield joined him there.

'Ah, Norroy. Madame Fahmy safely enhanced in Holloway?'

'Snug as a bug in a rug, guv,' the Inspector assured him. 'Returning to the scene of the crime?'

'Sort of.' Lestrade was measuring up angles. 'You stand there. You're Cabin, the night porter. There's actually a dog misbehaving itself against your shin, but you can forgo that pleasure. Now, I . . .' he darted back to the Fahmys' door, 'I say to you . . . walk towards me . . . I say "Look at my face. Look what she did to me" or words to that effect. You tell me to shut up.'

'I wouldn't dare, sir.'

'Oh, come on, Macclesfield,' Lestrade stamped. 'You must have played charades at some time in your life. Enter into the spirit of the thing, man.'

Macclesfield did. 'Look, do you mind shutting up, sir? You'll wake the whole hotel.'

'Right, right.' Lestrade doubled back, clutching his throat and gabbling nonsense.

'Guv?' Macclesfield shook him. 'Guv, are you all right?'

'I'm being Madame Fahmy, Norroy,' Lestrade explained with what little patience he could muster.

'Oh, sorry, guv.' Macclesfield let him go. 'It's just that, well, I saw you in the desert, remember.'

'Yes,' sighed Lestrade. 'Can I ever forget it? Now, you turn and walk away. I go back inside and "Bang!". You turn. Bang. Bang. You run back; no, to me, to me. You look down.' Lestrade staggered against the doorframe, clutching his chest. 'The Prince is lying here, still breathing. Barely alive.' He stood up sharply. 'Madame is in there,' he opened the door, 'gun in hand. No.' He brought his hand to rest on the back of his neck. 'No, it doesn't make sense.'

'Why not, guv?'

'All right.' Lestrade was talking to himself. 'All right. So I'm distraught. My millionaire playboy husband has been treating me like camel shit ever since he married me *and* demanding unnatural practices . . .'

'Oh?' Macclesfield raised an eyebrow.

'I'll tell you when you're older.' Lestrade scotched the Inspector's train of thought. 'But even so, why don't I wait 'til I'm in the bedroom to kill him? Or at least the vestibule? Why do I do it in the doorway?'

'Light?' Macclesfield suggested. 'It *was* the middle of the night.'

'No.' Lestrade shook his head and flicked on the electric light switch. 'This is the roaring twenties, Norroy. If anything it's brighter in here than it is out there on the landing. I don't suppose you did anything silly and handed in the gun to Forensics, did you?'

Macclesfield hit his forehead with his hand, then smiled and produced the automatic from his jacket pocket.

'Good boy,' Lestrade beamed. 'God,' he clicked back the mechanism, 'stiff as a day-old corpse. Could she have handled this, do you think?'

'I was wondering that, guv. She's not a very big lady.'

'Get it to Orange Street, to Bob Churchill. He'll tell us. Come on, Norroy. Had your lunch? We've got to get to Charing Cross Hospital. Got a corpse to have a look at.'

'Mr Lestrade?' A tall, rather suave man with a centre parting and lots of maccassar stood before the policemen.

'Yes?' Lestrade said, not at all caring for the cut of the man's spats.

'I am Sylvester Alexander, the hotel's band-leader. I understand you wanted a word.'

'Indeed, Mr Alexander. Walk this way, would you?' Lestrade sensed that the musician was a little alarmed by the gun in his hand so he slipped it into his pocket. 'I understand that you spoke to Prince and Madame Fahmy Bey at dinner last night.'

'To Madame Fahmy, yes,' Alexander said.

'What did you say?'

'I asked her if she had a particular request for a tune.'

'And did she?'

'No, sir. She said that her husband had vowed to kill her that night and she wasn't much in the mood for music.'

'I see,' Lestrade said. 'To which you replied?'

'I naturally bowed and expressed my hope that we would see Madame Fahmy today. I now gather that we won't.'

'Indeed not. Norroy, why are we walking down these stairs when we could have taken the lift? And what did the Prince say to that?'

'The Prince said nothing, sir, but Mr Weigall found it very amusing.'

Lestrade and Macclesfield stopped dead on the stairs. 'Weigall?' they chorused.

'Arthur Weigall?' Lestrade continued alone. 'Plump bloke, crinkly hair, good tan?'

'Mr Arthur Weigall of the *Daily Mail*, sir, yes.'

'He was at the Fahmys' table at dinner?'

'Why, yes, sir.'

'And he found this comment of yours amusing?'

'Certainly, sir. So did the lady he was with.'

10

Lestrade was no stranger to Fleet Street. He'd crossed its western end many years ago just as they were removing Temple Bar, when he'd swapped his City helmet for a Metropolitan one. Its eastern end was well known to him too, where the Fleet River ran under those mean streets and the locomotives of the LNER chugged in and out of Blackfriars. It was here that old Corner of the Yard and Lestrade had hunted for Blackfriars Dan. Half-way up Ludgate Hill, he'd met Mr Gladstone, the Grand Old Man, to whom Lestrade was on escort duty. And the posters on the walls of the urinals to the north-west of St Paul's had been the first in the world to ask gentlemen whether they'd adjusted their dress before leaving. It was a question which was only ever likely to be relevant to a few – and most of them were well known in the not-as-other-patrons community.

The offices of the *Daily Mail*, that vast Empire of Truth created by Alfred Harmsworth – later Lord Northcliffe; later still, dead – stood about half-way along, on the left; or on the right, depending on which way you were facing.

Above the deafening roar of the presses, a spotty youth whose face looked all the more deathly under the green shade, showed Lestrade into the office temporarily assigned to Arthur Weigall. Little bits of Egypt were all over the place.

'Lestrade!' the rotund former Inspector of Antiquities was surprised to see the former Chief Superintendent.

'Working on the Fahmy case?'

'The Fahmy case?'

Lestrade tapped a finger on the *Mail*'s front page as he sat down. 'Your leader,' he said.

'Where?' Weigall was on his feet in a trice.

'No,' Lestrade explained. 'Your leading article. On the Fahmy shooting at the Savoy.'

'Oh, yes. Yes, of course. No.' Weigall was fluster itself. 'I thought you meant Lord Rothermere. He's a stickler, you know. No, no.' He tried to smile. 'My brief is archaeology, remember. That's all I'm paid to write about.'

'And Madame Fahmy's brief is Edward Marshall Hall,' Lestrade said flatly. 'He'll have a field day with you.'

'With me?' Weigall continued to play the innocent. 'Why me? God, it's deucedly hot, isn't it? Even after Egypt, I mean?'

'It'll get hotter at the Yard,' Lestrade assured him.

'Look, Lestrade,' Weigall's voice betrayed him, 'it's very nice to see you again, and I'm glad you're over the worst of your Egyptian experiences, but I really am most frightfully busy . . .'

'Tell me about the Savoy.' Lestrade was playing with his Panama.

'Er . . . the Savoy?'

'It's a hotel, Mr Weigall,' the old Yard man smiled, 'not a stone's throw from here.'

'Yes, yes. Oh, it's been years. I think I had luncheon there once . . .'

Lestrade leaned towards his man, invading his space, crowding his conscience. 'I think you had dinner there night before last.'

Weigall just blinked. 'Now, look,' he said. 'You don't have any jurisdiction here, do you? Any more than you had out in Egypt?'

'None,' smiled Lestrade, leaning back. He'd played the cat-and-mouse game before. 'Except in so far as we all have jurisdiction – the right of citizen's arrest.'

'What can you possibly arrest me for?' Weigall's laugh was bordering on the hysterical. 'I haven't done anything.'

'But you had dinner with the Fahmy Beys,' Lestrade said quietly.

'Nonsense!' the *Mail* man snapped, getting up out of his swivel chair. 'Who said I did?'

Lestrade looked his man in his dancing, dark eyes. 'That really doesn't matter, does it?' he said. 'Let's just say that my source has no reason to lie and his evidence puts you squarely in the frame.'

'But she did it,' Weigall almost screamed, waving the morning's *Mail* around his office.

'Who says so?'

'Everybody!' Weigall shouted. 'Look,' his finger jabbed the front page, 'our Crime Correspondent, John Paulson. He's nobody's fool. Madame Fahmy has confessed.'

'Isn't it time you did, then?' Lestrade asked him. Weigall stood there, silhouetted by the window, his jaw flexing. 'Arthur?' Lestrade got up from his chair and perched himself casually on the corner of the desk. 'You know you'll feel better if you do.'

There was a silence between them. They'd come through the Valley of the Kings together, the shooting galleries that were Shepheard's Hotel and Cairo Airport. In an odd sort of way, they were blood brothers.

'All right,' Weigall sighed, closing his eyes. 'All right. I was there.'

Lestrade sighed too, but his was the silent, internal sort. Never give a sucker an even break. He sat back down. 'Tell Uncle Sholto all about it,' he said.

'I know the Fahmy Beys,' the *Mail* man admitted. 'I met him years ago when he was buying his title.'

'Buying . . .?' Lestrade was lost already. That didn't bode well this early into a confession.

Weigall looked at his inquisitor. 'You didn't think the title was genuine, did you?'

'No,' Lestrade lied. 'No, of course not. I'm just cross-referencing.'

'No, Ali Kemal Fahmy Bey's dad was an engineer. Exactly how the family came by *quite* such a lot of money I don't know, but by giving a little of it to charity, they gave him the title of Prince. It's the same over here. The New Year's Honours List is littered with people who've given generously to the Conservative Party – you know, people like Ramsay Macdonald. Anyway, I got a telegram from Prince Fahmy.'

'Inviting you to dinner?'

'Yes. He wanted to discuss something.'

'What?'

'Buying the tomb.'

'What?' Lestrade's eyes narrowed.

'He wanted to buy the tomb.'

'He was interested in archaeology?'

'He was interested in possessions. That's really, I suspect, why he married Marguerite.'

'Why should he talk to you,' Lestrade said, 'about buying the tomb, I mean?'

'Apparently, he'd tried Carter already. Carter had passed him upstairs to Lady Carnarvon.'

'And she had said?'

'"No",' Weigall quoted. 'That was her exact word – "no".'

'Rather finite, I would have thought,' Lestrade said.

'Aha,' Weigall shook his head. 'You didn't know Fahmy Bey. He was pumping me over dinner as to how he could get round Lady C.'

'And what did you tell him?'

'Well,' Weigall frowned, 'it was a little difficult. I mean, I work for Carter indirectly – loathe the man though I do – and he works for Lady C. Admittedly, the Prince promised to keep me on, in the role of Director in fact – and ten per cent of the profits.'

'Sounds a good deal,' Lestrade thought aloud.

'Very good,' Weigall agreed. 'But there are some of us left, Lestrade, who have little things called principles.'

'Ah,' Lestrade smiled. 'So you turned down Prince Ten Per Cent?'

'Let's just say I was less than enthusiastic.'

'What of the dinner?' Lestrade asked.

'The dinner? Well, I had the Lobster Bisque, washed down with a very palatable Chablis . . .'

'No, I mean the Fahmy Beys,' the interrogator explained. 'How did they behave?'

'Oh, outrageously, as always,' Weigall said in a matter-of-fact sort of way. 'Whenever I've met them, it's been the same. Totally incompatible. I told you, Fahmy wants possessions, not people. He's got that crawling snake Ernani and that big black bugger Costa. People are chattels to Fahmy. To an extent, it's the Egyptian way.'

'Were they any worse than usual that night?'

'It might have been the storm,' Weigall wondered aloud, 'but it certainly seemed so, yes. Certainly, I had a lap full of broccoli at one point which I assume was intended for him.'

'Thrown by . . .?'

'Her, yes.'

'And what of your companion?' Lestrade asked.

'My . . .?' There was a falsettoness about that word that Lestrade would not have expected to find in an adult male of Weigall's maturity.

'The lady you were with,' he explained.

'No, no.' Weigall was the master of his larynx again. 'I'm afraid you've been misinformed.'

Lestrade smiled. 'I'm afraid you're lying, Mr Weigall,' he said.

'What?' the *Mail* man snapped. 'How dare you?'

'Where do you live?' Lestrade asked him.

'Kensington,' he said. 'Why?'

'And Mrs Weigall?'

'Hortense? Well, with me, of course.'

'So, if I were to ask her . . .'

'You can't!' The special correspondent's reply was like greased lightning.

'Why ever not?' Lestrade's eyes opened ever wider.

'Because she's not here,' Weigall told him. 'Her mother's not well. She's tending to the old goat in New York State.'

'So,' Lestrade said softly. 'I assume we can rule out Mrs Weigall as your companion.'

'I was alone,' her husband insisted.

Lestrade stood up. 'This John Paulson,' he said. 'The *Mail*'s Crime Correspondent – where would I find his office?'

'Her name was Trixie Dilnot,' Weigall suddenly volunteered. 'Of the Ships in the Night Escort Agency. Lestrade.' He was around his desk and practically draped over the ex-Yard man in the blinking of an eye.

'Yes, Mr Weigall?'

'This . . . this doesn't have to come out does it? I mean, I only had dinner with the woman. Honestly. It's just that . . . well . . . Hortense can be . . . difficult.'

'Difficult?'

Weigall shuddered. 'Let's just say . . .' he felt his throat close

203

and his lips dry, 'let's just say that she can do things with a kitchen cleaver that would bring tears to your eyes. For all she's American and these are the roaring twenties, there's a puritan streak in Hortense that's terrifying. Surely, surely, Lestrade,' and Weigall fumbled in his pocket for his wallet, 'none of this is relevant. I'll say again, "Madame Fahmy did it".'

Lestrade's fist clasped over Weigall's, wrestling with his pound notes. 'Please, Mr Weigall,' he said. 'Don't compound the felony. Anyway, you couldn't afford me. Where did you say the Ships in the Night Escort Agency was to be found?'

'I didn't,' Weigall said, recognizing ruin when he faced it. 'But it's Number Thirty-five, Greek Street, Soho.'

'Thank you, Mr Weigall,' Lestrade said. 'I'll see myself out.' He reached the door. 'Oh, by the way, I thoroughly enjoyed your articles on our Egyptian adventure, but there's a "t" in my name. It's not silent, any more than it is in "harlot".' And he disappeared around the door.

Weigall collapsed into his chair, trying to decide whether the letter opener or a hearty leap from his office window should be his next logical step. He was still deliberating when Lestrade's head popped back into view. 'Your wife,' he said.

'What?' Weigall screamed. 'Christ, no!' And he buried his head in his hands.

'Does your wife still bear the scars of her eye trouble?' the old Yard man asked him.

'What are you talking about?'

'The play you told me of,' Lestrade reminded him. 'The one at the amphitheatre back in 1909.'

'Yes, yes,' Weigall tried to concentrate. 'What about it?'

'You told me the fellahin believed that the gods in their wrath were stoning you all – that Hortense was struck in the eyes with the flail of Amon.'

'No, no,' Weigall frowned. 'You've got that wrong,' he said. 'Hortense had stomach pains. It was Joe Linden Smith's wife, Corinna. She had damaged eyes.'

'Oh, yes,' Lestrade smiled. 'So she did.'

Lestrade was no stranger to Greek Street. The opium dens and bordellos of his rookiehood had given way to night-clubs and escort agencies, but what they pedalled had changed but little. The former were full of Bright Young Things in cravats and blazers and Americans driven three thousand miles for a drink by their ridiculous Volstead laws. The Ships in the Night Agency was housed on the third floor of a dingy little Victorian house that might have been built for the purpose. It had the offices of Women Against Syncopated Jazz on the first floor, the Soho branch of the Ancient Order of Rechabites on the second and more ways out than the Hippodrome.

'Yes,' Trixie Dilnot told him. 'Mr Smith.'

'Smith?' Lestrade repeated.

'That's the name he gave,' she said, filing her nails. Well, it was her lunch-break. 'Needed an escort for dinner at the Savoy. He'd picked me up at seven for seven thirty.'

'This was the night before last?'

'Yes, that's right. Pass me that wassname, will you, love? No, the other one. That's right. Yeah, 'cos Monday it was His Royal Highness.'

'The Prince of Wales?' Lestrade blinked.

Trixie consulted her notebook. 'Well,' she chuckled. 'It might say "Mr Smith", but then, it would, wouldn't it? No, it was him all right – flat cap, plus-fours, knitted jumper, silly dog under his arm. I said they wouldn't let us in the Ritz looking like that, but would he listen? Not him as would. The manager took one look at him and said "I don't care whose son you are, you're not bringing that dog in here". Well, naturally, HRH thought he meant me and punched the bloke on the nose. I don't know, these Royals! What's the world coming to?'

'Yes,' Lestrade said. 'But I'm actually more interested in Mr Smith Mark Two.'

'Are you?' Trixie looked at him under her false eyelashes. 'Look, mate, I don't wanna get personal, but I think you want the Rugger Club Escort Agency along at Number Sixty-nine. They cater for your sort.'

'Tell me about Tuesday night's Mr Smith.' Lestrade refused to be ruffled.

'Well, he was a boring old fart, really. Kept talking about Egypt and archaeology and stuff. I did put my hand on his knee at one point – all right, so we were in the lift at the time – but he had a one-track mind, so I gave up.'

'You had dinner?'

'Yeah, not a bad bash. I kept to the breaded plaice.'

'Whose table were you at?'

'One of the Savoy's, I suppose.' Trixie paused briefly in mid-file. 'It was in the hotel dining-room, after all.'

'No,' Lestrade said. 'I mean, who was with you?'

'Some Egyptian bloke. Prince Whoever-he-said-he-was. Rubbish dancer. Had feet like steamrollers. Had wandering hands, too.'

'Really?'

'Yeah. He'd undone me bra three times and the band hadn't even struck up by then.'

'While you were sitting down, what did you talk about?'

'Me? Nothing,' Trixie told him. 'Well, you see, in my line of work, there's three topics really – the weather, how I lost my virginity and what sort of corporal punishment I like. It depends on the client as to which one I use.'

'And on that night?'

'Well, the blokes – Prince Not Very Charming and Mr Smith – they were talking archaeology all night. She – stuck up cow, she was; nice frock, though – didn't speak English at all, so that was that. When I wasn't dancing with His Nibs, I danced with his secretary. I ask you, what sort of bloke has a bloke for a secretary? Mind you, he was very interested in the sort of corporal punishment I like. Said his master would be delighted and was I free on Thursday?'

'To which you replied?'

Trixie winked at Lestrade. 'I told him "I'm never free", ducky, and I'd have to consult my social calendar.'

'Tell me, Miss Dilnot,' Lestrade held his hand out while she peeled off an eyelash, 'did anyone else join you at the dinner table? An American lady, perhaps?'

'Nah.' Trixie shook her head. 'Only that band-leader blokey, came over to ask for any requests.'

'What time did the party break up?'

'Ooh,' Trixie frowned, 'now you've asked me. It must have been nearly one, 'cos I said to Mr Smith, "My place or yours?" and he didn't seem to know what I was talking about. Not that I mind, really. A night off you-know-what *and* three quid in my knickers; can't be bad, can it? By the way,' she leaned towards him, peeling off her other eyelash, 'what's your *real* name, Mr Lestrade?'

He winked at her. 'Smith, of course,' he told her.

'I've had a woman on the phone today,' Fanny said, pouring tea for them both.

'That's not possible, surely.' Her husband was reading the obituary in *The Times* of Prince Fahmy Bey, courtesy of Percy Merton, formerly their man in Egypt and soon to be so again.

'Miss Marie Corelli, no less,' Fanny beamed. 'You know, the novelist.'

'Do I?' Lestrade muttered, dunking his toast into his tea. 'Oh, yes. Raddled old trout, prosecuted for hoarding food during the war.'

'Oh, I'm sure that was all a misunderstanding. Sholto . . .'

'Sorry, dearest.' He surfaced from the paper. 'What?'

Fanny looked at the man she loved, then she folded her napkin and laid it carefully on the table cloth.

'What's the matter?' He took her hand.

'Oh . . .' she fluttered, as though to dismiss it.

'Don't "oh" me,' he warned. 'I know you too well, Fanny Lestrade. We've been together now . . . how long is it?'

She hit him with her buttered toast. 'Not so long that you should have forgotten,' she said.

'Quite.' He wiped his ear with his napkin. 'But long enough for me to know when something's wrong. Now, what is it?'

She bit her lip. She felt the tears start. It was tearing at her heart and had been since that mad, terrible day of the Cup Final when they'd brought his Emma home. She'd kept it from him; for the best of reasons, it was true, but she'd kept it nevertheless. It had become an albatross round her neck. In the event, she didn't have to say anything.

'It's Emma, isn't it?' he said.

Fanny nodded, feeling her eyes hot and wet.

'Something about her wound,' he went on, still holding her hand. 'Something about her walking . . .'

'She can't, Sholto,' Fanny sobbed and she fell into his arms.

He held her for a moment, then lifted her head. 'What do you mean?' he frowned, 'can't?'

'The doctor said', she sniffed, 'the knife has probably damaged her spinal cord. It's half real and half in her mind, he says. She tells me she has no feeling in her legs.'

He stood up, letting her arms fall. 'You should have told me,' he said slowly.

Fanny was nodding, looking up at him, at the parchment face, the dark-circled eyes. 'Oh, Sholto,' she sobbed, 'what shall we do?'

She saw his head lift, his shoulders set. 'What we've always done,' he said. 'We'll manage.' And he left the room.

There was something in his stride, something in the way he carried himself, that frightened her. She hadn't often seen her husband go into action, but when she had, she'd had the same feeling. It was the feeling she'd got when he was still at the Yard, facing anarchists' bullets or maniacs' knives. An empty feeling of terror and loneliness. She heard him bound up the stairs, two at a time. It was as well she didn't hear him resting at the top. Briefly, he braced himself outside Emma's room, then Fanny was aware of her door crashing back and half closing.

'Daddy . . .?' she heard her stepdaughter say.

Fanny heard her husband's voice too, but it didn't sound like her Sholto at all.

'Have I ever told you', she heard him ask as her foot trod the first stair, 'about my oldest memory?'

'No,' Emma said. 'I don't think . . .'

'They told me later it was the day the Light Brigade charged,' her father said. 'I was nine months old. And I took my first step.'

'Gosh.' Emma tried to lighten the mood. She'd never seen her father look so serious. 'That's early.'

'You know why I did it?' Fanny, on the fourth stair now, her heart in her mouth, heard him ask.

'No.' Emma's voice was small, distant.

'Curiosity,' Lestrade said. 'The will to do it. I don't remember, but I'd presumably been flopping about all over Pimlico before that day. It was night, actually. It was sixty-eight years ago, but I can still remember it as if it was yesterday. I can smell my mother's hands, warm and red and wet from the washing she took in. And I can see my old dad . . .'

Emma was trying to smile, but she couldn't. She couldn't because her old dad wasn't.

'. . . You'd have liked him, Emma,' he went on, backing to the window. 'I can see the buttons on his tunic and the letters on his collar, flashing in the firelight. Of course, I couldn't read them then, but I wanted to touch them. Had to touch them. As if . . . as if they were life itself.'

Fanny noticed that their bedroom door was ajar too. Yet she'd closed it just before tea. Madison was shopping in the village. That meant that Sholto must have gone in for something. She saw too that their wardrobe door was open wide. And she knew what it was. 'Here, Emma,' she heard her husband say. 'My old tunic. The old H Division. Whitechapel. Two point eight square miles of hell. Come on, Emma Lestrade. This is life. Here. Not stuck in that bed feeling sorry for yourself. Here. Now. Come and get it!' He was shouting at her, shaking the tunic like a matador's red cape.

She shook in the bed, her eyes blinking back the tears. 'Daddy,' she said, 'I can't. I can't.'

'Emma,' Fanny heard her husband growl, 'you can. You will. Now stand up!'

Fanny staggered back against the flock of the wall, the pounding in her heart almost painful. She'd never heard her husband yell like that, not in this house, not anywhere. She listened as the bedsprings jerked, the bedclothes being thrown back. She heard a silence she'd never heard in her life before.

'Come on, Emma,' Lestrade said. 'You can do it. That's it. That's it. Good girl. Come and get it. Come on. Life. Life. Come . . .' but he never finished his sentence, because there was a sudden scream that filled Fanny's heart.

She ran up the stairs that remained, three at a time, and flew into Emma's room. There was a tattered old police tunic on the floor, its collar numbers still bright in the afternoon sun. And a girl and an old man stood by the window, holding each other and crying.

'She did it, Fanny,' he said, grinning rather stupidly through the tears. 'My little girl did it.' He was kissing Emma's hair again and again; she was wrapping herself in his arms supported fully on her own feet.

Fanny dashed over to them and they wrapped their arms

around her too. 'You both did it,' she cried. 'You *and* your little girl.'

Sir Edward Marshall Hall had seen some strange sights in his time, but the one before him now was the strangest.

'Er . . . I rang the bell,' he said. 'And knocked. I'm not intruding, am I?'

They sat together in Lestrade's study, the greatest defence lawyer in the country and the world's second greatest detective. Outside in the summer sun of early evening Fanny and Emma were hobbling around like schoolgirls as the feeling came back to Emma's legs and Fanny marked out a hopscotch pitch.

'You mustn't mind them, Sir Edward,' Lestrade said, drying his eyes again on the curtains. 'It's been a rather peculiar afternoon.'

'Not as peculiar as my morning,' Marshall Hall assured him.

'Oh? Can I offer you tea, by the way?'

'No, thank you,' the lawyer said. 'What I have to impart is too serious for such an insipid beverage. Got any brandy?'

'Of course.' Lestrade poured for them both, glancing up every now and again as Fanny and Emma cackled anew at some sudden hilarity in the rhododendron bushes.

'Do I have your full attention?' Marshall Hall asked. 'It's about the Fahmy Bey case.'

'You have my full attention,' Lestrade assured him.

'I won't beat about the bush, Lestrade' – although the Lestrade women clearly were – 'I'm putting my career on the line visiting you like this.'

'I'm all ears, Sir Edward,' Lestrade confessed.

'I wouldn't normally break a client's confidentiality and talk to the opposition,' Marshall Hall assured him.

'I'm glad to hear it,' Lestrade said. He knew the rules of the game as well as anyone.

'The question is,' the lawyer closed to his man, 'can I trust you, ex-Detective Chief Superintendent?'

'As far as I can trust you.' Lestrade leaned in to him. 'Besides, I don't know about opposition; aren't we both on the same side – in the search for truth, that is?'

Slowly, the glimmer of a smile broke over the flat, regular features. 'Good answer, Lestrade,' he said. 'Very well. My client has told me a tale so fanciful . . . Well, it's nonsense, of course. I can't use it in court.'

'How fanciful?' Lestrade asked.

'More fanciful than a British jury can stomach,' Marshall Hall told him. 'My French, as you know, is second to none, but lest I miss a nuance here, a *je ne sais quoi* there, I have employed a French lady, herself a lawyer, to act as second interpreter for me. We have elicited from Marguerite Fahmy the following fantastic story and I, with all my vast powers of cross-examination, cannot shake her from it.'

'I remain a gog,' Lestrade said, his glass untouched.

'As you will have gathered from others by now, no doubt, dinner on the night in question was a stormy affair in more senses than one.'

'Indeed,' Lestrade nodded. 'The broccoli.'

'Quite. At a little before one thirty, the Fahmys said goodbye to their guests . . .'

'Arthur Weigall and Trixie Dilnot.'

'Really?' Marshall Hall made a hurried note of that. 'And then retired. They were both in a pretty foul mood. She remained in her evening gown. He undressed, cleaned his teeth, put on his pyjamas and walked the dog.'

'Walked the dog?'

'Just along the fourth-floor corridor, you understand.'

'Ah.'

'When he returned, she asked him for money to go to Paris for her operation.'

'For her piles?'

'Really?' Marshall Hall made another note. 'Then, he made an indecent proposal.'

'Really?' It was Lestrade's turn to pose that question, though he didn't bother making notes.

'Something else I can't expect a British jury to stomach,' Marshall Hall said.

'Er . . . how indecent?' Lestrade persisted, sensing, rightly, that he could cope with a great deal that a British jury could not.

'As Madame Fahmy put it to me,' Marshall Hall answered, '"I will do anything for love, Sir Edward, but I won't do that."'

'Ah.'

'Anyway, she wasn't having any. And therefore, conversely, neither was he. Which meant in turn, of course, that she wasn't either – any money, that is. She hit him.'

'And?'

'He hit her, grabbing her seconds later round the throat.'

'Upon which?'

'Upon which he dashed out of the room, although quite why I don't suppose we'll ever know, and collided with Cabin, the night porter.'

'Then she came out,' Lestrade took up the tale as he understood it, 'rabbiting away in French, presumably. And then the dog came out . . .'

'. . . Barking mad,' Marshall Hall filled him in.

'I've heard nothing new,' Lestrade felt bound to tell him.

'So far, no,' Marshall Hall nodded, pausing in mid-brief for a swig of Lestrade's brandy. 'But here, my dear ex-Chief Superintendent, all common sense and probability fly utterly out of the window.' They both glanced across to where Fanny and Emma were playing leapfrog over the croquet hoops.

'Madame Fahmy – Marguerite', Marshall Hall continued, 'grabbed hubby's gun.'

'The Browning automatic.'

'Which she can't fire.'

'It *was* a bitch mechanically,' Lestrade agreed.

'Marguerite knows nothing about guns. The cover was jammed and she tried to shake out the bullet. When that didn't work, she squeezed the trigger. A bullet whizzed out through the open window.'

'And then?'

'Then, not understanding an automatic's mechanism, she assumed the thing was empty. Whereas you and I know the next bullet had clicked into the firing position. She turned it on hubby, who was still hopping mad and screaming at her and . . .'

'. . . Shot and killed him.'

'No.'

'No?' Lestrade's left eyebrow rose. Then, on a moment's reflection. 'Well, she would say that, wouldn't she?'

'Lestrade,' Marshall Hall said. 'May I remind you who I am?' The lawyer produced an envelope from his inside pocket.

'What's this?' Lestrade said.

'It's an envelope, Lestrade,' Marshall Hall explained as patiently as he knew how. 'Be so good as to read it.'

Lestrade did.

'Aloud, please.'

'"The Greatest Lawyer on Earth".'

'Quite,' Marshall Hall beamed. 'A coquettish little device, but a useful one.'

'Someone thinks highly of you,' Lestrade said.

'*Everyone* thinks highly of *me*, Lestrade,' Marshall Hall put him right. 'But I fear you are missing the point. What, likewise, is missing from that envelope?'

'Er . . . the address?'

'Exactly. I wrote it to myself,' the lawyer confessed. '*With no address*. And still, it reached me at my chambers. Now *that's* the measure of my brilliance, Lestrade.'

Lestrade refused to be impressed. 'So you have a fan in the GPO,' he shrugged.

'The point I am making', Marshall Hall persisted, 'is that I've interviewed more clients than a dog has fleas. And I have *never*, repeat *never*, Lestrade, come across one I believe more totally than I do Marguerite Fahmy Bey.'

'All right,' Lestrade was prepared to play along, 'so she didn't shoot him. Who did?'

'Person unknown.' Marshall Hall sat back.

'Pardon?'

'Where was Fahmy Bey when he was shot?' the lawyer asked.

'In the suite doorway,' Lestrade said. 'Standing next to . . . ah . . .'

Marshall Hall positively beamed. It was an unnerving experience. 'The lift,' he said.

'Don't tell me.' Lestrade covered his face, seeing Macclesfield's case being blown sky high.

'I fear I must,' Marshall Hall said. 'Marguerite was pointing

213

the gun when there were three shots fired from behind her. Over her right shoulder. All of them hit the Prince and he dropped like a brick.'

'There was someone in the lift,' Lestrade said.

'Of course.'

'But Cabin, the night porter . . .'

'Turned at the sound of the first shot, yes. Remember that corridor on the fourth floor? I do, I've spent the last hour before luncheon walking up and down it. There's a kink half-way along. The lift is three quarters on. From where he was standing, Cabin couldn't possibly have seen the lift doors; whether they were open or closed; if anyone was standing there.'

'But he'd have heard the lift moving, surely?'

'In a perfect world, yes,' Marshall Hall conceded. 'But he'd just seen a man shot in front of him. And a woman holding a gun. Given that situation, I wonder how many of us would hear the whirrings of a lift?'

'True,' Lestrade nodded.

'Besides, it didn't move. Not for a while.'

'What?'

'Fahmy Bey had been shot with a Browning. The exact same gun that Marguerite owned.'

'So?'

'So that wasn't enough, was it? Even an average forensic scientist could discover that the bullets didn't match. And Robert Churchill would certainly elicit that – probably in seconds.'

'What are you saying?' Lestrade asked.

'I'm saying that our friend in the lift switched weapons. Oh, it probably wasn't part of the original plan, but it fell into his lap, so to speak. In the shock of what she thought she'd done, Marguerite dropped the weapon. While she was being hysterical, cradling the dying man in her arms and Cabin was chasing his own posterior in panic, chummy calmly snatched up Marguerite's pistol, substituted his own and nipped back inside the lift again.'

'But her prints.' Lestrade clicked his fingers. 'Madame Fahmy's prints were all over the gun.'

'Of course they were,' Marshall Hall leaned back, 'because

214

she picked it up again. We have the testimony of Arthur Mariani, the Night Manager, for that. He it was who took it off her.'

'I see,' said Lestrade.

'I'm glad you do,' said Marshall Hall, rising and crossing to the window. The women were still there, laughing and pushing each other as the shadows lengthened and the croquet hoops became little white ghosts in the gloom. 'Because I can't use any of it.'

'The great British jury?' Lestrade asked.

'Of course. No, I'll pursue the line that Marguerite did it.'

'Er . . . I'm sorry, Sir Edward.' Lestrade frowned. 'I was under the distinct impression that you were the *defending* counsel in this case.'

'So I am,' Marshall Hall yawned. 'I'll put that slimy tove Ernani on the stand and imply that he is not as other secretaries. That he and his master and that black chappie connived to lead poor Marguerite a terrible dance.' He suddenly crouched by the casement, an evil glint in his eyes. 'Picture', he growled, 'the wily Oriental, ready to spring on this defenceless creature. She, innocent and abandoned, sold into white slavery and subjected to unspeakable and unnatural vice. He was abnormal and a brute with the vilest of vile tempers and a filthy, perverted taste. Why was this woman afraid?' He suddenly straightened, pacing Lestrade's carpet as though it were Number One Court at the Bailey. 'Was she afraid of the hirelings of this man who would do her to death? The curse of this case is the atmosphere which we cannot understand – the Eastern feeling of possession of the woman . . .' his face was a livid crimson in the half light '. . . the Turk in his harem, this man who was entitled to have four wives if he liked, for chattels . . . it is something almost unintelligible, something we cannot deal with.'

'Sir Edward . . .'

'Imagine', the greatest lawyer in the world was in full flight, 'the effects of that storm on a woman of nervous temperament who had been living such a life – terrified, abused, beaten, degraded . . .'

'But . . .'

'In sheer desperation – as he crouched for the last time, crouched like an animal, retired for the last time to get a bound

215

forward – she turned the pistol and put it to his face and to her horror, the thing went off.'

Marshall Hall's face fell, his right hand came down and he visibly slumped into the corner before 'coming to', as it were. 'Then, I'll probably drop the gun, invoke the sunshine streaming in through the window – you know how it does in Number One Court – and ask for an acquittal.'

'And an Oscar?' sighed Lestrade, only now coming out of the great web of magic that Marshall Hall had woven.

'Oh, I expect there'll be the usual howls of protest from the Egyptian government,' the lawyer yawned, flopping down into his chair again. 'But what's that in the scheme of things? We certainly made the buggers back down at Tel-el-Kebir – or was it Omdurman?'

Actually it was neither, but it wasn't Lestrade's place to say so.

'No.' Marshall Hall finished his brandy. 'I just thought you ought to know, as someone who is attached, but vicariously, to the Yard, what *really* happened. Oh, and you might be interested in this.'

He rummaged again in his inside pocket and produced another envelope. This one was addressed clearly enough, to Madame Fahmy Bey, c/o the Savoy Hotel.

'It's in French,' Lestrade realized.

'Of course,' Marshall Hall said. 'That's the language the lady speaks.' He snatched it back from Lestrade. 'It says – and I quote – "Do not return to Egypt. A journey means a possible accident, poison in a flower, a subtle weapon which is neither seen nor heard."'

'Poison?' Lestrade repeated. 'That's a far cry from a Browning automatic.'

'Not a far cry from a few deaths in the Valley of the Kings, though, is it, Lestrade?' Marshall Hall raised an eyebrow.

'You've been reading the *Mail* again.' Lestrade clicked his tongue, shaking his head.

'Only mine and Madame Fahmy's,' the lawyer said.

'May I keep this?' Lestrade asked.

'Of course,' said Marshall Hall. 'I've never seen it, have I, ex-Chief Superintendent? No, I'll stick with the wronged wife ploy. I'd like twelve women on the jury, but old Percy Clarke

216

will never wear that. He might, however, settle for three . . . Well,' the lawyer heard Lestrade's grandmother striking from the hall, 'I must away. Thanks for the brandy.'

'Thanks for the information,' Lestrade said.

'Look, Lestrade.' Marshall Hall was staring out of the window. 'Those women . . .'

'Don't worry about them,' Lestrade beamed. 'Touch of the sun, that's all. I'll see you out.'

Marie Corelli, it transpired, had a theory. Lestrade knew that. The *hoi polloi* of Fleet Street knew that. But the lady had been so insistent and so mysterious and had, after all, got Lestrade's home number from *somewhere*, that he felt – well, actually, Fanny felt – that he ought to go. When the persistent lady said Stratford, that was fine. Lestrade caught a Circle Line and off he went. Having paced the length and breadth of the old K Division all morning, he eventually asked a policeman. It was perhaps lucky for Lestrade that he'd met the only genuine reader on the Force.

'No, sir,' the constable had told him. 'If it's Miss Corelli you're after, you're looking for Stratford-upon-Avon, not Stratford-at-Bow. It's up a bit and across a bit from here. I've got all her books, you know; from *The Romance of Two Worlds* to *The Secret Power*. Rattling good reads they are too. I think *The Murder of Delicia* is my favourite – but then, it would be, wouldn't it? Have a nice day.' And he saluted and was gone.

The municipal borough and market town of Stratford-upon-Avon is pleasantly situated on the river of the same name twenty-four miles south-east of Birmingham. The Americans had intruded even this far into the leafy heart of the country, claiming, somewhat spuriously, that John Harvard's mother hailed from there. Another American, G. W. Childs, had erected a fountain for reasons best known to himself, in the Memorial Park.

It was neither of these edifices that Lestrade had journeyed north to find, however, but Mason Croft, the home of one of the most read and least loved writers in history. Arriving by the back gate, he did happen to catch sight of what appeared to be three or four tons of granulated sugar, care of Messrs Tate and Lyle, piled high in the great novelist's back passage.

'I *do* intend to make jam with it all, you know,' a hideous old bat shrieked at him. 'To be distributed among the poor, together with a free copy of one of my books. Are you from the council, you vulgar little man?'

'No, Madam,' Lestrade told her. 'I'm from Scotland Yard.'

'Ah.' She clapped her hands gleefully. 'Would you be Chief Superintendent Lestrade?'

'*Ex*-Chief Superintendent,' he corrected her. She looked a litigious old bat, as well as a hideous one, and he didn't want to risk being caught impersonating a police officer.

'Tsk, tsk,' she scolded, leading him by the arm. 'One's former glories always stay with one. I, for instance, haven't written anything truly great, I will confess, since last Thursday, but the memory lingers on.'

'Would you be Marie Corelli?' He thought he'd better check.

'If I had my time all over again, you mean? Oh yes,' she nodded sagely, leading him towards the river that ran, sluggish and brown, at the bottom of her garden, 'yes, there's no one in the world that I would rather be. I often think I've been me before, you know. Signor Esparto!' She clapped her hands and a sour-looking little Italian glided out from under a trailing willow, a striped shirt over his upper body and a beret on his head. In his hands he held a long pole and under his carefully balanced feet, an ornate, gilded gondola cut through the water.

The great writer leaned to Lestrade. 'This is Signor Esparto,' she whispered. 'He used to be a grass to the Warwickshire Constabulary, but I reformed him and now he gondoles for me only.'

The little Italian twisted his left foot and the boat slid to a halt beside Miss Corelli's little jetty.

'Come with me,' she said to Lestrade. 'In my gondola.'

He helped her in with the aid of the gondolier and wobbled aboard himself. After the de Havilland Hercules, the slender, badly-balanced craft held no terrors for him. After all, should there be a mishap, he could always swim for it. Had he fallen out of the de Havilland, however, flying might have been problematical.

'Eyesore, isn't it?' She scowled at a large white and brick-red building to her right.

'Er . . . yes,' he agreed. 'What is it?'

'The locals refer to it as the Shakespeare Memorial Theatre.' She waved her talented right arm at it. 'I call it a brewer's vat, for obvious reasons. Well, if I confide that it was designed by two no-hopers called Dodgshun and Unsworth, I suspect that that will speak for itself. George Bernard Shaw has intimated to me, in one of his saner moments, that although he would not himself burn the place down, he would certainly send a telegram of congratulation to anybody who did.'

'Fascinating as this discussion on theatrical architecture is, Miss Corelli, I am a very busy man and you did mention something about a solution to the recent deaths in Egypt.'

'Ah, yes, indeed. Turn right here, Signor Esparto, I want to lob a brick at the mayor's house.'

Lestrade lowered himself still further in the boat and pulled his Panama down over his eyes.

'It's poison,' she said triumphantly, as though she'd just solved the riddle of the universe.

'Yes, Madam,' Lestrade couldn't believe it, 'I had got that far myself.'

'Had you?' The ancient writer blinked. 'Oh. Oh, well, why didn't you say so?'

'I didn't exactly have the opportunity,' Lestrade said. 'I believe you spoke to my wife.'

'Well,' she trilled, 'you could have telephoned me back. You have my number.'

'I certainly have, Madam,' Lestrade scowled. 'I have also come rather a long way for no purpose whatsoever.'

'I would hardly say that,' Miss Corelli gasped. 'You have spent the last few minutes in the company of greatness.'

'What sort of poison?' Lestrade ignored her.

'Arsenic,' she chortled. 'Obviously.'

'Obviously,' Lestrade growled. 'Signor Esparto, can you turn this thing round? I have a train to catch.'

'Do as he says, Signor,' Miss Corelli snapped. 'If you're not interested in my solving murders for you, that's your loss. I have plenty of other things to do. I was up to my eyes researching Ralph Holinshed when you pestered me . . .'

219

'Who?' Lestrade sat upright.

'Ralph Holinshed,' the great researcher repeated.

'Who's he?'

'*Was* he, Chief Superintendent,' Miss Corelli corrected him. 'He's dead.'

'Not poisoned, was he?' Lestrade was suddenly all attention.

'I really don't know,' she said. 'I've never thought about it. Ralph or Raphael Holinshed was an English chronicler. He worked for a printer employed by Good Queen Bess. Shakespeare drew heavily on his histories . . . Mr Lestrade, you've gone rather a strange colour.'

'Miss Corelli,' Lestrade knelt up in the boat. 'May I be permitted to say that I believe you are probably the greatest writer in the history of the world.' And he planted a kiss on the old bat's forehead.

'Oh,' Miss Corelli blushed. 'How nice of you to say so. What marvellous taste you have. And what jocund company you're in. Both the late Mr Gladstone and the late Oscar Wilde have said as much; though neither of them, for different reasons, ever, as far as I can recollect, kissed me on the forehead.'

Lestrade could believe that.

11

'Would you say that again, please, Norroy?' Emma Lestrade said, gazing into his dark eyes.

His face resembled a beetroot by now and the muscles in his neck, still not fully restored after his altercation at the Mosque El-Muayyad, were rigid as a dirigible.

'I said,' he just about managed to repeat, 'will you m . . .'

'That's enough of that!' A whirlwind in a sodden jacket and a dripping Panama hurtled past him.

'Daddy?' Emma broke free of the Inspector's clutches.

'Guv?' The Inspector broke free of hers.

'Sholto?' Fanny put her head around the door. 'Are you all right, dear? You appear to be steaming. I know it's July, but . . .'

'Shut up, woman, and pass me that shirt.'

She did, while he hauled at button and stud. 'If you want to know, I fell in the river.'

'Daddy, are you all right?'

'You turn your back, young lady,' her father snapped, down to his combs at this point. 'God, you'd think I'd have dried out by now, wouldn't you? It was standing room only on the train, even if everybody else was standing upwind of me.' He grabbed his old bowler, out of season though it was. 'Don't ask me how it happened.' He put a hand on each of his ladies' shoulders. 'If you ever smell this smell again,' he said, 'you'll know it's Avon calling and if you've got any sense, you'll run like merry hell. I'll have to borrow your copper, Emma. Got your station wagon, Norroy? Good, I can use your considerable powers of arrest.'

And then he was gone.

'Oh, Fanny.' Emma stood there, staring after Macclesfield's exhaust.

Fanny put her arm around the girl's neck. 'He'll be back,' she said. 'I promise you.'

It was a little after ten that the Yard men, past and present, knocked on the door of the suite at the Grand. It was opened to them by a sultry-looking woman in dark glasses.

'Mr Lestrade,' she said. 'Mr Macclesfield, how nice!' And she kissed them both. 'I'm afraid Jack's not here at the moment, but he shouldn't be long.'

'It's not Jack we came to see,' Macclesfield told her. 'It's you, Tilly.'

'Oh.' Her smile froze. 'How lovely. Do come in. Can I get you a drink?'

She showed them into an opulent lounge, Art Deco lamps illuminating the walls, slashed with hideous Art Deco wallpaper.

'Matilda Holinshed,' Macclesfield said, 'I am arresting you in connection with the murder of Alain Le Clerk on or about . . .'

'What?' Her shriek cut Macclesfield's sentence short. 'What the devil are you talking about?'

'Poison, Tilly,' Lestrade said. 'Hyoscine. Though how you passed yourself off as a man to obtain it I'll never know.'

'If that's a compliment to my femininity, Mr Lestrade,' she said archly, throwing her head back, 'I thank you for it. Are you seriously suggesting that I killed . . . what did you say his name was?'

Lestrade sat down uninvited. 'His name', he said quietly, placing his bowler on the table beside him, 'was Alain Le Clerk. It's my guess you met him in Cairo and when you told my daughter you were visiting the Fahmy Beys in Damietta, in reality you were accompanying Le Clerk to the Valley of the Kings.'

'Was I really?' There was cold hatred in her voice and she sat down too.

'What you didn't bargain for was Harry Burton and his camera. He took a snap, didn't he? A photograph of you and Le Clerk quite obviously not getting on. And that was odd.'

'It was?'

'Oh, yes,' Macclesfield said. 'You see, Monsieur Le Clerk got on with anybody in a skirt. Except you.'

'We had to work out why,' Lestrade said. 'It's my guess that you poisoned him over luncheon. Slipped henbane into his coffee and then, for whatever perverse reason I can only guess, told him you had.'

'Enough to cool any man's ardour, I would think,' Macclesfield said.

'You can't prove it,' she said levelly.

'We can have the photograph blown up, Mrs Ralph,' Lestrade said.

'Who?'

'The sobrickay you used when you visited the Valley of the Kings. Oh, I must confess I've been up a few blind alleys over the past months. Hortense Weigall, the archaeologist's wife; Corinna Smith, the archaeologist's wife . . . even Madame Fahmy . . .'

'. . . the dead bugger's wife,' Macclesfield chipped in.

'Quite,' Lestrade said. 'Thank you, Norroy. But you gave yourself away by using the name "Ralph". I'm not much of a Shakespearean scholar, I will admit, but the world's greatest living writer told me only this morning who Ralph Holinshed was – and everything fell into place.'

'How nice for you,' she scowled. 'You're clutching at straws, Lestrade.'

'No, I did that this morning,' he smiled. 'Or was it lilies? Would you take off your glasses, Miss Holinshed? I'm sure you don't need them in this subdued light.'

She looked at them both, her interrogators, her inquisitors and she did as she was asked.

'Matilda Holinshed,' Macclesfield said, 'I am arresting you also for the malicious wounding of Emma Bandicoot-Lestrade,' and he blushed crimson at the name, 'and the attempted murder of Almina, Lady Carnarvon, at Wembley Stadium . . .'

'This is preposterous!' Tilly was on her feet, still elegant, still cold, lighting a cigarette with a slightly shaking hand.

'There's a little boy I know,' Lestrade said quietly. 'His name is Algie. Observant little chap. I think he'd know those eyes anywhere. Those weak eyes that had to be kept out of the sun.

Those poor, dear eyes that my daughter assumed were so badly sunburned. But they're not sunburned, are they, Tilly?' Lestrade was leaning forward, whispering. 'They're tattoos. Dr Smith, the legal doctor in Cairo told me it's a custom, especially among high-born Egyptians. Mr Macclesfield here has the power to arrest you under any name you like, but it would be nice to have your real one.'

'Smenkhkare,' a voice thundered behind them.

'Jack!' Lestrade called, but he was too late. There was a crash of gunfire and Norroy Macclesfield went down, a dark red stain spreading over his shirt, his left arm flailing uselessly.

In a second the muzzle of the gun was inches from what was left of Sholto Lestrade's nose. 'Not Jack,' its firer hissed. 'Horemheb.'

'Let me go to him,' Lestrade asked.

'Let him bleed to death,' Holinshed growled. 'You'd better sit down, Lestrade. I'd hate you to go to your grave only partially aware of why I'm sending you there. Smenk, the door.'

She ran past Lestrade, flicking the lock.

'If you're wondering why no one's come to investigate that shot', Holinshed smiled, easing himself back on to the settee as the gunsmoke cleared, 'you have to realise that we are on the fifth floor. Our suite occupies all of it – a rather discreet penthouse. There's also a Ball on the ground floor,' he flicked his expensive evening-dress lapel, 'which is why I was late.'

'You can't have expected us.' Lestrade frowned, trying to see how Macclesfield was.

'No,' Holinshed conceded. 'No, we didn't. But', he waved the gun, 'we were ready.'

'Ah, yes,' Lestrade nodded. 'Madame Fahmy's Browning automatic. Which one of you did that?'

'I did,' Tilly said, pouring a drink for Jack and herself. 'I always had a stronger grip than dear, simpering Marguerite.'

'Are you going to tell me why, then?' Lestrade asked, sinking his back against his chair.

'You wouldn't understand,' she said icily, passing her brother a scotch.

'I don't know,' Holinshed said. 'Perhaps he would. You've

been there, Lestrade. To Egypt. To the Valley of the Kings. *Our* Valley.'

'*Your* Valley?' Lestrade frowned.

'Our country, right or wrong,' Holinshed said. 'It must be a long time since you were in school, Lestrade, so I hope you won't be bored by the following little lesson in history.'

'Ooh, goody,' Lestrade said, without smiling. 'History! My favourite.'

'Once upon a time,' Holinshed began, 'there was a great Pharaoh called Akhenaten. Oh, he was a heretic, but a great one. Unfortunately, he had a feeble-minded son whom he called Tutankhamun . . .'

'He of the tomb,' Lestrade said.

'I'm glad you're following this,' Holinshed grinned, 'because I shall be asking questions later. Tutankhamun, the likeness of the living God, was only fifteen or so when his skull was caved in by the boy-king's personal tutor, Ay, who was also his step-grandfather. I suspect that had we allowed Carter to get any further with his digging, he'd have found a hole in the mummy's head.'

'I'm riveted so far,' Lestrade told him.

'When Ay killed the rightful king and usurped his throne, there was a faithful general, away fighting to the south of Thebes.'

'General Horemheb.' Tilly had crossed to her brother and draped her long, sinewy fingers around his neck.

'He was a great warrior,' Holinshed said, sipping his whisky. 'His victories are emblazoned all over the inner chambers of Tutankhamun's tomb. He fought his way north, and hacked off, according to legend, the bald head of Ay and his son, Nakhtmin. This was some time around 1319, before the birth of your Christ. Horemheb founded the Nineteenth Dynasty, and all trace of Ay and his cursed line was destroyed for ever. Rather like you and Macclesfield,' Holinshed smiled, 'it was as though they never existed.'

'There's a comforting thought,' Lestrade nodded soberly. 'I don't see where you and Tilly fit in.'

'"Jack" and "Tilly" were just convenient labels,' Holinshed said. 'As was the surname. The world turns, Lestrade. Three

225

thousand years ago, the world was Egypt. Now, it's Britain.' A mocking smile crossed the man's face. 'I note however that the Empire is cracking. The Union Jack will cease to flap over a quarter of the earth soon . . . to be replaced by . . . who knows? The stars and stripes? The hammer and sickle? When Smenk and I were young, our parents, like ourselves Guardians of the Gate, taught us to be English. We went to the British School in Cairo, then I to Harrow and Smenk to Roedean. We even dyed our hair to make us more British. And our thorough immersion into your Shakespeare gave us the name of the chronicler Holinshed. And it worked . . .'

'. . . Except for the eyes,' Lestrade reminded him.

'Except for the eyes,' Holinshed acknowledged. 'It was the custom among the Pharaohs and has been among people of our class for generations. We were waiting, Smenk and I, for the world to turn again. For the time we could take our rightful places on the thrones of Upper and Lower Egypt.'

'Where does Zagloul fit into this?' Lestrade asked. 'And isn't there some sort of Sultan chappie?'

'There is a king, yes,' Holinshed growled contemptuously. 'But Fuad the First is in reality Ahmed Fuad, a jumped-up little nobody who has been placed on the throne by you British – a puppet of a dying Empire. As for Zagloul, he is the worst of hybrids – an Egyptian in his preparedness to kill and to scheme and to lie, but an Englishman in that he is prepared to embrace democracy.'

'We', Tilly said, running her hands around Jack's face, 'are the rightful rulers of Egypt. My brother, my husband and I.'

'There are three of you?' Lestrade appeared to have missed something.

'According to the old laws', Holinshed smiled, 'we Pharaohs take our sisters to wife. That way the line runs pure.'

'I see,' Lestrade said, remembering Marshall Hall's rhetoric in his study that all this was something difficult for an Englishman to understand. 'Then Carter found the tomb.'

'Yes,' Holinshed's Browning had not wavered one iota from Lestrade's head, for all the ex-Yard man hoped it would. 'And that at once opened old wounds and posed problems. Who would have thought that the very grave of the boy-king so defiled, whose death led to Horemheb's rise to power, would still be there, unviolated? But it was an Englishman who found it and an Englishman who financed the finding.'

'But Carter – and Carnarvon come to that – intend to keep the finds in Egypt,' Lestrade said. 'You wouldn't have lost them.'

'If the infidel looks on the trappings of the boy-king,' Holinshed said, 'then that is defilement. It is not where the trappings go that is important, but the very fact of their going. Carter will prise out the body of Tutankhamun from its sarcophagus. He will unwind the winding sheets, the resin-soaked linen, with their secret amulets and he will bare the boy-king's corpse to a greedy and alien world. Lindsley Hall will draw it; Burton will take his cheap, tawdry pictures. The sanctity and the heart of Egypt will have gone.'

'So . . . Carnarvon had to die?'

'Anyone connected with the tomb,' Tilly said. 'Although some were more important than others. Without Carnarvon, the money would dry up. Even then, we hoped that his death would end it. That they would reseal the tomb and leave Tutankhamun in his slumbers.'

'So you killed Carnarvon with henbane?'

'Yes,' Holinshed said. 'But he wasn't our first victim.'

'Ah,' Lestrade nodded. 'Albert Weez, the nightwatchman at St Bart's.'

'Precisely. We chose henbane because it grows so freely in Egypt – is the most common form of poison there, in fact. But I needed to have a readily usable form of the stuff. I'm no chemist.'

'You obtained it from Pargetter, the pharmacist.'

'Correct. He was suspicious, but corruptible. Every man has his price, Lestrade. Pargetter's was one hundred pounds.'

'But Weez disturbed you?'

'The silly old duffer wanted to know what I was doing there, at that hour. The hospital was too busy during the day and Pargetter insisted that I come to get it myself.'

'Because he intended to blackmail you,' Lestrade said. 'And having you on his premises gave him an extra edge.'

'Correct again. I suppose I panicked and I smashed in Weez's skull with a lead pipe. Then I smashed a window to make it look as though I'd forced an entry. I dragged Weez's body away

227

from the pharmacy to confuse the issue. But there was no confusing the blood-stain on the floor. It was obvious where he'd died. Pargetter said he'd smash the cabinet too, to make it look like a break-in and he'd falsify the records so that it appeared that something other than hyoscine had been stolen.'

'He doctored the records, all right,' Lestrade said, 'but he didn't break the cabinet.'

'Why not?' Holinshed asked him.

'I don't know,' Lestrade said. 'Perhaps he intended to throw suspicion on a colleague, a doctor perhaps. All it did, of course, was to throw suspicion on himself. He was trying to be too clever. But what I don't understand is how you were able to get out to Egypt and back again to engage me.'

'Simple,' Holinshed smiled. 'Remember the curse of the Pharaoh – "And death shall come on soft wings . . ."? The soft wings were mine. Fahmy Bey didn't have a monopoly on money, Lestrade. Our parents left us nicely provided for. I have a yacht and a plane.'

'Soft wings,' Lestrade nodded.

'Precisely. I flew out to Egypt. I'd known Carnarvon for years. Smenk had been to school with his daughter, remember. Odd that, Evelyn not telling you we were Egyptian; that was something that bothered us rather. Still, she's rather a daffy girl, I'm glad to say, and all was well. I borrowed Carnarvon's razor one morning and smeared it with the hyoscine I'd got from Pargetter. The hyoscine and something else.'

'Ah yes,' Lestrade said. 'The something else. What was that?'

'It need not concern you,' Tilly said, perching beside her husband-brother. 'It is a concoction of the ancients, handed down through the centuries. It is not for infidels to know of it.'

'I may not be a chemist, but I knew how to mix the two,' Holinshed went on. 'It is the most ancient poison that causes the delirium, the madness. I wanted Carnarvon to suffer before he died.'

'As you wanted me to suffer,' Lestrade said.

'You were a pawn, Lestrade,' Tilly dismissed him. 'A mere shuttlecock in our game.'

'I didn't, at that stage,' Holinshed continued, 'want any other

228

poison to be detected. So I wiped the razor clean and resmeared it with hyoscine only.'

'That's why it was still in Carnarvon's tent in the Valley of the Kings,' Lestrade realized aloud. 'You were playing cat and mouse with me.'

'I took the razor with me after Carnarvon had opened the old mosquito bite. He had others, should he be able to shave in the days left to him, so he wouldn't notice the disappearance of one. I kept it, ready to slip back into his tent later. The schedule was punishing, but I made it. I probably set up a new flying record in getting back to England in time to meet you and Emma at Highclere.'

'I sent the telegram,' Tilly said, 'as though from Evelyn. We knew you wouldn't be able to resist.'

'I still don't understand,' Lestrade said. 'Why engage me at all?'

'Remember we'd planned a number of deaths.' Holinshed crossed to the table to pour himself another scotch. Still the gun did not waver. 'Oh, the gullible might be frightened away by superstitious nonsense about the Pharaoh's curse, the Kiss of Horus, guardian of the tomb; but the Parquet? Scotland Yard? That wasn't likely. We knew of you, as we said we did, from Evelyn Herbert. If we had a famous detective, albeit a private one, and slightly gaga, working on Carnarvon's death and those of the others, then something could be seen to be done. A string of "accidents" would only provoke suspicion and we'd have God knows how many policemen trampling everywhere, snooping. We had to show it was murder – hence the hyoscine smeared back on the razor. The hyoscine that would point in *any* direction in a land of henbane poisonings.'

'But then . . .'

'But then,' Tilly said, 'you got too close. So did Alain Le Clerk. He was entering into a deal with Carter. He'd promised him the backing of the French government if he signed over the tomb's treasures to him. He was boasting of this openly in Cairo. As Mrs Ralph, I knew of his proclivities. With his revolting, clammy hands all over me, I accompanied him to the Valley, having doctored his drink in the morning with our potion. During the day, he became so nauseating that I cracked.

229

I told him what I'd done, that he was dying. He had been kissed, not by me, but by Horus, and his only hope was to leave the Valley fast. He did. And he rode to hell.'

'We had the plane waiting at Luxor,' Holinshed said. ' "Mrs Ralph" got there by donkey and we flew to Highclere as you've heard.'

'And Aaron String was next?'

'Another interloper,' Holinshed said. 'This time he offered to buy the tomb outright with his ill-gotten millions. Carter had refused, but he was a desperate man. He couldn't be sure that Lady Carnarvon would continue to finance the expedition, so he might have given way. After all, he'd already shown himself susceptible to the blandishments of Le Clerk. I laced his drink.'

'And he nearly blew my head off.'

'That would have saved us a great deal of trouble.' Holinshed sat back down on the settee. 'You see, the hyoscine I'd stolen from St Bart's was running low. Clifford Hanger was posing a threat because he was preparing to cheapen the find, selling his repulsive little Carnarvon razors and Tutankhamun propelling pencils. He was to die first and then the insufferable Merton of *The Times*.'

'And the insufferable Lestrade of the Yard?'

'Smenk and I split the dosage. We hoped it would be enough to kill you both. Unfortunately, it wasn't. It merely caused delusions. Delusions from which you both recovered.'

'So you used a gun,' Lestrade said. 'Nearly gave yourself away there, didn't you?'

'How so?' Holinshed raised an eyebrow.

'Well, you knew all about Aaron G. String's brace of Colts in the Valley of the Kings when he blew his brains out, then suddenly, in Shepheard's Hotel, you knew nothing about powder burns or bullets or anything else.'

Holinshed laughed. 'Point taken,' he said. 'I will concede that I was working under pressure. Hanger had discovered I'd been out to the plane.'

'To doctor the de Havilland's engines.'

'Yes. The perfect way to stop Carter once and for all.'

'Tell me,' Lestrade leaned forward, trying to see how Macclesfield was from the corner of his eye. 'Did you kill Hanger with that gun?'

'With my Browning, yes. This', he clicked back the hammer, 'is Marguerite Fahmy's, remember.'

'How could I forget?' Lestrade sat back again.

'Unfortunately, of course, in all the hoo-ha at the airport, I couldn't defend myself with it. It might, even in those hysterical moments, have given the game away.'

'But then', Lestrade said, 'you were on the plane, forced there by Zagloul's boys. And the plane was due to stop in mid-air.'

'So at that point', Holinshed admitted, 'I had to suggest to Mainwaring that we release the prop.'

'And having your own plane, you knew this was possible. And having brazenly passed the Sirdar's troops the night before on some pretext of checking the aircraft, you knew exactly how to put right what was wrong.'

'Of course.'

'But you were thoroughly rattled by this time,' Lestrade smiled. 'Come on, Holinshed, admit it. Your cool poisonings had given way to messy gunshots,' he glanced at Tilly, 'and feeble attempts at stabbing.'

'Smenk did her best,' Holinshed defended his sister-wife. 'You kept Lady Carnarvon and Carter well under protection. A veiled Egyptian woman in a crowd under the VIP awning, though – well, that might work. It was unfortunate that Emma moved at just the wrong time.'

There was a moan from Macclesfield.

'Oh dear,' Holinshed frowned, 'I must be slipping.' And he swung the Browning sideways.

'Then', Lestrade shouted, 'Pargetter got greedy, didn't he?'

His heart sank a little towards the right place when he saw Holinshed's gun muzzle swing back to him.

'He did,' the English-Egyptian said. 'He'd read those busy-body accounts in the papers by Merton and Weigall. He'd put two and two together. My name was there, together with mention of hyoscine. It didn't take a genius.'

'So you went to see him?'

Holinshed nodded. 'Taking my trusty lead pipe.' He smiled. 'Pargetter thought I was reaching for my wallet. You've never seen a man look so surprised.'

'Fahmy Bey was the riskiest of all, wasn't he?'

'In a way,' Holinshed nodded. 'But he had to go.'

'He was another despoiler of tombs,' Tilly said, her arm lolling round Holinshed's neck. 'You see, I *did* visit the Fahmy Beys when I was in Cairo. And he told me of his plans to force Carter to hand over the tomb's contents which he, Fahmy, would then sell to the highest bidder.'

'We knew how he treated Marguerite,' Holinshed said. 'The man was an animal. Ernani told us . . .'

'Ernani,' Lestrade frowned. 'You mean . . .'

Holinshed nodded. '*I* was the third man,' he said. 'The Shadow of the Shadow of the Light. I got as close to Fahmy Bey's secretary as Egyptian custom would allow – I'm sure you wouldn't want me to be too graphic on that score. And I discovered that the Fahmy Beys were bound for London. Ernani handled all the bookings. He even arranged the row on the night of 10 July with his usual insidious remarks to Fahmy about his wife's behaviour. All Smenk had to do was await her opportunity. I must admit, their row on their front doorstep, as it were, did play right into her hands.'

'We knew that Marguerite had a Browning automatic,' Tilly said. 'Horem bought one just like it in Cairo, waiting for a chance to use it. Marguerite knew nothing about guns. It was perfect.'

'But this,' Lestrade waved his hand to the fallen Macclesfield, 'this is far from perfect. How are you going to explain two dead policemen in your suite? After all, Horem . . . this isn't the Valley of the Kings or some back alley in the Old Native Quarter. This is the Grand.'

'You broke in,' Holinshed said. 'Barged your way through. Smenk was alone. You bullied her, making outrageous claims and accusations. Macclesfield became abusive. He hit Smenk and in a blind panic she retaliated, with the gun she keeps, like Marguerite Fahmy Bey, for her own protection.'

'A British jury will never wear that,' Lestrade said.

'With Marshall Hall as Smenk's defending counsel, they will.'

'Well,' Lestrade saw the sands of the desert running out before his eyes. 'That all depends on how realistic you can make it, doesn't it?'

'What do you mean?' Holinshed asked.

'How well Tilly . . . er . . . Smenk . . . can act and how convincing her injuries are.'

A cruel smile burst over Holinshed's face. 'We'll see,' he said and slapped her hard across the cheek. It was exactly the moment Lestrade had been hoping for – the moment when, almost for the first time, the Browning's muzzle left him. He launched himself at the younger man, throwing all his weight against his gun arm. The Browning erupted, the second bullet in the automatic's chamber crashing into the doorframe. Then the gun, knocked from Holinshed's grip, slid across the floor.

Lestrade could give Jack Holinshed thirty years or more, but the latter had more height, more strength, the will of the born fanatic. While Tilly was still reeling from her brother's slap, Holinshed and Lestrade struggled together on the Axminster.

'Get the gun!' Holinshed roared, grabbing Lestrade's hair and battering his head down on the carpet.

Tilly dashed for it, but to do so she had to cross the fallen Macclesfield and with whatever strength remained to him, the fallen Macclesfield swung up an arm and Tilly went down. It was all he could manage, however, and the next instant she'd knelt upright, steadying the gun Lestrade knew she knew how to fire. The room was spinning, his spine jarring with each successive crunch of his head on the floor. With one desperate lunge, he clawed free his brass knuckles and drove them up under Holinshed's rib-cage. There was a crash of gunfire and the English-Egyptian straightened, his eyes glazing, blood oozing from his mouth and nose.

Lestrade could hear Tilly gasp behind her dying husband-brother. He knew that she still had the gun in her hand, and Jack Holinshed, the last of the Horemhebs, toppled forward on to Lestrade's legs.

The ex-Yard man lay slumped against the wall, one murderer pinning him to the floor, the other still kneeling, facing him across the room. His brass knuckles were still in his fist. Could he hope to throw the switch-blade inside them across to Tilly before she fired? He'd never followed his science lessons at school, but in his heart of hearts even he realized that the velocity of a bullet was likely to be faster than anything he could manage.

'It isn't over,' he heard Tilly growl. 'We have a son, Horem and I. He is now the Guardian of the Gate. What we have begun, he will finish.'

Lestrade closed his eyes, waiting for death. It was the way he'd rather go, if he had to go at all that is, come wind, come wrack, with his knuckles on his fist and his Donegal on his back. Except that it was a balmy July night and he'd left his Donegal at home. He didn't expect to hear the shot that killed him, but he did. And the odd thing was, it didn't hurt at all. The even odder thing was that he was still able to open his eyes. Tilly, Smenk, whatever the harsh world would choose to call her, was lying against the door, a neat black hole in her right temple. Her blood was trickling through her curly blonde hair and running down the doorframe to form a widening puddle on the floor.

'Guv,' Lestrade heard Macclesfield say, 'are you all right?'

Lestrade hauled Holinshed off his legs and crawled across to the Inspector. 'Tsk, tsk, Norroy,' he said. 'Lying down on the job again.'

Inspectors Hambrook and Fabian solved the Old Fogey Murders between them that summer. The torn warrant card had belonged to Inspector Dicky Tickner of P Division after all and after his trial, while he was trying on various types of straitjacket in Broadmoor, he explained to Percy Merton of *The Times*, just before the journalist went back out to Egypt with Howard Carter, how he'd just about had enough of old people. They were always shopping when he was. Always bought the last cream doughnut he'd got his eye on. Always in the post office picking up their pensions. He'd have got even more of them if he'd had time, but Merton, he was sure, knew how it was. With a full-time job and all, there just weren't the hours in the day. But Tickner was one of their own. And so it was that neither Hambrook nor Fabian, when they came to write their memoirs years later, mentioned him at all. Neither, because of a certain few days spent in the Souk El Khasher, did they mention their adventures in Egypt.

The Carter expedition went ahead and the following year an astonished world looked for the first time in three thousand years on the golden face of the boy-king, the living image of God, Tutankhamun.

The Bandicoots came back from their extended safari in

Africa, just in time to attend the wedding of their adopted daughter, Emma Bandicoot-Lestrade to Inspector Norroy Macclesfield of Scotland Yard.

'Thank God,' Lestrade had gasped when Macclesfield had come to him to ask for his daughter's hand. 'I thought you wanted to borrow some money.'

Sir Edward Marshall Hall got Marguerite Fahmy Bey off in September, as he said he would. There were three women in the jury and the usual howls of protest from the Egyptian government. The greatest defence lawyer in the world had a broad back. He could cope with that.

No one noticed, over the years, how the Kiss of Horus lingered on. As Madame Fahmy Bey went to trial Aubrey Herbert, Carnarvon's younger brother, died, quite suddenly. An X-ray specialist sent out to photograph Tutankhamun's sarcophagus died *en route* to Egypt. Arthur Mace, working at Carter's right hand, died before the tomb was fully cleared. Carter's secretary, Richard Bethell, died in the Bath Club in 1929; his father, Lord Westbury, committed suicide soon after. And at Westbury's funeral, the horse-drawn hearse collided with a little girl and killed her.

Others lived longer. Carter fell in 1939; Burton the photographer, a year later. Lady Evelyn Herbert, one of the first to enter the tomb, died in 1980.

These deaths were widely scattered, in place and time, from the Valley of the Kings. The stories of the curse of the Pharaoh died away, in the face of science and rationalism. No one really noticed the brown-eyed, fair-haired boy who grew into a brown-eyed, fair-haired man. '*So* good looking,' some said, and Evelyn Herbert, before she died, did confide to her diary: 'That charming man who poured me a Bucks Fizz at Stringfellows the other day . . . I wish I could think who he reminds me of . . .'